Illustrated Battles of the
Napoleonic Age

Illustrated Battles of the
Napoleonic Age
Volume 3—1812-1813

Badajos, Canadians in the War of 1812,
Ciudad Rodrigo, Retreat from Moscow,
Queenston Heights, Salamanca, Leipzig,
Fight Between the Chesapeake & Shannon,
Chrystler's Farm, Dresden and Lutzen

D. H. Parry, Arthur Griffiths,
Herbert Russell
and Others

Illustrated Battles of the Napoleonic Age: Volume 3—1812-1813:
Badajos, Canadians in the War of 1812, Ciudad Rodrigo, Retreat from Moscow,
Queenston Heights, Salamanca, Leipzig, Fight Between the Chesapeake & Shannon,
Chrystler's Farm, Dresden and Lutzen
by D. H. Parry, Arthur Griffiths, Herbert Russell and Others

Leonaur is an imprint of Oakpast Ltd

Material original to this edition and presentation of the
text in this form copyright © 2014 Oakpast Ltd

ISBN: 978-1-78282-245-5 (hardcover)
ISBN: 978-1-78282-246-2 (softcover)

http://www.leonaur.com

Publisher's Notes

The views expressed in this book are not necessarily
those of the publisher.

Contents

The Taking of Badajoz by D. H. Parry	7
Canadians in the Field by Angus Evan Abbott	37
The Capture of Ciudad Rodrigo by Major Arthur Griffiths	59
Napoleon's Moscow Campaign by D. H. Parry	77
Queenston Heights by Angus Evan Abbott	129
Salamanca by Major Arthur Griffiths	153
The Battles Round Leipzig by D. H. Parry	173
Fight Between the "Chesapeake" and the "Shannon" by Herbert Russell	203
Chrystler's Farm by C. Stein	217
Dresden by C. Stein	231
Lutzen by C. Stein	251

April 6, 1812
The Taking of Badajoz

D. H. Parry

On the 16th of March, 1812, when the poplar trees that fringed the Guadiana were bending under a tempest of wind and rain, a British force some 15,000 strong, with a battering train of fifty-two guns, reached Badajoz—a strongly-fortified Spanish town near the frontier of Portugal—the bugles of the "95th" playing "St. Patrick's Day" as they faced the furious equinoctial gale. About a year before, the scoundrel Imas had delivered up the place to Marshal Soult, whose clubfoot did not prevent his being one of the most active men and fearless riders in the French service; and although we had made two attempts to retake it, we had failed on each occasion after heavy losses, our battering train being shamefully insufficient, and the enemy very much on the alert; the third time we were successful, and it is of this I am about to tell.

Badajoz was the *pax augusta* of the Romans, and a granite bridge with twenty-eight arches, dating from Roman times, still spanned the sluggish river on the north-west; but, save that the town had been frequently taken and retaken by Moors, Goths, and Spaniards, and was the birthplace of Morales, the painter, there was nothing very remarkable about its quaint, crooked streets and massive cathedral beyond the natural strength of its position, rising some 300 feet above the marshy plain, with eight bastions and their connecting curtains to protect it from attack.

It remained for Philippon and his gallant garrison, and our veteran troops under the Earl of Wellington—as he was then styled—to render Badajoz immortal, and bring a flush of pride and a thrill of horror to future generations who may read the tale.

G. Ortegal
Corunna
GALICIA
ASTURIAS
Minho R.
Vigo
LEON
Medina de Rio Seco
Vallad
R. Douro
Oporto
Douro R.
Salamanca
OLD
Almeida
Ciudad Rodrigo
Busaco
R. Mondego
Fuentes d'Onoro
Mondego Bay
Sabugal
Castella
Talavera
Toledo
Almaras
Alcantara
Tagus
Obidos
Rolica
Vimiera
Torres
Vedras
Cintra
Lisbon
Santarem
NEW
Cadajoz
Olivenza
Albuera
R. Guadiana
PORTUGAL
ESTRAMUDRA
R. Guadiana
Cordova
R. Guadalquive
ANDAL
Seville
ALGARVES
St. Vincent
Malag
Cadiz
Barrosa
C. Trafalgar
Tarifa
Gibraltar

The General of Brigade Philippon, colonel of the 8th of the French Line, and member of the Legion of Honour, commanded in Badajoz with a force of 4,742 men—composed partly of the 9th Light Infantry, the 88th Regiment, the Hesse-Darmstadt, some dragoons and chasseurs, artillery, engineers, and invalids, and seventy-seven Spaniards who ought to have been fighting on the other side.

Although somewhat short of powder and shell, Badajoz presented a formidable task to a besieging army, being protected on one side by the river, 500 yards wide in places, and having several outworks, or forts, notably one called the Picurina, on a hill to the south-east, whose defenders could be reinforced along a covered-way leading to the San Roque lunette close to the town walls.

Philippon had, moreover, taken every means possible to strengthen his post: mines were laid, the arch of a bridge built up to form a large inundation, ravelins constructed and ramparts repaired, ditches cut and filled with water, and that he should have no useless mouths to fight for, the inhabitants were ordered to lay up three months' provisions or march out there and then.

Such was Badajoz when Picton's 3rd, or "Fighting," Division; Lowry Cole's 4th—or, as they were nicknamed at the close of the war, " Enthusiastic"—Division; and the Light, known as "*The*" Division, invested it in the rain. The rest of the army watched Soult's movements closely, and prepared to oppose the relief of the town if that should be attempted, and the 5th Division was on its way from Beira to assist the siege.

As soon as darkness had fallen on the night of the 17th, 2,000 men moved silently forward to guard our trenching parties, and, with mattock and shovel, we began to break ground, 160 yards from the Picurina, the sentinels on the ramparts hearing nothing, as the howling of the wind drowned the sound of digging, and the sputtering rain fell incessantly into the works. So well had the volunteers from the 3rd Division laboured, for we had no regular sappers, that the light of the misty March morning revealed 4,000 feet of communication, and a parallel 600 yards long, on perceiving which the garrison opened a tremendous fire of cannon and musketry. The deafening roar of the heavy guns and the crack of rifles and smooth-bores continued with

little cessation for many days, increasing as we finished battery after battery and brought them to bear upon the doomed town. The condition of our siege artillery would hardly be credited were it not borne out by the unanimous published statements of credible witnesses.

Of the fifty-two pieces, some dated from the days of Philip II. and the Spanish Armada; others were cast in the reigns of Philip III. and also John IV. of Portugal, who reigned in 1640; we had 24-pounders of George II.'s day, and Russian naval guns; the bulk of the extraordinary medley being obsolete brass engines which required seven to ten minutes to cool between each discharge, lest the overheating should cause the muzzles to drop.

The ammunition was little better, and an engineer officer tells us that his 18-pound shot was of three distinct sizes, which had to be sorted out and painted different colours, while it was often possible to put a finger between the ball and the top of the gun, when the former was placed ready for ramming. Yet, with this miserable materiel we were expected to fight the most intelligent army in Europe!

Wellington learned from his spies that the garrison were to make a sally on the 19th, and at 1 o'clock the Talavera Gate suddenly opened, a little body of horsemen jingling out, followed by 1,300 infantry, who concealed themselves in the covered trench connecting San Roque with the Picurina. The cavalry pretended to skirmish, and, dividing into two parties, one pursued the other towards our lines, where they were challenged, and allowed to pass, on replying in Portuguese.

There was some excuse for the conduct of our pickets, as the French dragoons, in consequence of the difficulty of procuring new uniforms from France, were allowed to use the brown cloth so general all over the Peninsula, and were thus easily mistaken for our Portuguese allies, some of whom also dressed in brown. But we were soon undeceived, for the troopers dashed at the engineers' park, cut down some men, and galloped off with several hundreds of the entrenching tools, for which Philippon had offered a large reward.

Simultaneously the infantry sprang out of the covered-way with a part of the Picurina garrison, and, rushing forward, began to destroy our works. We drove them back almost to the walls of Badajoz, killing thirty and wounding 287. But we lost heavily, for it was a sharp encounter; and, unhappily, our chief engineer, Colonel Fletcher, was badly hit, a bullet striking a silver dollar in his fob and forcing it an inch into the groin, confining him to his tent until the latter end of the siege, the Earl going each morning to consult about the day's operations.

Our movements were by no means faultless, Wellington having great difficulties to contend with in many directions; in fact, during the whole of the Peninsular War he may be said to have fought the French with one hand, and Spanish pride, obstinacy, and selfishness with the other—fortunate indeed in possessing a genius which was ever at its

best the more trying the emergency. We stationed a cavalry regiment to prevent any further surprises, and continued our digging, the pitiless rain slanting unceasingly on the trench guards in their grey overcoats and oilskin *shakoe*-covers, while the working- parties shovelled and measured, and piled up long ridges of earth, standing ankle-deep in the water which filled the saps and trenches.

Many a man of the 3rd Division spun round and fell on the wet ground, for the enemy kept up a steady fire, and one shell dropped, fizzing, into a parallel and exploded, killing fifteen of the workers in a moment.

The Guadiana, too, rose in full flood and tore away the pontoon bridge which connected us with our stores at Elvas: it was replaced, however, and the garrison of Badajoz saw us creeping nearer and nearer to their walls, until, at last, our men finding the fire from the Picurina terribly galling, it was decided to storm that fort on the 24th.

The rain had ceased, and the dark mass of the fort, held by some of the Hesse-Darmstadt Regiment, loomed up, stern and silent, as five hundred of Picton's Division mustered before it about nine o'clock on a fine night.

A hundred men were kept in reserve, while the remainder, divided into two bodies, were to advance against the right and left flanks, also securing the communication with San Roque to prevent any succour coming from the town.

Scarcely had the word to march been given, when soaring rockets went up from the ramparts, port-fires illuminated the darkness in places, and the stillness became a babel of sounds, as shells came hissing towards us, drums rolled, and the bells of Badajoz rang wildly amid the deep booming of the heavy cannon. Red flashes streamed through the openings in the palisading, the Hesse-Darmstadt opened a murderous fire, but we swarmed irresistibly up the rocks and groped for the gate, the pioneers of the Light Division leading with their axes.

Down in the communication our fellows repulsed a battalion coming to the rescue, but it seemed for a time as if we had been baffled; the sides of the hill were dotted with our dead. Oates, of the Connaught Rangers, three engineer officers, with Majors Rudd and Shaw, who commanded the attack, and many a private soldier had fallen there. But as Powis, of the 83rd, brought up the reserve and forced the palings in front, the pioneers discovered the gateway on the town side, and, battering it down, rushed in with a shout.

Nixon, of the 52nd, was shot two yards within the entrance, and we fought with gun-butt and bayonet against a most heroic resistance; but at last they were overpowered, and half the garrison slain. One officer and thirty men floundered through the inundation and gained Badajoz in safety, but brave Gaspard Thierry, with the eighty-six survivors, were compelled to surrender, and the death-dealing Picurina was ours. The firing from the town ceased at midnight, but with the dawn of day they turned their guns on to the captured fort, driving us out and crumbling it to pieces.

Philippon had hoped to have held the work for four or five days, while he completed certain partially-finished defences, and its capture and destruction were a severe blow to him. But he urged his garrison to fresh efforts by reminding them of the English prison-hulks, which, as Napier justly says, were a disgrace to our country.

Three breaching-batteries were now constructed, one against the Trinidad bastion, another to shatter the Santa Maria, and the third—which consisted of howitzers—was to throw shrapnel into the ditch, and so prevent the garrison from working there. We had been eleven days before the town, and in spite of all the obstacles had made considerable progress, although latterly a bright moon had interfered with our nocturnal operations.

Overcoats were laid aside, and our men appeared in the well-worn scarlet *coatee* with white-tape lace, and the black knee-gaiter, which was the dress of a British-infantry private at that time. Pigtails had been done away with four years previously, and the well-known grey trousers were not issued to the troops until the following September. The Rifle Corps wore dark green, and used a wooden mallet to drive the ball down the grooved barrel; fusiliers and the grenadier companies of the line had bearskin caps, and light infantry were distinguished by green tufts in their felt *shakoes*, while our Portuguese friends were mostly clad in blue or brown, with green for the *caçadores*, or riflemen, each man carrying—including knapsack, accoutrements, kit, and weapons, etc.—a weight of seventy-five pounds twelve ounces, or ten pounds more than their opponents. The soldiers were enraged at the inhabitants of Badajoz for admitting the French, a sentiment which boded ill to them if we took the town. But, in the meantime, many instances of pluck on both sides were exhibited. One morning, early, before the working-party arrived, a brave fellow crept out of Badajoz and moved a tracing-string nearer to the walls, so that when we began digging in fancied security, their guns suddenly opened and bowled the men over like nine-pins. Another time, two of our officers and some men stole forward in the night, gagged a sentry, and laid barrels of powder against the dam which confined the inundation, and got back in safety; but the explosion did not have the desired effect.

At last, the stones began to fall from the Trinidad bastion, amid clouds of dust, as ball after ball went home with terrific force; the Santa Maria also crumbled under the cannonade, but, being casemated, it resisted better than the other, which, by the 2nd of April, yawned in a manner that must have dismayed the garrison, for they commenced to form what is known as a retrenchment, or second line of defence, within the walls, by levelling houses behind the growing breach. In places where the fortifications had not been completed the energetic Frenchman hung brown cloth which resembled earth, and his men were able to pass freely along; they also made a raft with parapets and crossed the inundation to our side. But all their efforts were useless: the breaches became larger as masses of stone and rubbish fell like mimic avalanches into the fosse below; and, on the 6th, a tremendous gap showed in the ancient masonry of the curtain between the two bastions which had not been renewed when the bastions themselves were rebuilt about 1757.

Then came a moment's pause. Soult, Drouet, and Daricau were advancing: a battle was imminent, and would need all our forces. In twenty-one days we had expended 2,523 barrels of gunpowder, each barrel containing ninety pounds, and we had fired 35,346 rounds of ammunition. Badajoz must be taken at all risk; and orders were now given for the most terrible of all species of warfare—*the night-attack by storm!*

Wellington's commands were precise and to the point, but they

were terribly eloquent to those who read them. I have extracted a few paragraphs from the original memorandum, and give them word for word: "1. The fort of Badajoz is to be attacked at 10 o'clock this night (6th of April). 2. The attack must be made on three points—the castle, the face of the bastion of La Trinidad, and the flank of the bastion of Santa Maria. 3. The attack of the castle to be by escalade; that of the two bastions, by the storm of the breaches. . . . 20. The 4th Division must try and get open the gate of La Trinidad; the Light Division must do the same by the gate called the Puerta del Pillar. 21. The soldiers must leave their knapsacks in camp. . . . 24. Twelve carpenters with axes, and ten miners with crowbars, must be with the Light, and *ditto* with the 4th Division."

The time had been altered from 7.30 to 10 o'clock, and during that interval the French placed the celebrated *chevaux-de-fris*e of sharpened sword-blades in the gap we had made in the connecting curtain; piles of shot and shell were laid along the ramparts, with beams of wood, old carriage-wheels, and every conceivable missile that their ingenuity could devise; each soldier had three loaded muskets beside him, and, as the unusual stillness in our trenches warned them that something was in preparation, an officer tried to reconnoitre us with a little escort of cavalry, but we drove him back, and all was quiet once more.

It was the calm before the storm, and men grew silent and thoughtful as the time drew near.

Letters were written home by hands that would never use pen again; absent friends were talked of in hushed voices, wills hastily made as in the presence of death; the married soldiers lingered in their quarters till the last moment, and then gave it out that they were "going on guard"!

The April day drew into evening; a grey mist rose from the river and stole among the trenches and the marshy ground, where frogs piped dismally and field-crickets kept up their perpetual chirp; then night came, still and cloudy, not a star visible, but here and there lights flitted along the ramparts, and the challenge of the sentries could be distinctly heard.

There was no bustle to show that eighteen thousand men were forming for a desperate attack; company after company they mustered and got under arms silently, words of command being given in a whisper. Picton had been hurt by a fall, and his famous 3rd Division was led by Kempt in consequence. Its destination was the castle, whose walls were from eighteen to twenty-four feet high; and the regiments which formed it were the 5th, 45th, 74th, 77th, 83rd, 88th, and 94th British, and the 9th and 21st Portuguese.

The 5th Division, under Lieutenant-General Leith—composed also of English and Portuguese—had to make a feint upon the Pardaleras outwork to the left, and then march round and storm the San Vincente bastion in rear of the town, while General Power made a false attack on the bridge-head beyond the Guadiana.

The Light Division and the 4th, under Generals Colville and Barnard, were to tackle the trenches, and were composed of the following corps—the Light having the 43rd, 52nd, and 95th British, the 1st and 3rd Portuguese Caçadores; and the 4th Division, the 7th, 23rd, 27th, 40th, 48th, and 97th British, with the 11th and 23rd Portuguese, and the 1st Battalion of the Lusitanian Legion.

(The trench-guards and the "forlorn hope" fell in, and about 9 o'clock four companies of the 95th Rifles crept forward and lay down, under the crest of the glacis, within a few yards of the French sentinels, whose heads could be seen, passing to and fro, against the sky.

Not a word was spoken as they crouched, unnoticed, in the mist

that veiled their dark uniforms. They waited the arrival of the "forlorn hope" to begin the attack. At length a sentry peered over the parapet: something had caught his quick ear, for he cried "*Qui vive?*" and there was a moment of keen suspense.

Not satisfied, he again challenged, and, receiving no reply, fired

his musket into the darkness; and instantly the drums of Badajoz beat to arms. Still, for ten minutes more the riflemen lay motionless, until the "forlorn hope" came up, and then, each man sighting carefully at the heads above the rampart, they poured in a volley, and the attack began.

It was unfortunate— as it happened—for Wellington wished all our assaults to take place simultaneously, but it could not be undone; moreover the garrison threw a huge mass of combustibles, called "a carcass," from the walls, and by its powerful blaze they saw the 3rd Division drawn up underarms; so, "Stormers to the front!" was our cry, and we rushed on with an uproar of cheers and shouting.

The ladder-parties and those carrying the grass-bags ran forward, scrambling across the trenches and broken ground, and, filing over the Rivillas by a narrow bridge, reached the foot of the castle wall under a heavy fire.

Brave Kempt, who afterwards fought at for Waterloo, fell, badly wounded, and as they carried him back he met Picton hurrying to take command with his sword drawn.

The 3rd Division had only twelve ladders, and eighty to a hundred men were all that could mount at a time; but they reared them against the masonry, and fought with each other who should be first to ascend.

Stones, earth, live shells, beams, heavy shot, and a rain of musket balls poured down; those who reached the top were stabbed and flung on to the others behind them—here a cheer as a man grasped the coping—there a howl of rage as the ladder was hurled broken from the wall and all its occupants flung in a heap below.

"Forward the 5th Fusiliers—Come on, Connaught Rangers." A corporal of the 45th fell wounded on hands and knees, a ladder was placed on his back in the confusion, his comrades mounting above him, and he was found next day crushed to death, the blood forced from his ears and nose.

Several of the ladders were broken, and those that remained were

flung off" repeatedly by the garrison on the ramparts, until the French cried "Victory," and the 3rd Division retired for a moment, to re-form under the crest of the hill.

Meanwhile, the 4th and Light Divisions, after a double allowance of grog had been served out, marched quickly on to the breaches, and the trench-guard rushed at San Roque with such fury that they bayoneted its defenders and carried the lunette without a rebuff.

As the stormers of the Light Division moved off. Major Peter O'Hare—who had risen from the ranks to a commission in the 95th (a most unusual thing in those days), and who was, moreover, one of the ugliest men and one of the bravest in the army—shook hands with George Simmonds, of the Rifles, saying—"A lieutenant-colonel or cold meat in a few hours!" They found him next morning stone dead and stark naked, with nearly a dozen bullets in his gallant frame. Officers were divided into two categories by the Peninsular soldiers—the "Come on" and the "Go on." O'Hare was one of the former.

As the firing commenced at the castle, the heads of the double columns reached the glacis to find all quiet and the place wrapped in profound gloom.

The ditch yawned beneath them, and the stormers threw their grass-bags, which measured some six feet by three feet, into it, lowered the *five* ladders which did duty for both divisions, and the "forlorn hope" of the Light Division descended into the chasm, doomed to a man!

A musket-shot told them that the silence was a treacherous one; but none were prepared for the awful scene that followed. The ditch was crowded with the stormers, and men waited their turn to follow down the ladders, when all at once a tongue of flame lit up the darkness, a terrific explosion seemed to rend the earth itself, and five hundred brave fellows were blown into eternity under the eyes of their comrades on the glacis above them.

One second's space the Light Division stood aghast, the next, they were leaping, sliding, climbing, never heeding the depth, into the gory grave that lay between them and the breaches, with a roar that went echoing along the walls of Badajoz—a roar of fury never to be appeased until bayonet should meet bayonet on the towering ramparts, fringed with the foe, beyond.

Down poured the 4th Division and mingled with them: the ditch was full of shouting red- coats, all struggling, regardless of rank, to get at the French, who, yelling defiance in their turn, showered grape, round shot, canister, hand grenades, stones, shells, and buckshot upon them; rolling huge cannon-balls from the parapet, sending baulks of timber thudding into the tumult, and coach-wheels that acquired a fearful velocity as they bounded down the rocks into the living mass of British valour pent up in the death-trap below.

Bursts of dazzling light were succeeded by moments of intense darkness; for an instant the huge bastions showed, bristling with armed men, to be lost again in a Stygian gloom, re-illumined the next minute by the flashing guns—by wavering port fires, and trailing rockets. A hundred Albuera men of the Fusiliers were drowned in an unexpected water-ditch; the air was heavy with gunpowder smoke and the sickening stench of the stagnant pools; individuals and regiments alike surged and scrambled to find a passage; until at last, getting on to an

unfinished ravelin, mistaken in the confusion for a breach, both divisions were jumbled together, and great disorder ensued.

Wellington, watching from a hill, and seeing the pause, exclaimed repeatedly: "What can be the matter?" sending *aide-de-camp* after *aide-de-camp* to report progress, as the glare revealed the faces on the ramparts and the peculiar hollow booming reached him, caused by the garrison firing down into the cavernous depths of the ditch.

At length there was a rush for the great breach. Officers and men, having extricated themselves from the carnage below, rushed on, to find an impenetrable barrier of sword-blades fixed in wooden beams and set firmly across the opening, while the *débris* in front was strewn with planks covered with spikes: if a soldier trod on one of them it slid down, either throwing him on the spikes or sending him back on to the bayonets of his comrades; and, to crown all, the garrison rolled barrels of powder into the middle of us, which exploded with shocking effect, filling the nostrils with the smell of burning flesh and singed hair, and strewing the breach with scarlet figures in every conceivable attitude of agony and death!

Our gallant fellows charged madly in masses, in groups, and even singly, one private of the Rifles forcing himself among the sword-blades, where the enemy shattered his bare head with their musket-butts.

It was not until the cruel slaughter had lasted *two hours* that the diminished divisions withdrew to the bottom of the slope and stood furious and exhausted, but powerless to effect their aim, and still under a fire that was thinning their broken ranks, while the enemy cried mockingly down to them, "Why don't you come into Badajoz?" Captain Nicholas, of the Engineers, gathered a few men and made frantic efforts to force the Santa Maria breach, and he was joined by Lieutenant Shaw, of the 43rd, who collected fifty men from various regiments and struggled over the broken masonry with them, but, two-thirds of the way up a hail of balls and hissing grape-shot mowed them nearly all down, and the divisions remained stolidly confronting inevitable death, unable to advance, unwilling to retire, for the bugles sounded twice unheeded, while, strange irony it seemed, a bright moon shining peacefully overhead, the Santa Maria, or "Holy Mary," looking down upon them on the one hand. La Trinidad, "The Trinity," on the other, and all around an Inferno such as Dante never dreamed of! About midnight Wellington ordered them back to re-form for another attack, and in the meantime Picton's Division, whom we left also re-forming, had rushed forward again, led by Colonel Ridge, who placed a ladder against the castle wall, where an embrasure offered a chance of foothold. A grenadier officer named Canch reared a second one alongside it, and the two mounted together, followed by their men, securing the ramparts after a desperate hand-to-hand conflict, and driving the enemy out of the castle into the town.

The garrison sent a reinforcement, and there was a sharp passage of arms at the gate, our redcoats firing from one side almost muzzle

to muzzle with the blue-clad, square-*shakoed* French on the other; but we kept the castle, though, unhappily, the gallant Ridge was slain.

Our reserves found the two ladders still standing, the top rungs of one being broken; and when the 28th Regiment practised storming a dry bridge with these, a couple of months afterwards, they were even then covered with blood and brains!

It was about half-past eleven when the 3rd Division succeeded in their escalade, and, retarded by unforeseen obstacles, it was not until the same hour or thereabouts that the 5th Division, under Lieutenant-General Leith, came under the breastwork before San Vincente at the west end of the town. As the 1st, 4th, 9th, 30th, 38th, and 44th Regiments, with a Portuguese brigade, halted, undiscovered, a few yards from a guard-house where the French could be heard talking, the roar of a distant explosion sounded, and the men whispered among themselves, "It is at the breaches!"

All was intensely silent around them; the murmur of the river rose on their left, the fortifications showed clearly before them as the moon came out; they knew that their comrades far off on the other side of the citadel were engaged, and an eager thrill went through the ranks. A sentinel discovered the mass of men and the glint of the moonbeams on the bayonets at the moment when our engineer guide exclaimed "Now's the time!" and as he fired we ran forward against the gateway.

Seized by a sudden panic the Portuguese ladder-party bolted, but we snatched up the heavy ladders and our axemen chopped fearlessly at the gate and wooden palings that fringed the covered-way, while from the walls which towered thirty-one feet overhead, the same tempest of beams, and shot, and bags of powder showered down on the heads of the 5th Division.

We cleared the paling and jumped into the ditch, crossing the *cunette* with difficulty and finding the ladders too short for our purpose; the engineer was killed, and a small mine exploded under our feet, but, as luck would have it, the ramparts at San Vincente had been thinned of some of their defenders, who had gone off at the double to attack Picton's men in the castle, and we placed three ladders under an embrasure where there was a gabion instead of a gun, and where the scarp was only twenty feet high.

Hand over hand, the troops clambered up under a concentrated fire that dropped them off by dozens, and the topmost stormers had to be pushed up by those behind before they could reach the embra-

sure, as the ladders were all too short; but at last the bold fellows got a foothold, and pulled the others up alongside them, until the redcoated mass grew larger and larger, and half the King's Own charged the houses while the rest of the division went roaring along the ramparts. Brown Bess in hand, hurling the stubborn garrison out of three bastions in succession. There was a great shouting, mingled with the scream of the grape-shot and the whistling hum of shells; yells, howls, prayers and curses were drowned or half-heard amid the *boom* of cannon and the incessant *bang-bang* of the deadly muskets fired at close-quarters.

The awestruck watchers on the hill above our camp stood in an agony of suspense, spectators of the terrific struggle; the entire citadel seemed full of flame and noise, as mine after mine exploded, and fire-ball after fire-ball was flung over the walls to light the besieged in their heroic resistance: never had Napoleon's soldiers fought with more determined gallantry, officer and man vying with each other in their efforts to keep us out, and as we drove them from one defence they retired into another and stood once more at bay.

Philippon, and Vielland, the second in command, though both wounded, flew from rampart to rampart, sword in hand, encouraging their brave fellows by word and deed, while the solemn chime of the cathedral rang out unnoticed hour after hour of that night of horrors. A strange incident occurred at San Vincente when General Walker fell riddled with balls on the parapet: either by accident or design, he made a Masonic sign as he staggered backwards, and a brother-mason in the French ranks dashed aside the threatening bayonets of his countrymen and saved him: afterwards, it is said, the general found his preserver a prisoner-of-war in Scotland, and procured his exchange in remembrance of his chivalry on the ramparts of Badajoz.

The 5th Division had obtained firm hold, knowing nothing of what was happening at the castle or the breaches, and as a portion of them were pursuing the enemy along the walls they rounded an angle and came upon a solitary gun with one artilleryman, who flung a port-fire down as they approached.

Instantly there arose a cry of "A mine! a mine!" and our fellows retired helter-skelter, followed by a fresh body under Vielland, who drove them back to the parapet again and pitched several over into the ditch, but a reserve of the 38th, under Colonel Nugent, about two hundred strong, poured a volley into them, and we rallied and charged along the wall towards the breaches.

The King's Own had entered the town at the first onslaught of Leith's Division, and a strange contrast they found it to the uproar of the bastions, as, with bayonets fixed and bugles blowing, they filed through the streets, silent and deserted as the tomb; every door shut, lamps alight in many of the windows, but not a soul abroad, except some soldiers leading ammunition mules, who were promptly taken prisoners. Sometimes a window opened and was immediately closed again; voices were heard, but the speakers were invisible; a few shots came from beneath the doors, but they were unheeded, and the adventurous 4th continued its march into the great square, where the same silence reigned, although the houses round it were brilliantly lighted.

The renewed fury at the breaches turned their steps in that direction, and they hurried off to take the garrison in rear: the attempt was well meant, but they were met by a fire that repulsed them, and they continued their wandering down streets and lanes, but the French began to be disheartened as well they might.

The castle in our possession they could possibly have besieged from the town side, as there was only one gate by which the 3rd Division could have issued; the Trinidad and Santa Maria were also well-nigh impregnable in spite of their shattered condition, had the garrison been able to concentrate there, but the forcing of San Vincente had let us in *behind* them, and the struggle was only a matter of time; so, brave Philippon and Vielland, with their remnants, forced the bridge and shut themselves up in San Christoval across the Guadiana, sending a few horsemen on the spur to carry news to Soult, and, the bleeding 4th and Light Divisions scrambling up again and rushing the breaches, Badajoz was ours!

As the heavy firing died away towards morning, a mighty shout arose inside the walls, caught up and echoed far and nearby our victorious soldiery, "Hurrah! hurrah! the town's our own, hurrah!" and the carnage-maddened men, breaking from all control, began a wild orgy, which lasted for two days and two nights, indelibly sullying the glory of our triumph.

Churches and mansions were entered and pillaged; costly sacramental plate and silver money from the military chest strewed the rugged pavement of the town; wine flowed down the gutters as freely as blood had done on the ramparts, and men staggered along with their *shakoes* full of liquor. One bestrode a cask with a loaded musket and compelled officer and private alike to drink as they passed him; here a group fired aimlessly down a street, caring little whom they hit, others blazed away at the convent bells, while some masqueraded in court-dresses, in French uniforms, and monks' cowls, howling, singing, dancing, like men possessed.

Many of the wretched inhabitants placed lighted candles and flasks of *aquadienta* on their tables and sought to hide themselves, hoping the marauders would drink and go away; they drank, but every cranny of the house was ransacked before they took their leave, and things were done of which we cannot speak, for the sake of humanity and the honour of the army.

"The town is ours, hurrah!"

Women and children ran shrieking to the officers for protection, which, alas, it was not always in their power to afford. Many an indig-

nant subaltern risked his life among his own men in frantic attempts to recall them to order; an officer of the Brunswickers was shot while struggling for the possession of a canary bird; one party was seen tormenting a wounded baboon that had belonged to the colonel of the 4th French Regiment. And breaking open the jail, they liberated the prisoners, some of the 5th and 88th holding candles aloft as the scum of a Spanish prison poured out to add to the disorder. Wellington himself was surrounded by a mob of drunkards, who fired their muskets to his infinite peril, shouting as they brandished bottles of wine and brandy— "Will you drink, old boy? The town's our own, hurrah!"

At length a gallows with three nooses reared its ominous form in the square, and a man named Johnny Castles, of the 95th, was placed beneath it; but no one was hanged, and by degrees the troops were drawn out of the town, credited with having murdered eighty-five of the inhabitants—in actual fact, the number being thirty-two. In fearful contrast to the licence within the walls was the scene outside. Philippon had surrendered to the future Lord Raglan, and retired from the service, in 1816, a General of Division, Baron of the Empire, and wearer of the Legion of Honour and the Order of St. Louis. The ditch, the slope, from the edge of the glacis to the top of the bastions, resembled a huge slaughter-house, nearly 2,500 of our men having fallen between the Santa Maria and La Trinidad alone, within a space of a hundred square yards; the 43rd and 52nd, respectively the gayest and the most sedate regiments in Spain, losing 670 men between them, and the place presenting an unusually shocking appearance from the explosions which had taken place there.

In one place the wife of a grenadier of the 83rd moaned over the corpse of her husband; in another a little drummer-boy of the 88th lay with his leg broken beside his dead father; the most heartrending sights were witnessed as the women and children sought frantically for their dear ones amid thousands of bodies, and the mangled fragments of what had once been living men .

Amid the horror of it all, two Spanish ladies came out of the town and implored two officers of the Rifles to assist them: one of them, Donna Juana Maria de los Dolores de Leon, afterwards married her protector, who became Sir Harry Smith, of Aliwal fame, and was long a prominent figure in English society—a curious instance of the "romance of war."

We took the colours of the garrison and the Hesse-Darmstadt, but there were no eagles in the town. The first man to die at the Santa

Maria was a Portuguese grenadier, and there was a story current in the army that José de Castro, bugle-boy of the 7th Caçadores, had sounded the French "recall" at a critical moment, for which he received a hundred guineas from the Earl of Wellington: certain it is that when a very old man, gaining a bare living by teaching the cornet in the town of Golega, he was still petitioning the Portuguese Government for a pension.

Five generals wounded, five thousand officers and men fallen during the siege—that is the story of Badajoz. And when Wellington stood in the breach and looked around him, stern Spartan though he was, he burst into tears.

1812

Canadians in the Field:
Three Features of the War of 1812

Angus Evan Abbott

Many deeds of daring done during the War of 1812 are remembered in the history of North America. Indeed, the bitter struggle between the Americans and Canadians was rich in brilliant exploits, either side having to its credit a number of memorable events. The needless conflict, which began about nothing and ended in nothing, caused a great deal of bitterness to be harboured at the time in the hearts of both parties to the quarrel. But, fortunately, that bitterness has quite died away; and, although the two halves of the great continent occasionally do look a little black the one at the other, the difference is merely a family one, with small chance, indeed, of growing into anything more serious than a scowl.

The War of 1812 furnishes a rich field for the student of independent and disconnected fighting. It was more or less a guerilla war from start to finish. Small bands of soldiers did wonders. Battles were fought with such determination and bitterness that the killed and wounded were desperately out of proportion to the number of soldiers engaged. The troops of both sides were born riflemen, never wasting a shot and always shooting to kill. Many engagements took place in the woods, and the Indians, who served on the Canadian side, were as ever ruthless and cruel. There can be no gainsaying that America had good ground to complain of the red man's doings. On the other hand, the Canadians found themselves obliged to defend their homes against powerful armies of invasion. No help could be looked for from across the Atlantic, for the United Kingdom had to grapple with the greatest

danger she ever encountered in all her history. During the years the War of 1812 was dragging its course, Britain got ready to meet Napoleon, met him, and fought the Battle of Waterloo. Canada, meagrely populated, was thrown on her own resources. Against her she had a great Union, practically unlimited as to territory money, and men. She therefore had to use every card in her hand, and one of the strongest cards was the Indian. Under Tecumseh and the younger Brant the red man fought with all his wonted cunning.

This article deals with the exploits of Laura Secord, the Glen-

garries, and the great Shawnee chief Tecumseh. That these feats were all performed for the Canadians is in no way implying that the records of the United States army are barren in daring deeds successfully carried through. On most occasions the Americans fought with dash, and their greatest successes were made when matters looked blackest for them.

Laura Secord's name is revered by the Canadians in much the same way as is that of Grace Darling in England, or, still better illustration, for each was concerned in war, Jeanne d'Arc in the land of "dame and dance." Of her deed the verse-writers of Canada, and they are many have, one may say without exception, spun their rhymes; and no history of the wonderful north-land would be acceptable to the Canadians did it fail to mention her name and chronicle her heroism. Tales have been told, dramas woven, songs sung to her honour; and as time goes on, her memory is surely destined to be kept green by the warm-hearted people of the great Dominion. For with heroic determination she pressed stoutly on through dark woods and across swollen streams to save the little army of Canadians from surprise and annihilation.

Mrs. Laura Secord was a daughter of Thomas Ingersoll, a United Empire Loyalist who removed from the United States to Canada after the war for independence and founded Ingersoll, now a flourishing town of some five thousand inhabitants. Laura married Mr. James Secord, and at the outbreak of the War of 1812 the two were living in Queenston on the banks of the Niagara River. When news came to the Canadians that an army for invasion was being formed on the opposite bank, James Secord, like most Canadians able to bear arms, volunteered for the defence of his country. He ranked as captain when the first decisive battle, Queenston Heights, was fought. That he bore himself gallantly and fought with all his might there can be no disputing, for towards the end of the awful day his wife Laura, as she picked her way among the wounded and dead—while the war-whoops of the frenzied red men still rang from the cliffs where the invaders were clinging to the face of the rock, with above the savages and below the swirling river— she came upon her husband lying among the dead as one dead. The wife gathered the wounded volunteer into her arms, and made her way with as great speed as the burden would allow to their house. There she found that, although he had received two desperate wounds, he still breathed. All that winter she nursed and tended him, and when in June the secret of the invading army came into her possession, her husband was still a cripple, and she herself determined to risk all and make the long journey alone.

The battle of Queenston Heights—a decisive Canadian victory—cleared the Americans out of Canada, but in the spring of 1813 they obtained possession of a strip of territory along the Niagara River. Queenston and, of course, the Secord's home lay inside the territory occupied by the Americans, and James Secord and his faithful wife were cut off from all communication with the Canadian army. General Dearborn, leader of the American army, had secured a firm footing on Canadian soil. Once safely across the frontier, he attempted to drive his army like a wedge into the interior of the country, but the Canadians fought fiercely. For them everything was at stake. Indeed, this war was carried on more like a war of extermination than a fair fight such as one would expect between two peoples speaking the same tongue. Devastation and rapine everywhere, neither side having a monopoly of the blame; villages, homesteads, crops were all given over to the flames, and the capital of each country was in turn burnt. It was a cruel, heartless, revengeful war.

In his attempt to penetrate the country, Dearborn met for a time with success; but at length the Canadians managed to check him at two or three points, and forced him to retire to the Niagara again. This caused much dissatisfaction in the United States, for Dearborn's army was considered quite large enough for the enterprise, and the general found himself likely to be superseded in command should he not without loss of time pick up the evacuated territory and continue to advance instead of to retreat. Not only the people of the United States, but the soldiers themselves considered that there had been no cause for such a right-about-face, and were eager to get away from the river, on whose banks they seemed destined to linger. Retreating, the Americans were, to be sure, pressed closely by the Canadians, who, although scarcely strong enough to attack, hastened to take possession of all the strategical points in the country evacuated by General Dearborn. In doing this a body of the Canadians, commanded by FitzGibbon, a light-hearted Irishman who played an energetic and not altogether unhumorous part in the war, entrenched themselves at De Cou's house, a spot commanding a number of highways leading into the interior of Canada. Until FizGibbon and his men were driven from their stronghold. Dearborn could not move. Once De Cou's house was stormed and burnt, a highway into the heart of Canada would be thrown open before the invaders. Dearborn planned to surprise FitzGibbon. For this purpose Colonel Boerstler was given command of 600 men, including fifty cavalry and two field-guns, and with the utmost secrecy, as he thought at the time, marched off through the bush for De Cou's.

As a reward for the valiant part he had played at the Battle of Queenston Heights, James Secord had been granted by the Canadian Government a small tract of land, which lay some distance outside of the village of Queenston. On the farm he and his wife lived, himself crippled and sorely distressed; and to their house, on the evening of the 22nd of June, 1813, came two American officers, who demanded food. While awaiting for or partaking of this, they fell to discussing the situation and Dearborn's plans, and, most imprudently as it turned out, carried on their conversation in a tone of voice loud enough for Mrs. Secord, who was waiting on them at table, to overhear everything they said. Soldier's wife that she was, and patriotic Canadian as well, she quickly guessed that some decisive move against her country's troops was meditated, and she paid careful but cautious attention to everything that passed between her two unbidden guests. When they had finished their meal and departed, Laura Secord repeated to her husband all that she had heard, and he agreed with her that an attempt to surprise the Canadians would certainly be made. If the surprise succeeded, the whole of western Canada must fall. That night the husband and wife discussed the pros and cons of the situation, and, the husband being unable to leave the house, the wife decided to make an attempt to steal through the American lines, and thread, by a circuitous route, twenty miles of bush to warn FitzGibbon of his great danger.

Laura Secord arose at dawn. She had planned every step of her journey and arranged the strategy by which she hoped to pass the vigilant pickets, whom the American general had thrown out at the skirt of the woods to prevent the accomplishment of just such enterprises as she had undertaken. Dressing herself only in a jacket and short flannel skirt and without shoes or stockings, she took her milking pail in one hand, her three-legged milking stool in the other, and set out to where her cow was lying, not yet having arisen from her night's sleep. As soon as she quitted the house, she beheld the pickets at their stations all alert with the vigilance of a coming crisis. She had not gone a rod from her house before the soldiers detected her and although they would know that, on a farm, woman's first duty is to milk the cow (it takes precedence over everything, the object being to allow the beast to eat her fill before the scorching heat of day and the swarms of flies drive her to take shelter under a tree), they still kept strict watch over her actions.

But to all outward appearances the good woman's only ambition was to get the milking over as soon as possible, for she walked straight to the cow and, causing her to arise, set down pail and stool, and commenced to milk. The beast had always been a quiet one, but this morning something was wrong. The soldiers, as they looked on, saw the animal kick over the pail and run a short distance towards the woods before being brought to a standstill by the entreaties of the farmer's wife. Again Mrs. Secord settled down to milk, and again the cow kicked over the pail and ran still nearer to the dark forest. One of the Americans, no doubt himself born and bred on a rich New England farm where cows had often kicked and run, sauntered over and offered his assistance; but Mrs. Secord expressed a determination to master the brute if she had to follow her about all day. Then she sat down and once more slily pinched the astonished animal. In this way, by short and easy flights, and all under the observation of the unsuspecting and completely befooled pickets, the cow and the woman reached the edge of the wood, passed into the wood, far into the wood, and finally deep enough into the wood for the woman's purpose.

Mrs. Secord leaped to her feet. Flinging pail and stool aside, she

darted into the deepest gloom, and as fast as her bare feet would carry her, and with nothing but a vague knowledge of the lay of the land and the way, made off to warn the Canadians and their faithful allies the Indians of approach of a foe.

Those who have never traversed a Canadian wood can have but a poor conception of the difficulties that are encountered even in a short walk. Laura Secord's journey was both a long and an anxious one. For half her distance she was in danger of coming upon American scouting parties and pickets (the Americans held the country for that distance around Queenston); and, besides this, many creeping animals lay in her path, animals that a woman with bare feet does not like to encounter. On her journey that day Laura Secord met with a thousand harassing impediments.

Underfoot the beech roots raised their gnarled and knotted backs through the soil; fallen trees, their dead branches held up as if, like a drowning man, in appeal for help, lay at every angle to be scrambled over as best she could; tangled clumps of briars and scrubby thorn, interwoven underbrush and rank grasses, and limbs of standing trees so low that she found it impossible to proceed upright. Again and again she was under the necessity of driving the rattlesnakes from her path by slashing at them with a goad which she carried for the purpose. (Those venomous reptiles were once to be found in great numbers in the peninsula formed by Lakes Ontario and Erie and the Niagara River, the scene of the brave Canadian's exploit, and in the month of June are very active.) But without pausing or paying more than momentary heed to the promptings to return to her home which must have on occasions surged upon her, she pressed on; the soil, loosened by the long winter's frost, treacherous under her feet, the gloomy closeness of the woods causing the perspiration to run from her brow; down into deep gullies she passed and up their steep sides again, over rocks, through morasses and cold spring swamps, across rapid streams on the trunks of fallen trees, keeping an anxious look-out in front of her for sign;, of friend or foe.

Night falls early in the woods. Dimness in the clearing is blackness under the interlocked branches of the forest. Owls began to hoot from the tree-tops and to flit past her with the soft rustle of ghosts; strange sounds awakened on the air: warm, sweet, enervating smells oozed from the ground where lay the leaves of ages; the whip-poor-will cried sharply and clear. The passage through the woods had been terribly trying to her, and during the last part of the journey she made but little progress. Her clothing was torn, her feet blistered and bleeding, and her strength all but left her. So it was that when, with whoop and spring, a band of Indians pounced upon her, she could not have been entirely unthankful that at length her long journey was ended for weal or woe. It happened that the Indians were allies of the Canadians; and Laura Secord, woefully bedraggled, was carried before the commander, FitzGibbon. He heard her story, and had her carefully attended to, for she was in sore straits.

FitzGibbon and his Indian allies acted with promptitude and decision, and the result of Laura Secord's remarkable journey through the woods was the complete discomfort of the American army. FitzGibbon captured every man and officer.

When the Prince of Wales was in Canada he visited Mrs. Secord, then an old, old lady; and a few days later she received a handsome present from the heir to the Throne of England.

The Glengarries at Ogdensburgh

The storming of the old French fort Presentation at Ogdensburgh must be looked upon as one of the most curious and daring exploits of the War of 1812. The business was coolly planned, and carried out with irresistible dash. But then, what but valour and dash could be expected from men who had inherited the very spirit of self-reliant bravery from the same sources as they had inherited their sturdy frames and determined, if fiery, tempers? Highlanders of the real fighting stock, heirs to the deeds of a long line of valiant warriors, many of them the direct descendants of those hot-headed mountain men who poured down from the hills to be scattered at Culloden, and who, for their failure to win or to fall, were transported to the shore of the then savage continent, North America. The sons of those who had fought at Culloden again fought a hapless fight against Washington in his struggle for freedom, and when the war for independence ended they left their all in the United States and journeyed to Canada rather than live under any flag but the Union Jack. It was these men and their sons that stormed Ogdensburgh.

Anticipating the arrival of many United Empire Loyalists—as those were called who quitted the United States after the struggle for independence—the Government of Canada set aside a large tract of land along the northern bank of the St. Lawrence. In the county of Glengarry these Highlanders made their houses, taking up farms, and by their industry soon turned that part into the garden spot of Canada. They beat their swords into ploughshares, and were as successful civilians as they had been brave soldiers.

To the settlement thus formed, about 1803 came a very welcome addition. When peace with France was patched up in the first years of this century, the authorities in England, believing that war had run its course for a time, disbanded a number of splendid regiments. Among these was a Highland regiment, Roman Catholics all; a regiment that had been raised for Continental service by the individual exertions of a priest, Alexander Macdonnell, of Glen Urquhart. He was a fighting clergyman, one of the old sort, who could with equal faith lead his flock in prayer or into battle. In the regimental marchings to and fro, Father Macdonnell went with his men as chaplain of the corps with true paternal love in his heart and true fighting fire there as well. The Treaty of Amiens signed and orders issued for the disbandment of this regiment. Father Macdonnell applied to the British Government to be allowed to take his men to Canada. Not only did he obtain the desired permission, but he was also given the means for transportation; and the men with their priest at the head marched in to the highland settlement of Glengarry, no doubt one and all welcomed to the land of the maple and beaver. Probably when they settled down upon the banks of the St. Lawrence to clear their farms for the plough, they dreamed that their fighting days were past forever. If so, they were unfortunately mistaken.

The war broke out, Queenston Heights had been carried and re-taken, and the harsh winter of the northern zone of America came down and effectively put an end for a time to active hostilities. But long before this took place—in fact, at the first serious news from Washington—Father Macdonnell's fighting blood had stirred in him and the fiery cross was sent through the land. The Highlanders lay by their axes, donned their tartans, took down their broadswords from their places on the ceiling beams, and repaired to the rendezvous where Colonel George Macdonnell—"George the Red," as he was called, after the Highland manner of distinguishing one of a name from another by some personal peculiarity—was ready to drill the men and lead them afterwards. "George the Red" was a near relative of the priest's, and a fighting Highlander through and through. The men he gathered around him were called the Glengarry Fencibles, and during the war proved themselves sore stumbling-blocks to the ingenious and valiant Americans.

The Glengarries were given a great stretch of the St. Lawrence to guard, their headquarters being at Prescott, in Grenville County, Ontario. After their long schooling against the highly trained troops of France, it must have been a curious experience for these men to engage in the semi-guerilla fighting that took place in the War of 1812. On the American side of the river and directly opposite to Prescott is Ogdensburgh, a thriving place to this day. Between the Canadian and the American towns the St. Lawrence flows, at this point quite a mile and a quarter in width, a strait of beautiful waves in summer, but a mass of grinding ice-floes in early winter and early spring. In the depth of winter it presents a curious spectacle: a windswept plain, glittering in

the sunlight and eerily white under the moon, broken into rugged furrows and dotted here and there by air-holes—breathing-places an acre or more in extent, from which ascend, when the temperature is very low, clouds of vapour as if from huge caldrons. The freezing over of the great rivers of America is a gradual process, the ice growing out from either bank until one clear night the ice-floes are jammed, their ragged edges are joined, their giddy whirlings cease, and the grinding roar is hushed. As the days pass the ice becomes so thick that it can bear any burden that man ever places upon it. Such was the river in the month of February, 1813.

At Ogdensburgh stood an old French fort, and in this fort a Captain Forsyth held command with five hundred American soldiers and a proportionate number of artillery. Early in February, Forsyth, with a small company at his back, had crossed the river late one night on a foraging expedition. This audacious proceeding enraged the "Glengarries." Father Macdonnell and "George the Red" laid their heads together. The outcome was the order that Ogdensburgh must be stormed, and stormed without delay. The leader at once set about preparing for the action.

His plans were as simple as bold. A stretch of ice more than a mile wide, offering no shelter from shot or shell, lay between the Highlanders and their foe. From the walls of the fort eleven cannon looked over this ice-plain. But Macdonnell cared nothing for the strange footing, and hoped to reach the cannon before the cannon would have time to reach him. Morning after morning the red leader marched his men out upon the frozen surface of the river, and for hours at a time used the ice as a drill ground. To the Americans at Ogdensburgh, who at first watched every movement of their dangerous neighbours, it appeared as though Macdonnell was determined to keep his men in thorough training for the spring campaign. Not only did the Highlandmen march and countermarch, but they hauled with them a couple of ugly-looking field-guns. Day by day they ventured farther out upon the ice in their practice, until the centre of the river was reached if not passed.

On the morning of the 2nd February the Highlanders as usual turned out upon the ice. Four hundred and eighty of them there were all told, and the everlasting two old field-pieces dragging behind them like the tail of a beaver. From the walls of the fort at Ogdensburgh the usual number of soldiers took their places to watch the drill. Captain Forsyth himself watched the spectacle for a time, but having seen enough of it, hastened to his breakfast. As he sat over his meal an officer came to him and said that he thought there was something suspicious about the looks of the Highlanders this morning. Forsyth thought otherwise, and went on with his breakfast. The junior officer, unfortunately for the Glengarry men, felt uneasy and sceptical, and resolved to keep a suspicious watch over the goings-on on the ice. Not many minutes passed before his shout from the walls of the fort caused the soldiers to spring to their arms. The Highland hosts had suddenly rent asunder, and two columns dashed straight for opposite sides of the fort.

"George the Red" himself headed the left wing. His men held the ropes of the two field-guns. Foremost in the right wing ran Captain Jenkins, a Canadian born and bred. On they dashed for the fort, running as fast as legs would carry across a frozen river. But half a mile of ice is a long, long road to travel, and before the columns had progressed many hundreds of yards the first cannon-load of grape shot came sweeping across the field of ice to meet the oncoming columns. Another hundred yards forward and the musket balls began to drop in the ranks, and men leaped into the air to fall flat upon the glittering ice.

Macdonnell's men carried the guns. It was the leader's plan to plunge into Ogdensburgh, brush out of his way any opposition that might there be offered, and plant the artillery in a position to fire into the fort from the rear, in this way preparing a breach for Jenkins, who was to storm the fort at the opposite side. But Macdonnell had not counted on his movements being so quickly discovered, nor that he would encounter such obstacles when he approached the bank. His men reached the American shore, swept through the village with irresistible fury; but when they reached the chosen spot for planting the guns, the guns were not forthcoming. They had, it turned out, become buried in a great bank of snow and ice that skirted the marge of the river. It took a weary time to hoist them out of their helpless position, tumble them up the river bank, and plant them in a commanding position. Meanwhile the Americans, rare marksmen and cool fellows, did not let the minutes slip unprofitably by.

While Macdonnell's men were floundering in the snowdrift, poor Jenkins and his band were having a very bad time of it. No sooner had he started forward than seven cannon were pointed at him, and the grape played havoc with his men, momentarily throwing them into confusion. He himself had his left arm shattered by the very first shot from the fort, but calling bravely to his men they all sprang forward.

However, they had not gone many yards before a second shot struck the leader, this time on the right arm, completely disabling that also. Notwithstanding his terrible wounds—his left arm had to be amputated and his right was never afterwards of any use to him, although it hung by his side—the gallant Canadian pressed stoutly forward to inspire his men, but at length fell exhausted on the ice from loss of blood. His men, however, never lost heart. Leaving their commander where he lay, they breasted the fire from the fort, scrambled up the bank, formed in proper order, and charged over the breastworks, depending on their bayonets to carry the day. In the nick of time "George the Red" got his guns into position, and with a "Hurrah!" both wings made for the old French fort. Forsyth, seeing all lost, retired with those men who were able to follow him, escaping into the woods that surrounded the place. The Highlanders secured the fort, burnt four armed vessels that lay in the bay, carted a vast quantity of stores across the ice to Prescott, and having destroyed the fortification, retired to Canadian soil.

The Canadian loss in the gallant affair amounted to eight killed and fifty-two wounded, most of them struck down on the ice by the raking grape-shot.

Tecumseh, War-Chief of the Shawnees

A few tame buffaloes where once roamed countless thousands; a few patches of ragged forests where once waved a continent of forests; a few red men, tamed but not civilised, where once the smoke from many villages of *wigwams* and *tepee* curled through green branches and drifted into the blue sky. The triumph of the white man in North America has been won by the extermination of well-nigh everything indigenous to the continent. The very climate has changed. Europeans from Spain, France, Holland, and our own island kingdom set foot on American soil only to fly at the throat of all things un-European. Beasts, wild-flowers, forests—all have been dislodged; streams diverted, rivers bridged, railways set to crawl over the face of nature, land laid bare to the glaring sun, and a unique continent turned into a second Europe. But the most deplorable sacrifice to white man's convenience was the sacrifice of the forests and the Children of the Forests.

Some of the grandest figures in American history are Indians. Among these Pontiac and Tecumseh stand out in commanding proportions, and it is a strange coincidence that both of these mighty warriors, during the years in which their greatest deeds were done, had their wigwams pitched on the banks of the Detroit River. Pontiac, than whom no greater war-chief ever swung the tomahawk, personally directed the operations against Fort Detroit, then garrisoned by British soldiers, and conducted the greatest siege that is recorded in the history of the red man. Tecumseh, the next striking figure in Indian history, fought on the banks of the same stream side by side with the British, whom his great forerunner had attempted to expel from American soil. As a striking figure of the War of 1812, this Tecumseh may be placed shoulder to shoulder with Sir Isaac Brock, hero of Queenston Heights, whom he knew and loved. Tecumseh was a born leader, eloquent in speech, lofty in principle, and brilliant in war. His death in the battle of the Thames caused a thrill of sorrow to pass through Canada, sorrow only less intense than that which moved the Canadians when they heard of the death of Brock on Queenston Heights.

Tecumseh, war-chief of the Shawnees, was born about 1770. His earliest recollections were of war, for his people, turbulent and fierce, found themselves in unending trouble with the Americans. He was twenty years old when General Harmer, commanding a large body of American troops, was sent to punish his tribe. The Shawnees met the Americans, and the cruel fight that resulted was altogether disastrous to the white men. They were forced to fight at great disadvantage, and finally had to take to heels to escape a general massacre. Next year General St. Clair undertook to avenge Harmer's defeat, and the end of this expedition was that the Americans were again almost annihilated. This, of course, could not last. The United States Government, two years later, fitted out a column, giving the command to General Wayne. Ample troops for the war were placed under the general's care, and Wayne most effectively administered the punishment which in the previous attempts had failed to be given. The Shawnees lost a greater part of their territory and a large number of their best warriors.

The disaster to his people had a curious effect on the mind of Tecumseh. At that time a young and no doubt unimportant buck, the defeat rankled in his heart without in any way cowing his independent nature. A great hatred for the Americans grew in his breast, and he formed a determination to overwhelm them in the west and drive them east of the Alleghanies. To do this he saw clearly that he must not begin by leading one tribe to war against the soldiers, but that all Indians on the continent must be formed into a confederacy and made

to act in concert. It was a dream cherished by most of the great Indian chiefs, but none set about its accomplishment with clearer intelligence and sterner determination to surmount all obstacles than Tecumseh.

His resolve once formed, he without loss of time set out to preach the crusade among the neighbouring tribes. His oratory, rich in the metaphor which the Indian loves and thrilling with martial fire, touched the hearts of the restless warriors; and when in 1804 Tecumseh's brother, the then chief of the tribe, proclaimed himself a

prophet sent by the Great Spirit to lead the Children of the Forest back to their original ways of life and ancient heritage, and at the same time renounced the chieftainship in favour of Tecumseh, the young warrior found himself at the head of a splendid band of warriors, which his own and his brother's fame, ringing through the land, was causing to be increased every day by ambitious spirits from friendly tribes. So threatening did the movement among the Indians appear to the United States that the president instructed General Harrison, himself president in after years, to see Tecumseh and learn his intentions.

This was the first meeting between Harrison and Tecumseh. They last came face to face in the swamp-lands of the valley of the Thames in Canada, and Tecumseh, fighting like a mountain-cat, fell riddled with buckshot.

This first meeting threw into relief the character of the Indian war-chief. Both Americans and red men arranged to meet unarmed. Tecumseh at the head of his warriors appeared at the appointed place punctually. One of General Harrison's officers offered a chair to the chief, saying—"Warrior, your father, General Harrison, offers you a seat."

Tecumseh gazed into the sky before answering:

"My father! The sun is my father, and the earth is my mother. She gives me nourishment, and I will rest on her bosom."

Having spoken, he flung himself on the turf.

The interview was short and unsatisfactory. Tecumseh refused to relinquish his idea of forming a confederacy, unless the president, on behalf of the United States, undertook to keep the white man within the boundaries already occupied by him.

Immediately after the interview the Shawnee chief set out to preach his favourite scheme to the Indians of the south. During his absence his tribe got into further trouble with the troops, and were again sorely cut up and defeated. Tecumseh returned home, gathered around him the warriors who had escaped destruction, and, the War of 1812 breaking out, he hastened with his band to Detroit, there to place himself at the disposal of the Canadians. From that day to the day of his death he led his braves with a judgment and brilliancy scarcely equalled in the annals of Indian warfare.

To Tecumseh and his warriors fell the distinction of striking the first telling blow in the War of 1812. An American army commanded by Hull had crossed to Canadian soil, expecting to easily subdue the western part of Canada. Hull's army depended on the west for supplies, and Tecumseh, knowing this, beset the road leading from Ohio, and ambushed a large convoy under Van Horne. The Americans were taken by surprise, but held their ground bravely against Tecumseh and his warriors. A fierce fight followed, but the Indian chief had the advantage of position, and moreover his braves were used to fighting in the woods. Under green trees and among tangled underbrush, as in the marshlands, none could war so well as the Indian. After fighting the fight of despair, Van Horne's little army was scattered; most of the troops were killed and important despatches captured. At the news of this disaster Hull retired from Canada, and shut his army behind the stockades of Detroit, leaving Tecumseh to return triumphantly to Amherstburgh. This was a characteristic beginning to a war for the most part fought in the bush.

Fresh from his victory over Van Horne, Tecumseh, war-chief of the Shawnees, met for the first and last time Brock, commander of the forces in British North America. It is recorded that the two took a great liking to one another. Brock certainly looked upon Tecumseh as a remarkable man, in whom all trust could be placed. Un-Indianlike, the Shawnee chief scorned liquor. He had been a heavy drinker in his youth, but seeing how liquor was carrying off his people he renounced its use. In victory he refused to plunder, and his valour was above suspicion. Brock and Tecumseh planned the storming of Fort Detroit, although the force they had for the purpose was far weaker than that under Hull, who held the fort. Tecumseh undertook the cutting-off of the fort from all communication with the outside world, and with his thousand warriors completely surrounded Detroit, besetting every highway and path; and when Brock summoned Hull to surrender, Tecumseh drew in his circle of ferocious followers, and their war-whoops, ringing from the woods and re-echoing from the old stockade, hastened the American general's resolve to open the gates. From that day to the day of his death Tecumseh was looked upon by friend and foe alike as one of the great leaders in the war. The Canadians found him an invaluable ally, and the Americans a leader to be reckoned with. Few Indian chiefs ever had such responsibilities placed on their shoulders by the white man as had Tecumseh. It is scarcely too much to say that Brock looked to the Shawnee to hold the territory of Michigan and defend Western Canada from attack. Proctor, who commanded the few troops Brock could spare from his hard task at Niagara, no doubt held actual command, but Tecumseh was the fighting force. And right well he did his duty.

In January of 1813, Proctor and Tecumseh led out their small force and surprised a brigade of Harrison's army, killing close upon 400 men, and capturing Brigadier Winchester, three field-officers, nine captains, twenty subalterns, and more than 500 men. Considering the small armies in the field at this time, the number of killed was appalling. Unfortunately some Indians, losing control of themselves, commenced to massacre the wounded, and a number of unfortunate American soldiers were in this way done to death before the red men could be brought under control.

News of this action spread among the tribes of the forest and plain, and Tecumseh's band was swelled by volunteers from near and from afar—bucks anxious to see fighting or to avenge the blood of killed tribesmen. Proctor, elated with the success of his offensive operation, determined to pursue the forward policy, and with 1,000 regulars and militia, and 1,200 Indians, he in April laid siege to Fort Meigs. At this siege Tecumseh again distinguished himself by cleverly leading Colonel Dudley and 400 American troops into an ambush, with the result that half were slain and the remainder captured. Although Proctor found it impracticable to continue the siege, he managed during the operation to take 550 prisoners, and the slain of the American forces were estimated at about 500 men. After this General Harrison's army was strengthened to such proportions that the small army of Canadians and Indians found it impossible to act on the offensive with any success, and when Commodore Perry in a gallant action swept the upper lakes of the British fleet. Proctor found himself compelled to evacuate Fort Detroit and retreat towards Niagara. Against this movement Tecumseh protested in one of the finest examples of Indian oratory that has been handed down to us from a time not so long passed, but passed for ever, when the Indian was still a great orator and a sturdy warrior. In the course of his speech he protested strongly against any retreat not preceded by a defeat. To quote a few sentences from his oratory:—

"Father, listen! our fleet has gone out; we know they have fought; we have heard the great guns; but we know nothing of what has happened to our father with that arm. Our ships have gone one way, and we are much astonished to see our father tying up everything and preparing to run the other.

"Father, listen! the Americans have not yet defeated us by land; neither are we sure that they have done so by water; we therefore wish to remain and fight our enemy should they make their appearance.

"Father! you have got the arms which our Great Father sent for his red children. If you intend to retreat give them to us and you may go. Our lives are in the hands of the Great Spirit. We are determined to defend our lands, and if it be his will, we wish to leave our bones upon them."

The Great Spirit willed, and Tecumseh left his bones on Canadian soil.

Proctor began his disastrous retreat on September 28th. The country through which his route lay is as peculiar in its way as any on the North American continent. Once upon a time this tract of land was covered by Lake St. Clair, but through the ages the water receded from the face of the earth, leaving a great alluvial plain of waving reeds and coarse grasses, the paradise of the wild duck. Through this the Canadians and Indians made their way, and, coming to the River Thames, set out along its northern bank through an open forest.

Closely following on their footsteps came General Harrison with 3,500 men, 1,500 of these Kentucky riflemen mounted on horses that understood the woods as well as any woodsman. Proctor found it impossible to make much progress owing to the terrible state of the ground; and Harrison, with his mounted men, soon caught him up.

On October the 5th the little band of regulars and Indians was forced to halt and prepare for battle. The position he secured was a favourable one. On his left the River Thames flowed, deep and treacherous. On his right, in the security of a swamp, lay Tecumseh and his warriors, delighted at the prospect of another meeting with their foe. The small force of regulars were deployed from river to swamp, and all was ready for the appearance of Harrison.

Tecumseh held a position that appealed to the Indian heart. A tangled mass of underbrush, long grass, and gnarled swamp-oak hid him from view; underfoot the soil shook like jelly and scarcely would bear the weight of a *moccasin* foot, being quite impossible to horsemen. In such a place the mighty warrior awaited in all confidence the time when he might spring whooping from his cover to fall upon the flank of the Americans. The last words he spoke to Proctor as he was about to retire to the fastness of the marshlands were, "Father, have a big heart!"

Notwithstanding the telling position he had secured, Proctor neither took ordinary precautions to escape surprise nor did he or his men display valour in the fight. At the first charge of the American horsemen, and before the Indians had an opportunity to begin the battle according to the arrangements come to between Proctor and Tecumseh, the regulars broke and ran. In fact, many did not go to the trouble of attempting to escape, but threw their weapons on the ground and surrendered.

Tecumseh saw what happened, and his rage was great. He and his warriors might very well have withdrawn and saved themselves, for no army could hope to catch the red man in the woods; but instead of doing this he resolved to give battle, and at the head of his bucks sprang out of the morass and flew at the throats of the renowned riflemen. The Kentucky men, hunters and trappers every one of them, were familiar with Indian tactics, and used to fighting under trees. They met the Indian charge with great coolness, and although badly cut up, held their ground.

In the savage struggle that followed, the great Shawnee Tecumseh met instantaneous death, being riddled with buckshot. His death put a stop to all fighting. The Indians quickly melted away among the trees, leaving their chief dead on the banks of the muddy Thames.

Tecumseh's end was one after his own heart. Pontiac died from a tomahawk-blow delivered, It is said, in a drunken squabble; but Tecumseh died with tomahawk in hand, the heat of battle in his brain, and his face to the foe.

January 19, 1812

The Capture of Ciudad Rodrigo

Major Arthur Griffiths

All was ready for the attack. Major George Napier, one of the three illustrious brothers whose names are now household words, stood at the head of his volunteer stormers, taking his instructions from Lord Wellington himself.

"Now do you quite understand? Do you see the way you are to take so as to arrive at the breach without noise or confusion?"

"Yes, sir, perfectly," replied Napier.

Someone of the staff, who was standing by, then said—

"You are not loaded! Why don't you make your men load?"

"No," sturdily replied Napier; "I shall not load. If we cannot do the business with the bayonet and without firing, we shall not be able to do it at all."

"Let him alone; let him go his own way," remarked Wellington, interposing, and thus fully endorsing the view which Napier took of the work in hand.

A few minutes later Napier was shot down as he entered the breach at the head of his men. His arm was shattered, and hung helpless, but he disdained all assistance.

"Push on. lads, push on" he cried undaunted, still cheering his men. "Never mind me; push on—the place is ours"

And there he lay, till all had passed him, getting terribly bruised and trampled upon in the confusion in the darkness.

It was not till he heard the shouts of "Victory! Old England forever!" that he gave himself up to the surgeon for the amputation of his arm.

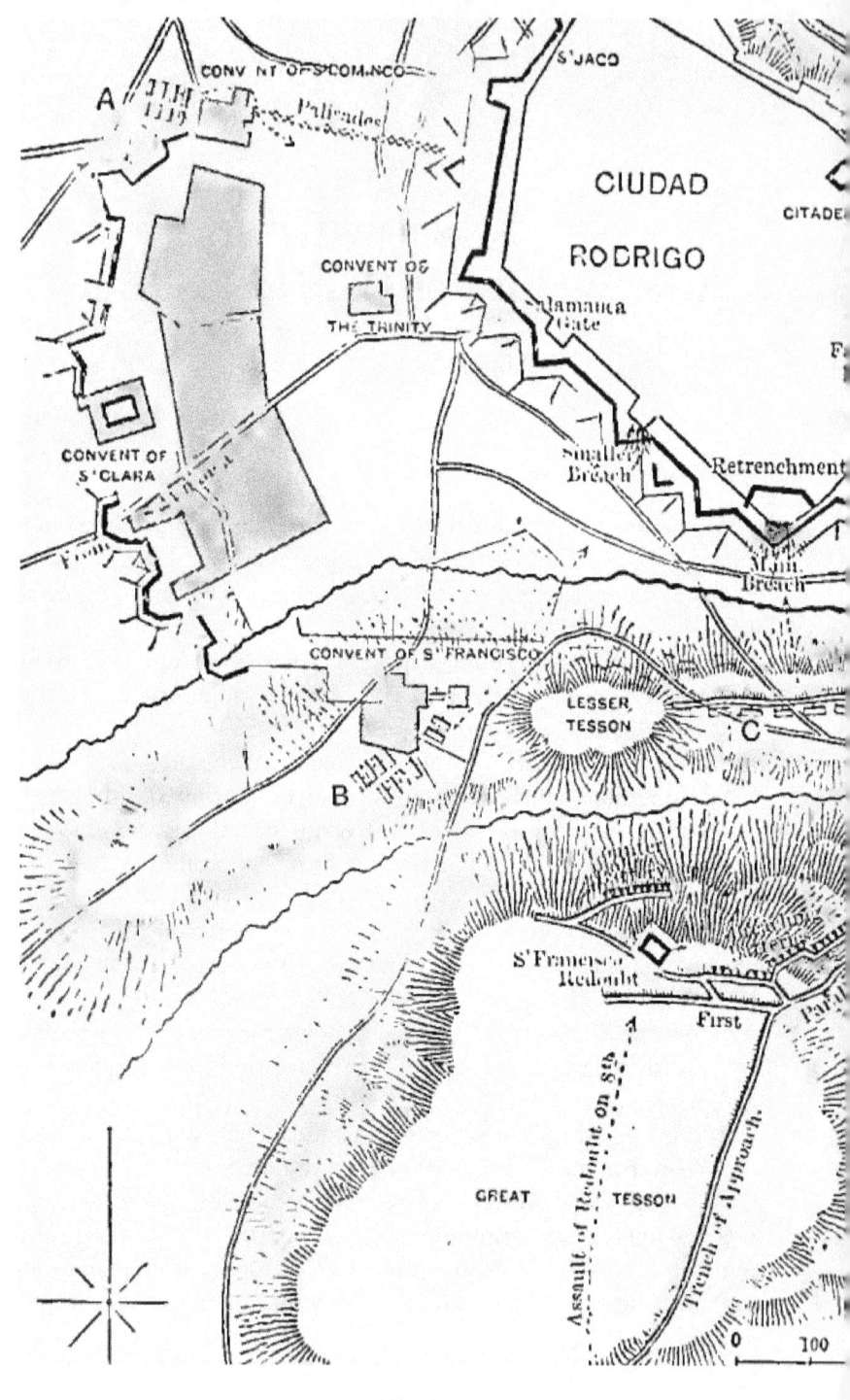

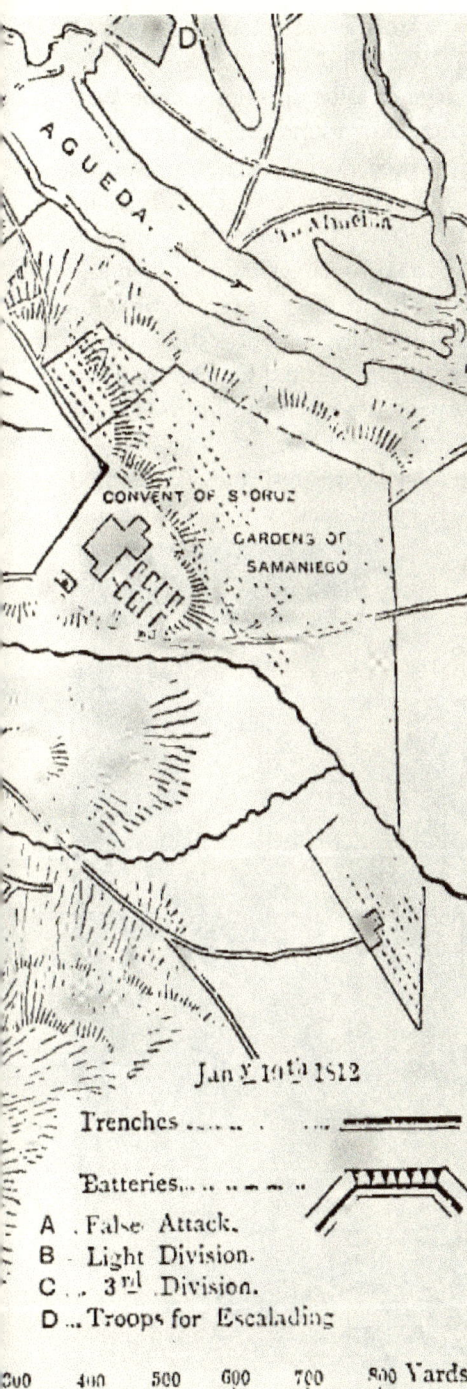

They were true heroes, these old Peninsular worthies; and there were few finer fellows than the Napiers—Charles, William, and George. But at Ciudad Rodrigo there were others who gained great fame: Generals Craufurd and Mackinnon, both killed at the breaches; Gurwood and Mackie, who led the forlorn hopes; Hardyman, a captain of the 45th, of whom it was said so gallant was his demeanour, so noble his exploits, that although three generals and seventy other officers had fallen, "the soldiers fresh from the strife talked only of Hardyman." The taking of Ciudad Rodrigo was indeed a splendid feat of arms.

Time was of vital importance. The French general, Marmont, was collecting his strength for its relief: the ground the besiegers occupied might at any moment be flooded, for it was the rainy season, and a night's downpour of rain would have ruined the trenches. The only chance lay in boldly attempting an assault, without waiting till the fortifications were ruined by bombardment. Heartless as it may sound, the only solution was to sacrifice life rather than time. This is what Wellington had meant when he prefaced his final orders by the announcement that Ciudad Rodrigo must be taken on a particular day. His men knew what was expected of them, and, without hesitation, they answered: "We will do it!"

It was no light enterprise, the siege of Ciudad Rodrigo; but Wellington undertook it on sound, reasonable grounds. In the first place, he was bound to do something just then. A real, substantial success was very urgently required. Great dissatisfaction prevailed in England at the prolonged inactivity of his army. The government at home was unpopular, and it passed on what it could to its general commanding in the field, finding fault, yet giving him no very generous or sufficient support. He stood practically alone—he must bear the brunt of all he did and all that came of it; but not the less did he reckon up his chances and consider the various operations open to him independently of their difficulty or the risk attending them.

The one he chose was that which lay nearest and yet seemed almost hopeless and impossible. Its very audacity was what really

made it feasible. Marmont was really misled by the many disadvantages that told against the English, and must prevent them, as he thought, from attempting any serious blow. It was the depth of the winter season; the weather was intensely cold, snow and frost alternated with heavy rains. The country around was so wasted and depopulated as to impede all military movements. The English army was in very poor case; the troops suffered greatly from ill-health, due to their long occupation of damp, low-lying ground; hundreds were in hospital, the rest were dispirited and badly found, their uniforms were ragged, their pay three months in arrear; supplies were scanty, and brought up with great irregularity; men were put on half-rations, and for three consecutive days they had no bread; the horses of the cavalry and artillery, the mules of the military train, were half-starved—chopped straw, the only food, was exceedingly scarce; and the muleteers, upon whom much depended, had been eight months without pay. Above all, the Portuguese, Wellington's allies, were apathetic, disinclined to co-operate in any forward and decided move.

Yet Wellington, nothing daunted, proceeded to gather up the threads and weld them together for his purpose. His troubles, after all, were working to his advantage: the enemy was aware of them and magnified them greatly. The dispersing of the British troops over a vast area was taken as a clear proof of the difficulties of subsistence, and as a certainty that they could not assume the offensive. Other small matters encouraged this false security in the French. Nothing, least of all a siege, could be contemplated, for it was firmly believed that the English had no battering-train. Again, the quartermaster-general, Murray, was granted leave of absence to go to England. No great operations could be near at hand when so prominent an official was suffered to leave the army. When Murray afterwards reproached Wellington for allowing him to lose all share in the coming birilliant exploit, the general laughingly replied that his absence had been of the greatest service to him, for Marmont had heard of it, and was in consequence satisfied that nothing much was about to happen.

Profound secrecy was a first condition of success in an operation which, as the historian puts it, needed extreme nicety, quickness, prudence, and audacity. Wellington was careful to divulge nothing, and only a masterful, self-reliant leader could have made such extensive preparations without betraying his purpose. He had begun them re-

ally the previous autumn when he had refortified Almeida, which had recently fallen into his hands, intending it as a secure place of arms, where he might collect his siege artillery. Large detachments of infantry had been practised in the business of military engineering, in the manufacture of gabions, fascines, and pickets in the digging of trenches and earthworks. He had also set the military artificers to build a great trestle bridge to be used in crossing the River Agueda, upon which Ciudad Rodrigo stands.

By the 1st January, 1812, he had brought up half his guns, had fortunately found ammunition in Almeida, and had begun to lay the bridge at Marialva below the town. Four divisions were to be employed in the siege—the 1st, 3rd, 4th, and Light; but as the weather was bitterly cold and the army had no tents, there was no cover or protection to the troops on the north side. It was ordered, therefore, that the regiments should occupy cantonments on the south bank among the villages. They were to cross over to their work from day to day as their turn of duty came round. In this way each division was to have one whole day in the trenches out of every four, taking with them their food, cooked, and their entrenching tools. The hardship of this service was great. It was necessary to cross the icy-cold River Agueda going to and fro, wading through water sometimes to the waist. No fires could be lighted, and their wet clothes often froze on to the men during the night. One of those who went through this siege describes how pieces of ice were constantly brought down by the rapid current, and so bruised the troops in fording the river that cavalry were ordered to form four deep across the ford, and under this living shelter the men crossed comparatively unharmed.

The fortress of Ciudad Rodrigo stood on rising ground in a nearly open plain with a rocky surface, but to the northward there were two hills respectively some 180 and 600 yards distant from the ramparts. The first of these, called the Lesser Tesson, was about on a level with the walls; the second, or Greater Tesson, rose a few feet above them. Upon the latter an enclosed and palisaded redoubt had been constructed, called San Francisco, and this prevented any siege operations on this side while it was in the enemy's hands. The town itself was defended by a double line of fortifications— one, the inner, an ancient wall of masonry, not particularly strong; the second, outside it, intended to cover the inner wall. The latter is known in old-fashioned fortifications as a *"fausse braie."* It gave but little defence, being set so far down the slope of the hill. Besides the foregoing, the suburbs of the town were defended by an earthen entrenchment hastily thrown up by the Spaniards a couple of years previously. But since the French had held Ciudad Rodrigo they had utilised three convents, large and substantial buildings, in the general defence, fortifying them and placing guns in battery upon their flat roofs.

Wellington, having resolved to attack from the north side, was compelled, in the first instance, to get possession of the redoubt of San Francisco on the Greater Tesson. This was effected upon the night of the 8th January in most gallant style by a portion of the Light Division, led by Lieut.-Colonel Colborne, one of the most brilliant of the soldiers who earned fame in the Peninsular War. Major George Napier, who has been mentioned already, had volunteered, but Wellington said the stormers should be commanded by the first field-officer for duty. Colborne's orders were given so clearly and precisely that it was impossible to misunderstand them. The storming party was to descend into the ditch, cut away the palisades, and climb over into the redoubt. They moved forward about 9 p.m., the watchword being "England and St. George;" and finding the palisades close to the outward side of the ditch, sprang on them without waiting to break them down. Then they rushed on "with so much fury that the assailants appeared to be at one and the same time in the ditch, mounting the parapets, fighting on the top of the ramparts, and forcing the gorge of the redoubt." Such undaunted courage was irresistible. The garrison of the redoubt were all killed or made prisoners, and this with only the most trifling loss on our side.

The capture of the redoubt was the signal for "breaking ground," as it is called, the digging of the first trench or parallel—the first of the series of zigzags or approaches—under cover of which the assailants creep up to a fortress which is being besieged. The work must be done at night, and quickly. A whole brigade covered this operation, and 700 men with pick and shovel laboured to such purpose that a trench three feet deep and four feet wide was dug by daylight. Once safely established at a height which gave a good view of the whole place, the English engineers proceeded to lay out batteries and improve the parallel. The work was continued the next night, and so on, 1,200 men being regularly employed in pushing forward inch by inch till a point was reached near enough to batter down the walls and make a breach in the place. Five days were thus fully occupied, the daily progress being always good, although the siege was marked with vicissitudes which tended to retard it. The enemy's artillery was powerful according to the ideas of those days—although now the heaviest would be thought a mere popgun—and their fire was often most destructive, both to the assailants- and their works.

On the night of the 13th the English batteries were armed with 28 guns; one convent—that of Santa Cruz—was taken and secured on the right flank. Next day the French made a successful sortie at the time when the guards of the trenches were being changed, and when the old relief did not wait for the new, but retired in a hasty and disorderly manner. The works being thus left unguarded, the enterprising garrison did them much mischief, and might have gone so far as to spike the guns, but the sortie was checked by the stout stand made by a few of the workmen collected together by an officer of engineers.

After this the battering-guns were directed upon the convent of San Francisco, and fired up with great vigour till dusk, when the building was forcibly entered and captured. Next day the fire was concentrated upon the ramparts at two particular points—one known hereafter as "the great breach," where the walls jutted forward at a very salient angle; the other upon a turret, within the inner line of defence, and this was called the "lesser breach." The battering continued fiercely and without intermission until the 18th January. Towards evening on that day the tower and turret were seen to be in a ruinous condition, and the opening at the main or great breach was yawning wide enough to justify an attempt to enter. This was the deadly work of just ten days. The outer wall, or *fausse braie*, was greatly shaken: there were two formidable breaches in the main wails, and sweeping discharges of grape and canister prevented the garrison from repairing them.

Then Wellington, ready to avoid unnecessary bloodshed, summoned the place to surrender. The French commandant, General Barrié, bravely refused, declaring that his emperor had entrusted him with the defence of the fortress, and that he could not give it up. The message ran:

"On the contrary, my brave garrison prefers to be buried with me under its ruins."

Assault became inevitable therefore, and Wellington at once issued his orders, prefacing them with the memorable words already quoted, that Ciudad Rodrigo must be attacked that evening. There is no more striking picture in our military records than that of the Great Duke seated on the reverse or inner side of one of the advanced approaches

writing out his orders with his own hand, after having made a close reconnaissance of both breaches. The minuteness of these orders, the mastery of intricate details, which in such a position he must necessarily have carried in his head, his strong grasp of the situation, and his unerring decision as to the method and best points of attack, show the great British general at his best.

There were to be two principal attacks, made by the two divisions on trench duty that evening—the night between the 18th and 19th January. These were the 3rd and Light Divisions. To the first was entrusted the assault upon the main breach, to the latter that on the lesser or breach by the tower. The brigade of General Mackinnon was to lead the first, supported by Campbell's brigade; Vandaleur's led, and Andrew Barnard's brigade supported, the second. Both were to be preceded by forlorn hopes and storming parties, with others carrying wool-bags and ladders to facilitate descent into the ditch and the escalade of the walls. The eagerness, the noble emulation, among British soldiers to be foremost in these, the most dangerous services in an assault, were well illustrated on this occasion. George Napier, who had obtained a promise from his general, the famous but ill-fated Craufurd, that he should lead the Light Division stormers, was directed to call for volunteers. The intrepid young major, addressing the 43rd, 52nd, and Rifle Corps, said:—

"'Soldiers. I want a hundred volunteers from each regiment: those who will go with me, step forward.' Instantly there rushed out nearly half the division, and we were obliged to take them at chance"

Such is Napier's own account of the affair written years afterwards.

Seven o'clock in the evening was the time fixed for the assault, which was to be led off by Pack's Portuguese. A regiment under Colonel O'Toole crossed the river and attacked the work in front of the castle, lending a hand to another column, which, issuing from behind the convent of Santa Cruz, and consisting of the 5th and 94th regiments, supported by the 77th, were to cover the attack of the main breach by Mackinnon's brigade. The latter were not slow to advance: even before the signal was given, and while Wellington in person on the left was instructing Napier how to move with the Light Division stormers, the 3rd division had rushed on to the breach. First came a party of sappers with hay-bags to fill up the ditch; then the stormers, 500 strong, under Major Manners, preceded by a forlorn hope; then the whole brigade. The whole space between the advanced parallel and the ramparts was alive with troops advancing reckless of the  iron tempest that ravaged their ranks. Already on their right the column from Santa Cruz had made good its entrance and scoured the opening between the two walls of defence, driving the French before them. This cleared the ground for Mackinnon's men, who pressed gallantly on; but they were met by a retrenchment, a fresh obstacle, a parapet and ditch constructed within the breach, and behind which the defenders offered a still stubborn resistance.

At this moment, while the assailants were vainly seeking to cross the ditch, a mine was sprung with a terrible explosion which proved fatal to many, including the brave Mackinnon. Still the remainder held their ground; and now Mackie, who led the forlorn hope, clambered over the rampart wall and dropped inside, to find there an

opening on one side of the main breach by which an entrance was possible. Climbing back, he collected his men and led them by this road into the interior of the place. About this time they encountered and joined O'Toole's Portuguese regiment, and, the whole of these columns of attack having made good their footing, established themselves strongly among the ruined fortifications, awaiting the result of their comrades' attack.

Meanwhile the Light Division, whose goal was the lesser breach, had also got down to serious business. The stormers, with their forlorn hope, were formed under the shelter of the San Francisco convent, and were there addressed by General Craufurd, the divisional general, whose fiery spirit kept him always in the forefront, and who intended now to charge at the head of the attacking party. Craufurd's name will long be remembered in connection with this Light Division, which by his unwearied efforts and his stern, relentless discipline, he had trained into one of the finest bodies of British troops that ever fought through a campaign. This was the last occasion, unhappily, on which he was to stand at the head of his men, and his short, stirring speech to the stormers were almost the last words he spoke. The words are so reported by one who heard them, he said:

"Soldiers the eyes of your country are upon you. Be steady; be cool; be firm in the assault. The town must be yours this night. Once masters of the wall, let your first duty be to clear the ramparts, and in doing this keep together."

A rocket was to be signal for the advance, and when its fiery track was seen in the black sky Craufurd added briefly, "Now, lads, for the breach!" and led the way.

He did not long survive. As the columns advanced he kept to their left, and, posting himself on a point of vantage, continued to give his instructions while his men entered the ditch. His voice, raised to the loudest pitch, drew down upon him a fierce fire of musketry at short range, and his situation was of such extreme peril that, not strangely, he was soon hit, and with a mortal wound.

There were some three hundred yards to cross under a murderous fire, but the men raced forward and, disdaining to wait for ladders, jumped down a depth of eleven feet into the ditch, which was swept with a storm of grape and musketry. Here some of the forlorn hope went to the left instead of to the right; the main body of the stormers took the proper direction, but were checked at the breach because the opening was so narrow. This crushed the attacking column into a compact mass, upon which the enemy's fire told with terrible effect. Just now George Napier, its leader, was struck down. The men halted, irresolute, and, forgetting they were unloaded, began to snap their muskets. Then their wounded chief, from where he lay disabled, shouted "Push on with the bayonet!" And the wisdom of his decision in the early part of the evening was plain, for the stormers answered the inspiriting command with a loud "Hurrah!" and pressed hotly forward. The breach was carried; the supporting regiments—Vandaleur's whole brigade—"coming up in sections abreast, gained the rampart, the 52nd wheeled to the left, the 43rd to the right, and the place was won."

All this had occupied but a few minutes in time. The battle was thus, practically, decided, but other successes contributed to the general result. The struggle at the great breach was still being maintained when three of the French magazines in this neighbourhood exploded, and then the 3rd Division broke through the last defences. The garrison still resisted, however, fighting as they fell back from street to street; but finally the castle, their last stronghold, was captured, and Lieutenant Gurwood, who had led the Light Division forlorn hope, received the governor's sword. The attacks on all other sides had prospered equally, both O'Toole's and Pack's, the latter having entered without opposition on the south-eastern front of the fortress.

It would be well if there was no more to be said of the capture of Ciudad Rodrigo. But unhappily the glory of this great achievement was greatly tarnished by the shameful excesses of the victorious troops. The French garrison, it is true, were spared; there was no cruel and unnecessary carnage where the men laid down their arms. This is proved by the fact that out of a total garrison of 1,800 men, 1,500 were taken prisoners. But the town itself was plundered, under the most wanton and brutal circumstances. Houses were ransacked and burnt, churches desecrated and destroyed; the wine vaults and spirit stores were broken open, universal drunkenness prevailed, and every species of enormity was perpetrated. No Englishman can read of the sack of Ciudad Rodrigo, and of other Spanish fortresses during that war, without a blush of shame at the madness which overtook brave men in the hour of their triumph.

It is pleasanter to think of their deeds of prowess or their cool courage in the face of danger. There is a story told of an old soldier, who during the siege treated a live shell in a way that would in these days have certainly earned him the Victoria Cross. A 13-inch shell had dropped into the trench, and everyone within reach had fallen flat upon his face as the custom was, for when shells explode the pieces fly upwards, and a recumbent position is the safest till the danger is over. But this one man ran up to the shell and knocked out the still burning fuse with a blow of his spade. Then he carried the now harmless projectile to his commanding officer, saying: "She can do your honour no harm now, for I've knocked the life out of her."

The capture of Ciudad Rodrigo had important consequences, for it paved the way to that still more brilliant feat of ours, the taking of Badajoz. It was a triumphant vindication of Wellington's iron and unquenchable spirit, for at the outset everything seemed against him—the season, the condition of the country, the state of his troops, the inferior quality of the siege material. The tools supplied by the British storekeeper were as bad as the bayonets so recently held up to public scorn, and the English engineers were eager to pick up the enemy's implements and use them whenever they could. At the moment of the

attack it was found that the army was unprovided with scaling-ladders. "Well," said Wellington quietly, "you must make them—out of the waggons. The transport has done its work, by bringing up ammunition and supplies: cut up the waggons."

JUNE-DECEMBER 1812
Napoleon's Moscow Campaign

D. H. Parry

One must go back through centuries of history to find anything approaching the horrors of the Russian War of 1812. Towards the end of June, 610,058 armed men and an enormous multitude of non-combatants—women and children—crossed the broad Niemen, joined afterwards by 37,100 more, making a total of 647,158; and on the 13th December—or rather less than six months later—16,000 alone repassed that river with weapons in their bruised and frozen hands, almost the sole remains of a magnificent army whose bones are to this day turned up by the plough of the Russian peasant.

******

The Niemen flows between Prussia and Poland; and in the forest of Pilwisky, behind the rocky heights on the Prussian side, a multitude of men lay concealed, speaking a score of tongues, and wearing a strange variety of uniform, many nations having sent their best and bravest to swell the ranks of the *Grande Armée*.

The famous Imperial Guard was sleeping in the green corn, dreaming of future conquests, and that mighty host awaited the word of one man to embark on a campaign whose disasters have had no equal—one little pale-faced man dressed now in a long grey riding-coat and a Polish cap—the man who, by the force of his own intellect and the marvellous power of using men and circumstances to his own ends, had ground the whole of Europe—England alone excepted—under the heel of his military boot!

At two o'clock in the morning of June 23rd Napoleon mounted

his horse and rode off to reconnoitre the river, his charger stumbling and throwing him on to the sandy bank.

A voice exclaimed in the darkness: "That is a bad augury: a Roman would go back." But no one knew who had spoken, and, after ordering three bridges to be constructed for the following night, the little party returned to its quarters, the words sinking ominously into their hearts.

Next evening some sappers, with their white leather aprons and keen axes, crossed in a boat, and were met by a Cossack officer, who rode forward alone to inquire what they wanted in Russia.

"We are Frenchmen," said one of the sappers, "come to make war upon you—to take Wilna—to liberate Poland!"

The solitary horseman disappeared without a word, and the sappers fired their muskets into the silent woods. For three whole days the tramp of men and the heavy rumble of guns filled the air as the army filed down to the banks, and poured across the bridges—grenadiers, *voltigeurs*, *chasseurs*, and dragoons, regiment succeeding regiment, corps after corps. Now the scarlet and green of the 8th Hussars; again the heavy squadrons of Sebastiani's *cuirassiers*, smart Polish lancers of the Guard and Line, *carabineers* with brass body-armour and snow-white uniforms, long trains of lumbering artillery, waggons and field-forges, carriages, and caissons, the sutler's cart jostling the *caleche* of the general officer, a sultry sun overhead, and the river dancing in merry ripples beneath them as the bridges trembled under the tread of the marching thousands.

Napoleon crossed at Poniemen with his Guard, the corps of Marshals Davout, Oudinot, and Ney, and Murat's dashing cavalry; Prince Eugène, with the army of Italy, passed at Piloni on the 9th; and Jerome Bonaparte's Westphalians advanced upon Grodno which they reached

NAPOLEON'S MARCH
From the Niemen to Moscow.
1812.

on the 30th. To the north Macdonald attacked Riga on the Baltic, and Prince Schwartzenberg marched through Galicia in the south; but it is the army of the centre, under the emperor himself, whose fortunes we shall most closely follow, omitting the marches of the thirteen divisions into which the invading forces were formed, and not pausing to notice the minor actions in which they were sooner or later engaged.

Hardly had Napoleon gained the enemy's side than a black cloud gathered in the sky, and a furious storm broke over the country for fifty leagues right and left. The rain descended with surprising violence, the air grew piercingly cold, and the flat land covered with tall black pine-trees became a swamp, through which they splashed dismally onward.

Ten thousand horses died, heated by the green corn which formed their forage, and then chilled by the rain as they stood shivering in their exposed bivouacs.

The bridge across the Vilia having been destroyed by retreating Cossacks, Napoleon impatiently ordered a squadron of the Polish lancers of the Guard to swim the swollen stream, and, clad in crimson uniforms, faced with dark blue and laced with silver, they gained the centre, only to be carried away by the current, and many of them drowned, crying "*Vive l'Empereur!*" as their heads disappeared under water.

Beyond Wilna, Octave de Ségur (brother of the historian) and his 8th Hussars drew first blood from the Russians, and were sadly cut up; but Oudinot drove Witgenstein back at the same moment, and, sending Murat in pursuit, the emperor returned to Wilna, to waste twenty days in raising unsatisfactory levies, and to disgust the Poles with disappointing hopes of liberty.

Russian proposals of peace were rejected by Napoleon, whose entire conduct during the campaign has baffled his friends and foes; and leaving Wilna at half-past eleven at night on the 16th July, he marched

to attack Barclay de Tolly, provided he could find him.

Two hundred and fifty thousand Russians had been formed into three distinct armies—the First Army of the West under De Tolly;

the Second, under Prince Bagration; and the Third, which was not then completed, under the cavalry general Tormasoff; 18.000 Cossacks being distributed among them, those of the Hetman Platoff especially destined to win a terrible renown. The infantry wore green, with slate pantaloons and mud-coloured great-coats, the officers affecting wasp waists, tremendous curled whiskers, and gold rings in their ears. The Cossacks of the line were dressed for the most part in blue, with fur caps and long lances; generally swarming with vermin, they were mounted on active little horses, which they urged on with whips, there being also bands of wild horsemen called Baskirs, who used *bows and arrows* with a precision that caused mourning in many a French home.

The war assumed a curious character: on through the swamps and lonely forests of Lithuania, interspersed here and there by deserts of choking sand, the long columns wound; the Russians burning their villages as they retired, the French in their turn destroying what the Russians had left, devastation and disorder marking every league of the way; the roads dotted with the bodies of dead men and horses, who had sunk with fatigue, and the rear-guard of the enemy disappearing as the French advance-guard came in sight of it.

Napoleon derided the foe as arrant cowards; but the persistent retreat was all part of a wise policy, originated by De Tolly, to draw them into an unknown country, far from their magazines, until hunger, forced marches, the burning heat of the days followed by nights of intense cold, and last of all the terrible winter of those latitudes, should crumble away the army and utterly destroy it.

The young blood of Russia naturally revolted at such a course and wished to fight, but results have justified its adoption, the significant fact remaining as additional proof of its wisdom, that in nearly every instance during the advance, where the two forces came into contact, the French proved victorious.

At Ostrowno the remnants of the 8th Hussars came up with three Russian cavalry regiments, and routed them in quick succession among the birch woods; Murat ordering some Poles of the line to charge, and being obliged to lead them, although, as commander, he should have kept out of danger.

The lances were lowered in a glittering row behind him, and the troopers, gay in blue and yellow, came thundering on. From the nature of the ground escape was impossible, so, making a virtue of necessity, the King of Naples flourished his famous riding-switch, galloped at their

head, and the charge was successful: the 106th took the Russians on one side, Piré's Hussars and 16th Chasseurs on the other. The French artillery resumed its fire; and falling back in disorder, the foe melted away into the forest that hid Witepsk.

At that place De Tolly made a stand, hearing that Bagration was about to join him; and Napoleon saw the sun glinting on the arms of eighty thousand men on a bright July morning, as two hundred *voltigeurs* of the 9th crossed a narrow bridge and formed in front of the Russian horse.

Murat sent the 16th Chasseurs-à-cheval at the enemy, without any support; but though their sky-blue facings had figured in almost every campaign since 1793, they had no chance single-handed on broken ground, and the Cossacks of the Guard put them to the rightabout, pursuing as far as a hill on which the emperor stood, and only being driven off by the carbines of his personal escort. On their way back the Cossacks attacked the *voltigeurs* with great fury, the army holding its breath and regarding them as lost; but the little band took post in some brushwood, and routed the lancers in full view of both forces, the French clapping their hands and cheering their comrades to the echo. Napoleon sending to inquire to what corps the heroes belonged.

"To the Ninth," was the reply; "and three-fourths of us are lads of Paris."

"Tell them that they are brave fellows," said the emperor to his *aide-de-cam*p, "and that they all deserve the Legion of Honour"—one account stating that every man received it.

Murat, Eugène, and Lobau rushed on the enemy's left, and compelled him to retire behind the Luczissa; but believing that De Tolly meant at last to stand his ground, Napoleon stopped the conflict, although it was only eleven o'clock, saying to Murat: "Tomorrow at five you will see the sun of Austerlitz."

The morrow came; the sun rose redly through the mists; but the wise Barclay had vanished, having learned during the night that Bagration had been worsted, the French discovering *one* Russian asleep in a thicket, and not a reliable trace of the direction the others had taken.

The expedition had never been popular, either with officers or men, and they began to grumble with good cause; for an army that had conquered Prussia in fourteen days, and whose standards were heavy with the gilded names of a hundred glorious victories, had now penetrated for more than a month into a land teeming with discomforts. Many of the regiments were shoeless, the cavalry horses died by dozens every day, the hospitals were full of sick; extremes of heat and cold, bad food and little of it, blinding dust, a draught of muddy water to wash it down—all this and more had been their daily lot since they crossed the Niemen, and there had been no great battle to revive their drooping hearts; besides which, the rye bread seriously disagreed with them, and dysentery and deadly typhus laying its wasting hand upon them, had already sadly thinned their ranks.

Their pride, too, sustained a shock when news came that the advance-guard had been repulsed at Aghaponovtchina; and at length awaking from a lethargic dream, the emperor sent the various corps into cantonments on the skirts of Poland, Russia proper still before them; and returning to Witepsk with his Guard, took off his sword and laid it on his maps, saying:

"Here I halt. . . . The campaign of 1812 is over; that of 1813 will do the rest!"

But his ambition gave him no peace. Murat came riding in from the front, his green *surtout* all laced and bejewelled, and urged his brother-in-law to action; and although Napoleon went daily to inspect the huge ovens, where 39,000 loaves of bread were baked at a time, and arranged that theatrical companies should come from Paris to enliven the dreary winter months, his suite soon began to find him bending down to his maps again, turning his eyes towards Smolensk and Moscow.

Soon afterwards he came across a proclamation calling upon Russia to rise and exterminate the invaders, and containing some very forcible home-truths which enraged him; and hearing, to his great chagrin, that Alexander had made peace with Turkey, he gathered up his legions in four days, left Witepsk to join them on the 13th of August, and rushed headlong into difficulties and disaster, from which neither he nor his army ever recovered.

By one of those masterly movements of his (so conspicuously absent during the rest of the war), he crossed the front of the Russian army unknown to them, and two days later fell unexpectedly on their left flank at Krasnoë.

Ney forced the town, to find General Néwérowskoi beyond it,

with 6,000 infantry and Cossacks belonging to Bagration, which formed into a square of such thickness that the French cavalry sabred its way far in without being able to break it, and the tall corn, now mellowed by Autumn's breath, saw some ghastly work as Néwérowskoi came to a strong palisade and had to halt; his rear ranks facing round to fire on the Wurtemberg Horse, while the front-rank tore down the obstacle; the body succeeding in their escape, although they left 1,200 dead, 1,000 wounded, and eight guns in the hands of the French, who fired a salute in honour of the victory, which happened to have fallen on Napoleon's birthday.

The good folk of Smolensk were coming out of church, where they had been returning thanks somewhat prematurely, when Néwérowskoi's fugitives poured panting into the city, closely followed by Marshal Ney, who, receiving a ball in the neck, lost his temper, and led a battalion at the charge against the citadel, under a hail of musketry that slew two-thirds of them.

Falling back to a hill whence he could reconnoitre, he conducted Napoleon thither, who exclaimed, "At last I have them!" as several immense columns of men were seen hastening towards them on the other side of the Dnieper, being nothing less than Barclay and Bagration with 120,000 troops, coming on at a run, after learning how the emperor had outwitted them, and arriving out of breath to succour the threatened city.

Some sanguinary fighting took place, and a great battle was expected for the next day; but the wily De Tolly again retreated, his black columns being discovered on the opposite bank marching swiftly away, to the mortification of the invaders.

Even the fiery Murat tired of the campaign, and at length urged Napoleon to stop; but the emperor persevered, and the King of Naples, exclaiming prophetically as he strode out o Napoleon's tent, "Moscow will be our destruction!" galloped to the front of a Russian battery, flung himself from his horse, and waited for a ball to kill him.

A violent attack was made on the city; twenty-two men fell by a single shot from a Russian gun, while Murat, who courted death, was unhurt. The gorgeous artillery of the Guard pounded unceasingly. An attempt to storm the place was baffled by the defenders, and when night descended, Smolensk was seen to be in flames, the army finally entering the city to find it a heap of smouldering ruins, and the state of the army itself truly terrible.

General Rapp, who had ridden post to join Napoleon, and who

consequently followed their route, gave a vivid recital of the misery and devastation he had witnessed in the rear. Sebastiani revealed the condition of affairs in the heavy cavalry, and the emperor could close his eyes no longer.

"It is frightful, I am fully aware," he said. "I must extort peace from the enemy, and that can be done only at Moscow."

At the hill of Valoutina a shocking conflict was waged by the gallant Ney far into the night, both sides fighting with terrible fury. Ju-

not, Duke of Abrantes, the Emperor's old companion-in-arms, showed symptoms of the insanity that caused him to commit suicide not long after; and failing to charge at the right moment, the enemy saved his baggage and wounded. General Gudin was killed, the whole army mourning the loss of as gallant and good a man as ever fell in action.

Lieutenant Etienne, of the 12th, took the Russian General Toutchkoff, in the middle of his troops. Napoleon gave eighty-seven crosses to Gudin's regiments, and presented an eagle to the 127th with his own hands; but the misery of the troops outweighed the glory they had gained: they had seen seven hundred wounded Russians left untended for three days at Witepsk, and the French surgeons tearing up their own shirts for bandages; at Smolensk, fifteen large brick buildings saved from the fire were then full of groaning men, Lariboissiere's gun-wadding and the parchments in the city archives being used to dress their wounds. There, also, a hospital containing a hundred sick was overlooked for three days, until Rapp discovered it by chance. Eleven thousand Bavarians had been *marched* to death without firing a shot, and discipline was so lax that at Slawkowo the Guard burnt for firewood the only bridge by which the emperor could continue his route next day.

Many *cuirassiers* rode on native ponies, regiments straggled along and pillaged without check, Davout's corps alone preserving anything like its usual order: the popular impression that the French disasters began with the winter's snow is utterly false; the Army of the Centre alone, under Napoleon in person, having lost 105,500 in fifty-two days, and advancing on Moscow with only 182,000, after deducting 13,500 left at Smolensk.

Everything pointed to a decisive battle to restore the *morale* of the *Grande Armée*, and Napoleon seemed for the moment to pull himself together, if we may be permitted a homely phrase. Countless orders were despatched, every carriage was to be destroyed that was likely to retard the advance, and meeting with that of his *aide-de-camp* Narbonne, he had it burned before his eyes, without allowing the general to remove a single article.

A change came over the Russian tactics at the same time: all ranks clamoured for a leader who would fight and not retreat, and consequently De Tolly was replaced by old Kutusoff, who, notwithstanding his defeat at Austerlitz, was a Russian, and beloved by the army for his superstitious practices, and an affectation of Suvarrow's eccentricity of manner.

The French advanced in three columns, and troops of Cossacks began to hover round them threateningly. Beyond Gjatz, Murat became so annoyed at the hordes of those filthy, unkempt horsemen, that he rushed forward, and standing in his stirrups, with the very sublimity of conceit, waved them back with his sword, and they retired in astonishment and admiration.

But soon the high road debouched on to a natural battleground, and dark masses of troops were seen drawn up in solid bodies, there

being no longer any doubt that the Russians intended fighting to cover "The Holy City," Moscow, a large field-work commanding the road itself, bristling with cannon in a threatening manner.

The army attacked without delay, and drove the foe back to a range of hills. General Compans leading the 61st, with bayonets fixed, against the fortification.

Three times they took it, and three times they were dislodged; but at length, other positions being forced in their rear, the brave garrison evacuated the bloodstained ramparts, and Compans retained possession.

Among the heaped-up slain inside, a Russian artilleryman, decorated with several crosses, lay beside his gun, grasping it even in death with one hand, and clenching the hilt of his broken sword with the other; while next day, when Napoleon reviewed the survivors of the 61st, he asked, with surprise, what had become of the 3rd Battalion.

"It is in the redoubt," said the colonel grimly. A cold drizzle began to fall that night, and Napoleon, through the striped curtains of his tent, pitched in a square of the "Old Guard," saw a great semicircle of fire from the Russian bivouacs.

He slept little, and went early in his grey riding-coat to reconnoitre once more, afraid even then that the foe might retreat; but when morning came the huge force was still in position, extending for six miles, the flanks retired, and the centre advanced towards him.

Its right was protected by a marsh, its centre strongly entrenched, a strong redoubt mounting twenty-two guns frowned near the left centre, and the entire left wing was on lower ground, terminating on the old Moscow road, with two more redoubts before it. To turn that left wing, storm the works, and drive the Russians into the marshes on the opposite flank was the emperor's plan, the battle proving one of the most murderous ever fought by the *Grande Armée*, and known afterwards by them as the "Battle of the Generals," from the number who fell there, or, officially, the Mosqua, from the river flowing near— the Russians naming it after the village of Borodino, where some of the hardest fighting took place.

Marmont's *aide-de-camp* arrived with the news of that marshal's defeat at Salamanca, but the disaster was forgotten in another incident— namely, the unexpected receipt of a portrait of Napoleon's little son, the King of Rome, which he showed to the grenadiers at his tent door.

A proclamation was issued to the army, beginning: "Soldiers! behold the battle which you have so ardently desired! Victory now depends on yourselves," and concluding with the words, "Let it be said of you—'he was in the great battle under the walls of Moscow'"; but being distributed late, many regiments went into action without reading it.

It was the 7th September. A sky of cloudless blue stretched over the amphitheatre of hills, where the leaves were already falling, and at six o'clock Count Sorbier opened fire. Pernetty and Compans were in full march; the Russian processions of priests in glittering vestments that had chanted hymns and invoked the aid of Heaven retired precipitately, and an hour later Davout had his first horse killed under him as the fighting became general.

Compans' division found itself before one of the enemy's works,

and Charriere, colonel of the famous 57th, gave the simple command, "To the redoubt!" the regiment running briskly forward up the slope with a shout.

Compans fell wounded, Dessaix had his arm broken a little later, and Rapp took command.

"Grape shot, grape shot—nothing but grape shot!" cried Belliard to the artillery, as a heavy column of Russians poured down to resist the attack. Within sixty minutes Rapp was hit four times, the fourth time on the left hip—the twenty-second wound received in his exciting career; and while Poniatowski struggled with his weak corps among the pine-trees on the Russian left, Delzon advanced with drums beating, on the village of Borodino, where Plauzonne was killed at the head of the 16th, and where the 30th had to fight its way out, leaving General Bonnomy badly wounded, Morand's eighty guns tearing the dense mass before him, and Ney seizing the heights of Chewarino.

The fiercest conflict raged about the redoubts. Two were retaken by the Russians, and the third was in danger, when Murat dismounted and, waving his plumed cap with one hand, laid about him with a private's musket.

So terrible was the carnage that one colonel ordered his men to retire, and Murat, seizing him by the collar, demanded what he was doing.

"We can stay here no longer," said the colonel, pointing to half his regiment dead on the trampled ground.

"I can stay here very well myself," exclaimed Murat.

"*Eh bien*," replied the officer, looking steadily at him: "soldiers, face to the foe—*to be slain!*"

Rapp, carried wounded before the emperor, had said to him, "The Guard is required to finish it," but Napoleon shook his head, saying, "No, I will not have that destroyed—I will gain the battle without it."

It was noon, and though the Russian left had been forced, they still stood their ground obstinately. Murat sent four times for the Guard, but Napoleon paced slowly up and down, always returning to his chair, some cannon shot rolling almost to his feet; and it was obvious that he was not himself, he saying repeatedly during the day that "he did not see the moves clearly on his chess board," the old activity of mind and body having apparently forsaken the greatest warrior that Europe has ever produced.

The thunder of a thousand guns boomed and echoed far and near, the French alone firing ninety thousand rounds and many *millions* of ball cartridge.

The Russians re-formed for the third time, and General Montbrun, at the head of the heavy cavalry, was killed by a ball from the great redoubt.

"Do not weep," said Auguste Caulaincourt, who took command,

to Montbrun's *aides*. "Follow me, and avenge him!" and crying to Murat, "You shall see me there immediately, dead or alive!" he placed himself at the head of the 5th Cuirassiers, whose long swords gleamed in the bright sunshine, and turning to the left, entered by a gorge, and took the work, falling mortally wounded at the moment of victory, and dying within an hour. He was only thirty, and had left Paris to join the army on his wedding day.

Dense smoke clouded the heights, rolling into the ravines to shroud the wretched wounded; flames showed where villages were blazing, the crash of muskets and the shouts of 250,000 men only diminishing as they fell by thousands to redden the soil, or to crawl shrieking to the rear, where the surgeons, under Baron Larrey, were busy from morning until long after darkness came.

Kutusoff had made so sure of victory that he was feasting with his staff well out of danger, the bulletin announcing a French defeat already written, when officers came crying for reinforcements, the conceited old man at first refusing to listen to any details that differed from his own idea of what *ought* to be taking place, his long pigtail wagging incredulously the while. But the reports were true. The French had won the plain, and were battling for the heights with irresistible fury.

Eugène improved Caulaincourt's success; Belliard shattered the last Russian attack with the concentrated fire of thirty guns; Lauriston galloped up the reserve artillery, and did tremendous execution; and Grouchy— so well known in after years from the undeserved abuse showered on his brave head—had swept the high road and the plain beside it. The Russians, beaten in detail, retired to a second range of

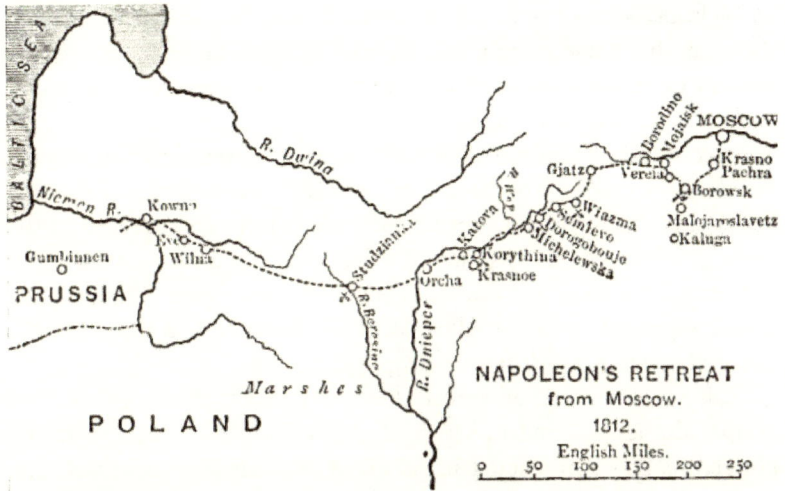

NAPOLEON'S RETREAT from Moscow. 1812.

heights, from which the army was too exhausted to dislodge them without the assistance of the Guard, and night saw the two battered and bleeding forces still facing each other amid a fearful *débris* of slain.

On the French side. Davout had been hit three times; Generals Montbrun, Caulaincourt, Plauzonne, Huard, Compere, Marion, and Lepel were killed; Nansouty, Grouchy, Rapp, Compans, Dessaix, Morand, Lahoussaye, and many more—some forty in all—had been hit; and of the soldiers 35,000 lay dead and wounded, mangled by the showers of grape and the large musket balls used by the Russians.

They, on their side, counted three generals, 1,500 officers, and 36,000 men killed and wounded, accounts varying greatly as to the number of prisoners taken by the French, some making them 5,000, others 700 or 800 at the most.

Riding slowly across the battlefield, when the surgeons and the burial-parties were doing their ghastly work, the hoof of Napoleon's charger brought a groan from a prostrate form, and one of the staff remarked in his hearing, that "it was only a Russian"!

"After a victory," exclaimed Napoleon severely, "none are enemies, all are men."

The army advanced and fought a sharp action at Mojaisk, where the emperor lay for three days, burnt up with fever, and compelled, notwithstanding, to transact enormous arrears of business—dictating to seven people at once, and. when his voice left him, explaining with difficulty by writing and signs.

He left Mojaisk on the 12th of September to join the advance-guard in that famous travelling-carriage which Londoners know so well, his legions reduced to 198,000; and two days later, having mounted his horse once more, he saw the goal of his ambition, the ancient capital of Russia, glowing in the light of the afternoon sun.

In the centre of a vast plain, and built, like Rome, on seven hills, the two hundred and ninety-five churches and countless magnificent buildings of the "city of the gilded cupolas," twenty miles in circumference, with a river meandering through it, burst on the view of the army as it crested the "Mount of Salvation," and a shout went up of "Moscow! Moscow!" as the soldiers cheered and clapped their hands; whole regiments of Poles falling on their knees to thank the God of Battles for delivering it into their grasp.

Fairy-like it stretched before them, dazzling with the green of its copper domes and the minarets of yellow stone. Oriental in its architecture, and constructed in Asiatic style with five enclosures one within the other, it was like some fabled city of the Arabian Nights, sparkling with brilliant colours, the famous Kremlin towering above the palaces and gardens.

The advance-guard under Murat mingled with bands of Cossacks, who applauded him for his known valour, and the king distributed his jewellery and that of his staff among them; but an officer arrived from Miloradowitch with a threat of burning the city if his rear-guard were not allowed time to evacuate it.

Napoleon stayed his march therefore, and the day wore on. When Murat at last entered by the Dorogomilow Gate, he found that Moscow was deserted: the streets were empty, the houses closed, a few loathsome wretches released from the prisons, and a handful of the lowest of the low, alone surged round their horses near the Kremlin; but the inhabitants were gone, in a cloud of dust that hid the retreating Russian army, towards Voladimir. The gates of the Kremlin were battered open by cannon shot, a convoy of provisions captured, some thousands of stragglers were afterwards taken, but that was all; and on the gate of the governor's mansion at Voronowo. the following notice was found in French:

"I have passed eight years in embellishing this retreat, in which I have lived happily in the bosom of my family; the inhabitants of this property, to the number of seventeen hundred and twenty, quit it at your approach, and I set fire to my house in order that it may not be defiled by your presence. Frenchmen, I have abandoned to you my two houses in Moscow, with furniture to the value of half a million of *roubles*. *Here* you will find nothing but ashes.—Rostopschin."

With the army singing the "*Marseillaise*" Napoleon entered at night, and appointed Marshal Mortier governor, saying: "No pillage—your head shall be responsible for it." And though several French residents acquainted him with the Russian intention of burning the city—that the senate had agreed to it with only seven dissentient voices, that all the engines had been removed, and they were treading on the brink of a volcano—he refused to believe it, and tried in vain to sleep.

At two o'clock in the morning they brought him news that Moscow was on fire!

When daylight came he hurried to the spot to reprimand Mortier and the Young Guard, but the marshal showed him that black smoke was issuing from houses that had not been opened, and the whole affair had evidently been carefully planned.

He went to the Kremlin—a vast structure, half palace, half castle, surmounted by the great Cross of Ivan, and built on a hill—from which he wrote overtures of peace to the *Czar*, overtures that received no attention.

In spite of the efforts of the soldiers the flames spread, a ball of fire had been let down into Prince Trubetskoi's palace, the *bazaar* was in a blaze, and the strong north wind blew towards the Kremlin itself, which, report whispered, was undermined.

Murat, Eugène, and Berthier urged the emperor to leave the city, without success: he had come there, and there he would remain—a conqueror in the very centre of the Russian empire. But the cry arose that the Kremlin itself was on fire: a police-agent was discovered near the burning tower, and bayoneted by the Old Guard almost in Napoleon's presence. There was no longer time for hesitation, or dreams of empty glory, and passing down the northern staircase, where the massacre of the Strelitzes took place under Peter the Great, he left the city for the castle of Petrowsky, a league on the St. Petersburg road.

The army also marched out, encamping in the fields, eating their horse-flesh from silver dishes and swathing their wounds with costly silks, the rain falling in torrents, and Moscow a sheet of fire for four days.

Much has been written of Napoleon's escape by a postern, of hurried wanderings through burning lanes, past convoys of powder, which the whirling sparks might have ignited at any moment, and various dramatic situations dear to the French historian. In point of fact, he ran little personal risk, and left the Kremlin by the great gate, returning thither when the flames had abated, and ordering the Guard to occupy the ruins of the city on the 20th and 21st.

About a tenth of the houses remained intact, especially in the

Kitaigorod, or Chinese quarter; many rich merchants' dwellings, and here and there a palace or church reared their barbaric forms amid the general chaos; gay flower-beds still bloomed in the suburbs, and the old red wall that surrounded' the Kremlin was comparatively unharmed; but the aspect of the place, which should have furnished winter quarters for the *Grande Armée*, struck a chill into the hearts of all, and caused the emperor to say that "the commerce of Russia was ruined for a century, and the nation had been put back fifty years." In *six*, however, a new Moscow had arisen and Napoleon was a captive in St. Helena!

Six thousand Russian wounded are said to have been in the city when the French entered: what became of them one dare not contemplate.

On the return of the troops universal pillage became the order of the day, and readers of the early French editions of Labaume's narrative will understand why I pass much over in silence. Some of the inhabitants had returned, others had been concealed in the vaults of churches and the cellars of their homes; but the grenadiers routed them out and committed unmentionable excesses.

In the camps and quarters all the wealth of the East lay scattered about underfoot: priceless carpets, velvet hangings, lamps of gold and silver set with gems, ecclesiastical vestments and works of art, became the prey of settlers and the riff-raff of Parisian slums; choice wines and liqueurs flowed like water; lace, linen, and ladies' jewellery were taken from carved chests and coffers of exquisite workmanship, for the household effects had been left untouched when the city was abandoned.

Drunken sappers lolled on sofas covered with costly satin, and muddy boots were cleansed on rich furs and Cashmere shawls of enormous value: seldom had an army, famed for its rapacity, had such an opportunity for its gratification, while, with the Russian forces, white bread was six shillings a loaf, sugar ten shillings a pound, and butter unprocurable at any price.

In the midst of this disorder, the real originator of it all dated his correspondence from the Kremlin Palace, and thought of pushing on to St. Petersburg. A march of nine hundred leagues, with sixty conflicts *en route*, had produced nothing, difficulties were increasing, winter was coming fast. Still the *Czar* kept an ominous silence, and although an armistice had been declared, the Russians daily cut off the foraging parties, and the peasantry rose to arms.

Rostopschin in his proclamation to them wrote:

"Take your three-pronged forks. A Frenchman is no heavier than a sheaf of corn!"

Murat, always to the front, had followed Kutusoff in his circuitous march round Moscow, and lay observing him between that city and Kalouga, fighting two sharp but indecisive actions—Czerikowo and Winkowo.

During the truce the Russian officers asked the French if they had not corn, and air, and *graves* enough in their own country; adding,. "In a fortnight the nails will drop from your fingers."

The little pale-faced man grew visibly paler with anxiety, and went on hoping against hope discussing poetry just arrived from Paris, drawing up regulations for the *Comédie Française*, and trying to reassure himself that the winter was still far off by poring over the almanacs for forty years back, and trusting to the hot sun that still shone in a blue sky above him.

Chef d'escadron Marthod, with fifty dragoons, of the Guard—*his*

Guard, so seldom defeated—had been cut off while foraging. A slight fall of snow lay white for a few hours on the plain—a foretaste of what was coming. No message arrived from Alexander, and one day, to crown all, while he was reviewing some troops, young Beranger galloped in with the alarming news that Murat had been overthrown at Tarutina, near Winkowo, two generals being killed, the king wounded, and the advance guard almost destroyed.

It was clearly time to go, and dismissing the troops, Napoleon issued orders for immediate departure, leaving Moscow late the same evening, October 18th, or, as some say, before dawn on the 19th. Marshal Mortier remaining behind with the Young Guard to cover the retreat and blow up the Kremlin.

*****

Where are the words that will paint that enormous and disorderly throng moving in a ragged column over the plain to the south of the ruined city? Coats and gaiters were patched and mended; shakoes assumed every shape but the regulation one; brass no longer shone, and steel had grown rusty, as the troops straggled onward, their knapsacks bulging with plunder; bearskin-capped grenadiers pushing wheelbarrows full of gold and silver plate, and the ambulance waggons creaking and groaning with costly brocade, household furniture, pictures, statuary, and every conceivable articles of value the pillagers could carry away.

Napoleon set the example; for the huge Cross of Ivan, torn down by his orders, lumbered along with many other trophies, under a strong escort, and miles of carts of every description thronged the road and the fields on either side. The French residents fled in the wake of the army; delicate ladies, clad in thin dresses and stuff shoes, peering at the strange procession from the windows of travelling-carriages; wounded soldiers jolted by lying on piles of loot, their aching limbs ill-tended amid the lavish profusion of spoil, for never has man's selfishness displayed itself more forcibly than during that terrible retreat.

Night fell, and the host halted only a league from the city. With the 103,000 men who marched, more than 500 guns were dragged by lean horses, the emperor insisting that they should not be abandoned; but at the present moment the bulk of them are ranged in rows in the great square of the Kremlin—a lasting memorial of that awful war.

Two roads led from Moscow to Kalouga, and Napoleon pushed along the old one, on which Kutusoff awaited him; but at Krasno

Pachra, the emperor turned off to the right and crossed the fields to the *new* road, in the rain, which hampered the artillery and lost much time; but once on the causeway, which they gained on the 23rd, they set their faces towards Kalouga again, trusting to pass Kutusoff undetected in one day's march.

Napoleon slept at Borowsk that night, and Delzons had occupied Malo Jaroslavetz, four leagues in advance.

In the early morning, however, Doctoroff, with the 6th Corps of Kutusoff's army, came shouting out of the woods, drove Delzons down the steep hill, and commenced one of the fiercest battles of the campaign.

At sunrise Delzons forced the town again, and the victory seemed won, but a ball through the head slew him. His brother tried to carry him out of the *mêlée:*, and another ball laid him lifeless. Guilleminot placed a hundred grenadiers in the churchyard on the left of the road, and for hours it became a mimic Hougoumont, the Russians alternately charging past it and being driven up again, exposed to a hot fire from the loopholed wall.

The whole of the 14th Division was engaged, and the fight surged along the high road, now on the heights, now in the valley by the river; the wooden town ignited by the howitzers, and burning the wounded, while the guns, breasting the hill at a gallop, scrunched the charred corpses, grinding the living and the dead into a sickening pulp.

The 15th Division, mostly Italians, attacked the burning town and suburbs, and took it for the fourth time, but were driven back to the foot of the slope, and as a last resource, Eugène advanced with his Guard. The 13th, 14th, and 15th Divisions rallying, and Colonel Peraldi charging bravely with the Italian *chasseurs,*, they gained the heights for the last time, and the Russians, 50,000 strong (some say 90,000), retired from their vantage ground before 18,000 men, who had fought *uphill* against the most stubborn resistance.

All the eye witnesses speak of the awful sight presented by the high road and churchyard. The brothers Delzons were buried in one grave, and the grenadiers of the 35th fired a salute over General Fontane; while Napoleon himself had a narrow escape as he hurried towards the sound of the cannonading.

The road was blocked by the baggage train: stragglers marched along in safety in the midst of the army, when the emperor, Rapp, Berthier, and a few officers, having outstripped the escort, saw bands of Cossacks darting out of the woods, between the rear of the advance-guard and the head of the *Grande Armée*.

"Turn back!" shouted Rapp; "it is they!" and grasping the bridle, he pulled the emperor's charger round.

Reining in by the roadside, Napoleon drew his sword, and they awaited the attack. Rapp riding forward to shield his emperor.

A Cossack's lance penetrated six inches into the chest of Rapp's horse and brought him down, but the staff rescued him, and unconscious of the prize within their reach, the Cossacks rode for the baggage waggons, until the cavalry of the Guard came up and drove them into the woods again. They were 6,000 of Platoff's men, and Napoleon's life had hung in the balance!

That night, in a weaver's hut, filthy beyond expression, an emperor, two kings, and three marshals of France held a stormy council of war, at which Murat and Davout quarrelled, as was their wont, and which Napoleon broke up by saying, "It is well, *messieurs*—*I* will decide," electing eventually to retreat by the most difficult road—that which the army had wasted" on its advance.

It was the last time that they had any option in the matter. A few days more, and the retreat became a disorderly rout—emperor, kings, marshals, and men glad to seize the first road that led them from their remorseless enemies.

On the 23rd, at half-past one in the morning, a hollow boom had startled their ears, even those who were expecting it. The *capitaine* Ottone, of the Naval Artillery, had fired his train. Mortier's orders were executed, and the Kremlin had been partially blown up by 180,000 lbs. of gunpowder, Mortier rejoining, to the surprise of all, at Vereia with 8,000 men, mostly dismounted cavalry.

At Vereia there was another brush with Platoff, and his son, mounted on a magnificent white Ukraine horse, was killed by a Polish trooper.

On a hill covered with sombre fir trees the Cossacks buried the dead boy, riding slowly round him with lances lowered, uttering wild cries of grief, and then filing silently away with vengeance in their hearts.

Every village at which the French halted was burned on their departure, each succeeding corps helping to complete the devastation, so that the route was marked by ruined homes, huge dogs from each hamlet following the army until they increased to enormous packs, *living on the dead* who lined the road, and adding a new terror to the retreating invaders.

At Mojaisk the sky lost its intense blue, and the landscape became gloomy, the cold wind sobbing and wailing down the avenues of melancholy pines, and the men drawing closer to each other as they marched. The columns debouched on to the field of Borodino, and sad memories were aroused at every step; for, although thousands of bodies had been burned by the Russians, the plain, the heights, and especially the redoubts were littered with broken weapons and innumerable accoutrements, the hands and feet of the hastily buried slain protruding from the sandy soil in all directions.

One ghastly incident, vouched for by the great majority of writers, occurred as the head of the army traversed the field. Cries were heard, and a mutilated spectre crawled towards the startled soldiers. It was a Frenchman, whose legs had been broken during the battle more than

seven weeks before, and who, unaided, had lived on the putrid flesh around him, sleeping in the stinking carcase of a disembowelled horse.

Taking him tenderly up, the army hurried on. The skeletons they were leaving behind grinned silently as the straggling band passed by. A little further on, the wounded at the abbey of Klotskoi held out their hands beseechingly, and an order was issued that every vehicle should carry at least *one* of them, the weakest being left to the tender mercies of the Russians. Every now and again a dull explosion came from the line of march as caisson after caisson was blown up when the horses became too weak to drag them; and a few miles on the road to Gjatz a terrible outcry arose as wounded men were found lying on the ground, having been thrown out of the sutler's carts in order that the vile wretches might save their plunder—one sufferer, *a general*, living just long enough to tell the tale.

As evening drew down and Napoleon approached Gjatz a fresh horror awaited him; for Russian dead, still warm, and with their brains battered out in a peculiar manner, were met with at every few yards. The escort of Poles, Portuguese, and Spaniards told off to guard the prisoners had chosen that method of ridding themselves of the weakly ones who lagged behind. A stringent order went forth, and the murders ceased; but every night the miserable captives were herded together like cattle, without fire, on the bare ground, a meagre ration of raw horseflesh served out to them, and when that failed the frantic wretches *turned cannibals and devoured each other*. The 4th Corps, under Eugène, meanwhile followed the Imperial column, and Davout commanded the rear-guard, five days' march behind.

Intense cold had now set in, and the land was icebound; violent winds fluttered the ragged uniforms, the fifteen days' rations brought from Moscow were exhausted, and the depth of misery seemed to have been reached. Yet all this was as nothing to the sufferings in store.

Napoleon waited thirty-six hours at Wiazma for the rear-guard to come up, and seeing no sign of it, left Ney there to relieve it, and marched for Dorogobouje on the 1st November; while Eugène and Davout, arriving at Wiazma on the 3rd, found Nay hotly engaged with Miloradowitch, the Russian Murat, who opposed further advance.

A battle ensued, lasting many hours. Great heroism was displayed, especially by the 25th, 57th, and 85th Regiments, and at length Eugène got away through the town; Davout, in his turn, retiring step by step before 20,000 men and the crashing fire of twenty-four guns, was met by another force in the winding streets, and only extricated himself after tremendous loss, the bulk of the Russians under old Kutusoff remaining motionless within earshot, in spite of all the efforts of Sir Robert Wilson to induce him to attack.

During the fourteen days since the *Grande Armée* left Moscow it had lost 43,000 men, reducing its numbers to 60,000; and its condition may be understood from the fact that the day after Wiazma a little flour, carefully measured out in a spoon, formed the only food of the officers of the 4th Corps.

The dogs howled round the tail of the straggling columns, croaking ravens followed in black flocks. When a horse fell the hungry soldiers rushed upon it and tore it to pieces before life was extinct; and on the 6th November the sun disappeared, a grey fog enveloped the

troops, the wind dashed them one against the other as they stumbled mechanically along, *and it began to snow!*

Whirled on the storm wind, the flakes shut out the country on either hand. No sooner had a waggon—a gun carriage—a decimated regiment gone by than it was instantly lost to sight. The road vanished, the hollows were filled up; one could pass within twenty yards of a log hut and not see it. Everything became white—a pitiless, monotonous, dead level of snow, and strong men sobbed struggling onward—as they hoped—towards that *Belle France* that not a third of their number were destined to reach again.

Napoleon was on the heights above Mikelewska when the snow began, and news of the most serious import reached him at the same moment. Count Daru arriving with the account of General Mallet's attempted conspiracy in Paris.

Surrounded by a circle of his *chasseurs*, shivering in their scarlet pelisses, the emperor listened to the startling narrative, the storm howling round him as he bent over the neck of his horse; and even when he retired into a post-house to digest the alarming intelligence his cup of bitterness was not full, for Colonel Dalbignac came from the rear-guard, which Ney had taken over, with a terrible report of the disorder that the marshal had discovered at Dorogobouje.

"I do not ask you for these details, colonel," said Napoleon; but some waggons arriving from Smolensk laden with provisions, he waved Bessières, who wished to keep them for the Guard, aside, and sent them on to Ney, saying, "Those who fight shall eat before the rest," begging him, if possible, to check the foe, and allow the main body some time to reorganise at Smolensk.

The bulk of the Russian spoil, including the great Cross of Ivan, had been sunk in the lake of Semlewo, and cannon were abandoned at every mile. Generals and staff officers marched in bands, without men, without thought of anything but their own preservation. Twelve to sixteen horses were required to draw a single gun up the slightest hill, slippery as glass, and with the thermometer registering twenty-eight and thirty degrees of frost, 10,000 wretched animals died in a single night—the terrible night of sixteen hours of darkness. In some Italian villages they still speak with horror of "the night of the fifteen hundred frozen"—that being the number of Italians that died on one occasion between sunset and sunrise.

Even the Russian Miloradowitch suffered from a frozen eye, and men who sat to rest a moment on the snow fell back in a stupor, a little blood gushed from mouth and nose, and their earthly woes were over.

Horrible the fate of those who straggled from the track and fell in with the villagers. Sir Robert Wilson at one place saw sixty naked Frenchmen laid in a row, their necks on a felled tree, while men *and*

women hopped round them, singing in wild chorus, and battering out their brains in succession with faggot sticks.

At Wiazma fifty were *burned alive*; at Selino the same number, still breathing, were *buried*, the dog belonging to one of them returning daily to the graveside for a fortnight before the peasants slew it.

Yet amid all this misery, his men wearing bed quilts, pieces of carpet, women's clothes from the baggage waggons which they began to pillage on the 7th November, and existing too often on the bodies of their comrades roasted by the flames of a burning log hut. Marshal Ney, well styled "the bravest of the brave," set his face to the foe, and fought for ten days and nights against Cossacks—artillery, horse, foot, and dragoons—and, worst of all, the terrible *Général Morizov*, as the Russians called the frost. Holding each wood, contesting every hill, knowing that he was virtually sacrificed to save the wreck of the army, his men deserting, despairing, dying, he fought on foot to give them courage, his face livid with the cold, and almost unrecognisable from the long red beard he had allowed to grow.

Some idea of the stubborn character of those wild Cossacks may be formed from one little incident. One of them came into the Russian camp, having ridden twenty miles after being hit by a cannon shot. His arm was taken out at the shoulder-joint by the famous Doctor Wiley, who afterwards amputated Moreau's legs at Dresden. During the operation, which lasted four minutes, the man never spoke, the next morning walked about his room, and drank tea, and, getting into a cart which jolted him fourteen miles over a Russian road, was afterwards heard of, many hundreds of miles on his journey homeward to the Don, doing well!

Small wonder, then, that the hoarse *hourra* struck terror into the fugitives, and that half a dozen of the barbarians would send a battalion of bleeding conscripts flying for their lives down the glittering aisles of drooping birches, whose fairy-like branches glistened with magic beauty in the wintry sunshine.

Eugène was attacked as his corps crossed the Wop with five or six thousand soldiers under arms, double that number of stragglers and wounded, and more than a hundred guns. The ford became blocked, the current was very rapid, and the river only partially frozen. A shameful pillage of the waggons took place, gold, silver, and costly plunder being scattered in the mud; and it was not until a brave Italian colonel named Delfanti crossed up to his waist in the floating ice that the others took heart and followed him.

Colonel Labaume tells us that he picked up a magnificent cup of splendid workmanship, drank some muddy water out of it, and flung it aside with indifference; but others, thinking only of gain, exchanged silver money for gold at a great sacrifice, secretly laughing at their comrades, who soon sank under the weight, while they escaped with the lesser bulk.

One officer, apparently lifeless, felt a man pulling off his boots, and exclaimed, "Ah, rascal, I have still need of them. I am not quite dead."

"*Eh bien, mon general,*" said the soldier, coolly sitting down beside him, "*I can wait.*"

Napoleon rested five days at Smolensk; but so neglected had been his orders that no meat was found there— only rye flour, rice, and brandy—and the army fought desperately at the doors of the magazines, killing many men, raging at the Guard, whom they accused, with great reason, of being unduly favoured, and breaking out into excesses of every kind.

On the 14th November, at four o'clock in the morning, the main column left for Krasnoë, leaving little or nothing behind them for Eugène, Davout, and the valiant Ney, who had instructions to evacuate the city with a day's interval between each corps, Ney to blow up the place when he took his departure.

Out of 37,000 dashing cavalry who had crossed the Niemen only *eight hundred* remained mounted at Smolensk, the 20th Chasseurs being credited with a hundred; and this remnant was collected under Latour-Maubourg, a brave and very popular officer, who, on losing a leg at Leipzig the following year, said to his weeping servant, "*Mon ami*, why do you grieve? In future there's only one boot to clean."

The army was now 42,000 strong, having lost 18,000 in the previous eight days; but it was estimated that 60,000 unarmed stragglers still impeded the march. Before leaving Smolensk, however, a reinforcement brought the force up to 47,000. to meet *four* Russian armies, one of them with 90,000, under Kutusoff, another commanded by Miloradowitch with 20,000 men.

The artillery of the Guard took twenty-two hours to do the first five leagues out of Smolensk. One company of sturdy Wurtembergers mustered *four* men, and when Eugène reached the abandoned city in a furious gale his men had to mount the slippery hill literally *on their knees*.

Beyond Korvthnia Miloradowitch opened on the Imperial column, and Napoleon rode in the centre of the grenadiers of the Old Guard. He seemed to bear a charmed life, for three times a certain Captain Finkein had penetrated Moscow to kill him, and he was often under fire during the retreat. This time, however, he had to pass a hill bristling with cannon, and the band struck up a then well-known air, "Where can one be happier than in the bosom of his family?"

"Stop," cried Napoleon, fearful of the memories it might raise in the minds of the men. "Rather play, 'Let us watch over the safety of the empire.'" And to that air they marched past the batteries, soon leaving the danger behind them.

When the column had gone, Miloradowitch descended from the hills, drew across the road, and cut off the rear corps, who had to fight their way through with terrible loss.

Eugène tried to force a passage, but failed; and leaving his fires burning—and what miserable fires they were!—turned the flank of the Russians, and got by in the night.

At the critical moment the moon shone out, and the wretched band was challenged.

"Hist, fool," whispered a Polish officer named Klisby in Russian. "Do you not see that we belong to Suvarow, bound on a secret mission?" And so, without interruption save from the Cossacks, the viceroy joined his stepfather at Krasnoë, where Napoleon made a retrograde march to succour Davout, who came in, his luggage gone, his marshal's baton taken, his men reduced to a few platoons, and with no news of Ney, who was reluctantly left to his fate, the army moving on Orcha,

Mortier and the wreck of the Young Guard retiring slowly in the rear, after holding Krasnoë as long as possible, Laborde saying to the troops, "The marshal orders the ordinary time—do you hear?—the ordinary time, soldiers," although under a heavy fire of balls and grape shot.

At Orcha Napoleon destroyed his papers. At Lubna the twenty-one staff officers of the 4th Corps crouched round a miserable fire in a cart-shed, with their horses behind them. At Krasnoë the brave

Delfanti limped along on the arm of Villeblanche. A round shot struck him between the shoulder blades, carried off Villeblanche's head, and they fell dead on the snow. Wherever one turned it was horror upon horror. Delicate women and little children lay by the roadside. The Cossacks stripped everyone they found.

Wilson has some dreadful details in his interesting diary. At one place a number of naked men sat round a burning hut, their backs quite frozen, when, turning to warm them, the fire caught the congealed flesh and roasted it in his presence.

Again, he saw four wretches huddled together, hands and limbs immovable, *but minds yet vigorous,* with two dogs snarling and tearing at their frozen feet; while nearly all the dead he came across seemed to have been "writhing with some agony at the moment their heart's blood congealed."

Woe to the man who lost his bivouac, and strayed to another fire. He was driven away with blows and curses from one after another until he sank and died. If anyone fell on the march, and implored a helping hand, the passers-by shook their heads and passed on, although many were still laden with plunder.

An awful thing occurred as Ney left Smolensk, showing the depths to which human nature can sink, a female sutler being seen to throw her little five-year-old boy off her heavily-laden sledge and leave him. Twice the marshal had him placed in her arms, and twice she flung the child from her, saying, "He had never seen France, and would never regret it, while she was resolved to see it again." The soldiers could stand it no longer. They carried the boy safely through the rest of the march, and left the unnatural woman to perish in the snow!

Ney's retreat with the rear-guard was one of the great events in French history, and has never been exceeded by any general for courage, determination, and self-reliance.

With barely 6,000 men, twelve guns, and 300 crawling skeletons—which it is a mockery to call horses—and burdened with 7,000 stragglers, whose wants and selfishness added greatly to the difficulties, he followed the traces of the *Grande Armée,* easily recognisable by the burnt-out bivouacs with their circles of dead—the white mounds that indicated where a cuirassier, a dragoon, a barefooted *voltigeur,* slept his last sleep, and the patches of trampled, bloodstained snow strewn with helmets and corpses, over which the dogs wrangled and the ravens croaked in the dull light that showed a battleground.

Beyond the plain of Katova, where, three months before, they had driven Newerowskoi through the cornfields, they were summoned by an officer in the name of Kutusoff; but while he was speaking forty guns opened on the French, and Ney exclaimed, "A marshal never surrenders—you are my prisoner," the astonished Russian marching with them for twenty-six days without attempting to break his parole.

Ney boldly attacked the *eighty thousand* men, heading his feeble band in person. They broke the first line, and were rushing on the second when the guns began again, sweeping the columns and killing some women in the waggons.

The French fell back in confusion, but Ney rallied them again, replying with his *six* remaining guns, and showing his teeth with the *two thousand* ragged wretches who kept their ranks. If Kutusoff had sent a single corps against them, not a man would have survived to tell the tale. As it was, when night fell Ney turned his back on them, and retreated towards Smolensk.

After an hour's dreary march they halted, Ney, as usual, in the rear; and breaking the ice on a streamlet to find which way the current ran, followed its course through the silent forests until they reached the Dnieper.

Guided by a lame peasant, they found a spot where the ice would bear them, although a thaw was setting in; and, after lighting fires to deceive the hovering Cossacks, the intrepid marshal rolled himself in his cloak and slept on the river bank for three hours.

At midnight they began to cross, the ice parting and letting many of them in as they crept in single file. An attempt was made to get the wounded over in the waggons, but the treacherous blocks gave way, and they were drowned with heartrending screams, Ney himself rescuing one survivor, an officer named Brigueville.

Using the cowardly stragglers as a shield, by placing them between his men and the foe, he pursued his way, taking advantage of the woods, surrounded by 6,000 Cossacks, and repeatedly played upon by cannon; lying in the forests by day, and marching when darkness had set in, until, with 1,500 men under arms, most of the stragglers slain or taken, and all his guns and baggage gone, he rejoined the wreck of the army at Orcha on the 20th November, Napoleon well saving before his arrival, "I have two hundred millions (*francs*) in the cellars of the Tuileries, and I would have given them all to save Marshal Ney."

Oudinot and Victor also joined the wreck about this time, bringing up the total number to 30,000 or thereabouts, the emperor's column mustering only *seven* thousand men and *forty* thousand stragglers, mingled with the enormous baggage train of the 2nd and 9th Corps that had escaped much of the previous disaster; and closely pressed on each flank by the immense armies of Kutusoff and Witgenstein, the doomed men prepared to cross the Berezina in the face of Admiral Tchitchakof, who lined the opposite bank.

Latour-Maubourg had only 150 horsemen left, and Napoleon

formed 500 mounted cavalry officers into what he called his Sacred Squadron, Grouchy and Sebastiani commanding it, and generals of division serving in it as captains; but in a few days this last romantic idea had crumbled away.

Corbineau, with the remains of the 8th Lancers and 20th Chasseurs, saw a peasant riding a wet horse, and compelled him to show them the ford opposite to Studzianka; and while the French made all the parade they could lower down the river to attract Tchitchakof's attention, the brave engineer Eblé arrived at Studzianka in the dark winter evening of the 25th November with two field forges, six chests of tools, some clamps made from waggon tyres, and a few companies of pontoniers, and began to make a bridge, the water rising, the ice floating in blocks, and the men working up to their necks without even a draught of brandy to protect them from the cold.

As the grey dawn broke, the first pile was driven; eight hours' work was required before the bridge would be practicable, and the haggard fugitives waited with agonised hearts for the cannonade that would destroy their last hope; but to the astonishment of all, the admiral was seen in full retreat on the farther bank, disappearing into the woods with all his guns.

A caricature exists, showing Kutusoff and Witgenstein tying Napoleon up in a sack, while Tchitchakof is cutting a hole in the bottom of it; clearly indicating the Russian view of that individual's conduct.

Napoleon wished to question a prisoner, and two officers swam their horses across, through the ice, Jacqueminot, Oudinot's *aide-de-camp*, seizing a Russian, holding him on his saddle-bow, and *swimming back with him*.

When an old man he mounted to the top of Strasbourg Cathedral, and hung fearlessly from an arm of the cross with hundreds of feet of space beneath him: it was natures like his alone that survived the retreat.

Chef d'escadron Sourd, with fifty men of the 7th Chasseurs, carried some infantry over behind them, and two rafts conveyed four hundred more across to defend the bridge head. A second bridge for artillery and baggage was finished at four o'clock; it broke twice during the night, and again the following evening: all was confusion and disorder. The Russians were expected any moment on the heights that commanded the low-lying snow-covered shore, yet the stragglers waited fatuously until the morning of the 27th, and then all attempted to cross at the same time.

When the remnant of the Guard was seen clearing a way for the emperor, there was a rush; the bridges were blocked—men, women, and children were crushed to death and many drowned. Yet that night—the panic over—thousands returned to the bivouacs of Studzianka, and the bridges were deserted again.

Victor, with 6,000 men, kept Witgenstein in check; Tchitchakof, a martyr to the cold, who had by that time warmed his toes thoroughly, returned to the opposite shore and began firing, and another terrible rush was made for the frail structures on the 28th, while Ney, across the river, was repulsing the admiral, and Victor fought all day long to give the wretches time.

The waggons and carriages were more than could have crossed in six days, said Eblé—who died soon after from exposure. Ney wished them burned, but Berthier, who was little better than a writer of reports and a species of machine actuated by Napoleon himself, opposed it on his own responsibility, and caused the death of a multitude of sufferers in consequence; for when the shot and shell began to fall in the river and splinter the ice, the drivers charged down on the bridges, tearing their way remorselessly through the living obstacle.

Sword in hand, single horsemen cut a passage for themselves; women, waist-deep in the water alongside, were frozen with their arms raised to preserve their children, who were too often left to freeze there by the passers-by.

The Countess Alesio—a young Italian bride of eighteen, who had accompanied her husband on that ghastly wedding-trip—survived all these horrors, and *lives*, as I write these lines, full of terrible memories of the retreat.

Selfishness and heroism went hand in hand. An artilleryman jumped from the bridge to save a mother and her two little ones, succeeding in rescuing one boy; others pushed their comrades off to find room for themselves. And even when the early night settled down, the Russians knew where to point their guns by the screams and curses that rang over the waste amid a fearful snowstorm.

When the 4th Corps reached the other side, their only fire was a miserable blaze lighted for Eugène, of wood begged from some Bavarians, and his officers ran about *all night* to keep warm.

The artillery bridge had long since broken down—hundreds being engulfed—and only one remained, leading into a marsh choked with carriages, guns, waggons, wounded, dead and dying; across which, at nine o'clock, Victor's shattered battalions had to force their way over with their bayonets.

One instance of remarkable coolness is recorded of an artillery officer named Brechtel. whose wooden leg was smashed by a cannon ball. "Look for another leg in waggon No. 5," he said to a gunner; and when it was brought, he screwed it on, and calmly continued his firing.

Ney's pay-waggons were crossing at the same time under the care of Nicolas Savin, a hussar who had been at Toulon in 1793, in Egypt with Bonaparte, at Austerlitz, Jena, and in the Peninsula; but through a breakage of the bridge he and his gold were taken by Platoff's Cossacks, and marvellous to relate, the veteran died in Russia, during the winter of 1894, at the extraordinary age of 127.

In vain Eblé urged the fugitives to fly—many still lingering on, until at half-past eight on the morning of the 29th, the engineer set fire to their sole means of escape on the approach of the enemy.

Heartrending was the scene; language fails to describe it, though many men of many nations have poured forth all their eloquence upon the theme. Snow, flames, round shot and shells; the half-frozen river, the army already passed on its way; France, friends, home, *everything* gone. A father on one bank, a mother on the other, never to meet again in this world; brothers, children, old men and young girls, the bridges blazing, and the hoarse "*Hourra!*" of the Cossacks as they tore down the bank among the forsaken crowd like vultures on a carcass.

A little while and the frozen land was still again; the wolves came out of the woods to sniff at the ghastly heaps; the white dogs, no longer lean and famished, wrangled with each other for the choicer morsels, finding the mother and the babe more to their liking, and leaving the war-worn veteran to the carrion crows.

When spring thawed the ice, *thirty thousand* bodies were found and burned on the banks of the Berezina; and happy they whose troubles had ended there. For the weather grew colder, the storms were more frequent, hundreds of miles had yet to be traversed; the Old Guard had lost from cold and missing a *third* of its diminished numbers, the Young Guard *half*, and the army was reduced to a wandering mob of *nine thousand*, twenty-one thousand having fallen in three days and four actions.

Over the marshes in the keen north wind they hurried, Ney still commanding the rear-guard; on the 30th, Oudinot, badly wounded, defended himself in a wooden house with *seventeen men* for several hours, and drove the Russians out of the village. The sun shone out to mock them; there was hard fighting almost every day; and at length, when the main body reached Smorgoni, the emperor resolved to put in practice an intention he had formed some time before of hurrying secretly to Paris to forestall the real truth of his disasters.

He has been unjustly accused of deserting his men when they were at their last gasp; but in reality no blame attaches to him, as his presence in France was absolutely necessary, and had he remained with the army he could have done nothing to restore it, for things had gone too far. To what extent he had contributed to those disasters is, of course, another matter.

After revising his 29th Bulletin, and appointing Murat to the chief command, he got into his carriage with Caulaincourt (brother of Auguste), Rustan the Mameluke, and Captain Wukasowitch sitting on the box, Duroc and Lobau following in a sledge, and escorted by some Polish lancers, drove off in the dark on the night of the 5th December.

Later on he exchanged the carriage for another sledge, the peasant

driver of which died in Bavaria as recently as 1887, preserving to the last some of the coins Napoleon had given him.

On the 18th the emperor arrived in Paris. The day after his departure the cold increased to a frightful degree; men lost their reason, and sprang into the burning huts. At Wilna, where there were great stores of food, they pillaged without check; and even the Old Guard paid no heed to the *générale*. All Napoleon's linen and his state tent were burned there, and the few remaining trophies, drawings being made of them before their destruction by his orders.

The Jews committed nameless cruelties on the French wounded, and although Durutte's division increased the army by 13,000, they died by hundreds, immense numbers having been frozen and suffocated at the gate of the city in their mad attempt to get in.

The day after their arrival the Russians were on them again. De Wrede's Bavarians were routed, Murat lost his head and bolted, and everything devolved on the heroic Ney, who volunteered again for rearguard duty, keeping Kutusoff at bay while the army retreated on the road to Kowno, the last Russian town before they could reach the Niemen, 4,000 men alone preserving an orderly demeanour under arms.

At the hill of Ponari the Cossacks fell foul of them, and, while under fire. Napoleon's private treasure was portioned out equally among such of the Guard as remained, every man who survived afterwards accounting for his share to the last coin.

The final scene may be summed up by a brief narration of the fabulous gallantry of Marshal Ney. It had been his invariable custom to halt and rest from five in the evening until ten, and then resume the march; but at Evé, near Kowno, he woke up to find his *fourth* rear-guard gone, their arms still piled, and glistening in the frosty night. When he overtook them they were in disorder, and could not be rallied, Ney entering the town attended only by his *aides*, but instantly setting to work to form a *fifth* guard. He found 2,000 drunken men dead on the snow, and the fugitives gone on to the river; but with 300 German artillery and 400 others, under General Marchand, he set about to defend Kowno.

The last remnant, having crossed the Niemen, were flying through the Pilwisky forest, from which they had issued five months before in very different plight, only 13,000 in reality mustering behind that river. Kowno was attacked on the morning of the 14th December, and hastening to the Wilna Gate, Ney found the German artillery had spiked their guns and fled.

In a towering passion the marshal drew his sword and rushed at the officer in command, who still remained there, and; but for his *aide-de-camp* averting the blow, would have slain him. The officer escaped, and Ney summoned one of his two weak battalions, also German, and after a spirited address, formed them behind the snow-capped palisade as the enemy approached, but fate was against him. A ball broke the colonel's thigh, and he blew out his brains before his men, who instantly threw down their guns and fled, leaving Ney alone.

Gathering all the muskets he could reach, the marshal fired them through the palisade—*one* man against *thousands*—until others came to his help; the town was attacked on the opposite side at the same time, and though he maintained his post with thirty ragged scarecrows until dark, he had to retreat step by step, through the town and across the Niemen, the last man, after forty days' and nights' incessant fighting with the rear-guard, to leave the Russian shore.

******

In Gumbinnen, Mathieu Dumas was sitting down to breakfast, when a man in a brown coat entered, his beard long, his face blackened and looking as though it had been burnt, his eyes red and glaring.

"At length I am here," he exclaimed. "Don't you know me?"

"No," said the general. "Who are you?"

"I am the Rear-Guard of the *Grande Armée*; I have fired the last musket-shot on the bridge of Kowno; I have thrown the last of our arms into the Niemen, and come hither through the woods. I am Marshal Ney."

******

Macdonald, in the North, was reduced by hardship and the defection of the Prussians; Schwartzenberg, in the South, had been obliged to retire, and the magnificent army of the Centre, led by masters in the art of war, under the emperor himself, we have seen dwindled down to 13,000 in less than six months. It was not altogether the Russians, it was not entirely the frost, although both contributed to its destruction: when all laws, physical and moral, are transgressed, when flesh and blood are tried beyond the limits of possible endurance, and wild ambition takes the place of common-sense, something will give, and disaster is certain in the long run.

By one of the most careful of contemporary computations it is concluded that 552,000 unfortunate creatures who had marched under the eagles of Napoleon never returned from that campaign, and the medal struck by Alexander to commemorate it, sums up the whole case in a sentence of singular piety.

On one side, in a triangle surrounded by rays, is the Eye of Providence, with the date beneath It; on the other, the inscription: "*Not unto us; not unto me; but unto Thy*

October 13, 1812
Queenston Heights
Angus Evan Abbott

A war that had for its tilting-ground the picturesque frontier of Canada, and for its period the opening of the nineteenth century, when, as yet, the great West was a mystery, and the forests of America stretched far beyond the white man's ken, could not but be one of infinite colour and romance. When all Canada—one-sixteenth of the land surface of the globe—contained a white population of less than 300,000 souls, and the United States, now the home of more than sixty millions of people, could only boast of a population of eight millions; when no express trains snaked their way across the mammoth continent, nor swift steamers trailed their smoke athwart the blue of the skies; when the bayonet still played an important part in the winning or losing of battles; when flint locks had not been bred into hammerless guns; when the ring of the long ramrod was heard where now is heard the snap of the breechloader; when cannon were few and small, and when an army was complete without a telegraph corps to weave a network of wire at its rear like the tail of a comet—in those days wars were longer drawn out, the dead were not counted by the tens of thousands, as now. Hand-to-hand lighting was still to be had, and it would seem that individual valour played a greater part in the result of the conflicts than can be the case in this the day of machine-guns and electricity. So it is that, although many wars of the century saw more troops in the field and larger armies confronting one another, few indeed are more romantic in their details than that which is known in Canadian and American history as "the War of 1812."

The opening battles of this unfortunate, this criminal war were

fought amidst some of the grandest scenery of the world. A broad blue river—the equal of which is scarcely to be found—bore on its bosom Tecumseh, fighting chief of the Shawnese, and with him General Isaac Brock, to the capture of Fort Detroit. The muffled thunder of the Niagara Falls smote upon the ears of the soldiers who met in the shock of battle at Lundy's Lane. The misty veil of the falling waters and the swirl of the river fresh from its maddening plunge were within sight of the Battle of Queenston Heights—hills, rocks, precipitous banks, wide rivers, lakes so vast as to be rightly termed inland seas, forests unending.

Then, too, the world had not as yet bestirred itself out of its picturesque stages. Times were still old-fashioned. Governments, generals, and people alike were in those days dependent for news of the outside world upon the sailing-vessels that battled their ways from port to port—a prey to adverse winds, uncharted currents, and unmarked rocks, and, worse than these evils, the ever-present danger of being swooped upon by one of those hawks of the sea, the privateer, of which vast numbers flitted to and fro on the bosom of the Atlantic. Nor were communications much less risky ashore. The courier with his coon-skin cap, his *moccasins* in summer and snow-shoes in winter, and flint-lock over shoulder, thrid the forest where lurked a hundred dangers.

But these strange features of departed days do not complete the list

Campaign in
CANADA, 1812.

of things that have been, but are never again to be. In "the War of 1812" the crasis—the "makeup" of the army for the defence of Canada—was such as can never again take the field. For side by side with the men of the 49th—"Green Tigers" the Americans nicknamed them at Queenston Heights for their ferocity in battle—stood the Canadian Militia, made up of farmers, village artisans and craftsmen, clerks, fur-traders, and such-like components of an army; stood United Empire Loyalists and French-Canadians; stood Indians, under Tecumseh and the younger Brant; stood, it is told at Queenston Heights, negro slaves as well as freemen—all joined together to defend the country against the invading American. A heterogeneous band, in all conscience, assembled to oppose an advancing army not quite so mixed in its *personnel*. In writing of the Battle of Queenston Heights, it will be as well to refer to the defenders of Canada as Canadians; for, notwithstanding the presence of British troops, pure and simple, the bulk of the antagonists which the Americans encountered were Canadian volunteers—Canadian white men and Canadian red men.

It is unnecessary here to go into the question of blame for "the War of 1812." But this may be said: the struggle was an unpopular one in the United States. Indeed, some of the most patriotic states in the Union—states that had stood firm for the cause of liberty in the struggle for independence—condemned the action of the President in declaring war on Great Britain. The legislature of Maryland denounced the war. The Governments of Rhode Island, Connecticut, and Massachusetts—three of the most important States in the Union—looked upon the struggle with so great a dislike that they at first refused their quota of troops. And many of the ablest men in the country cried out against the war as unrighteous.

But war, righteous or unrighteous, once begun, a country must stand by the central authority; and soon the full resources of the people of the United States were brought forward with the object of attaining a success. The United States were fortunate in so far that they had no other businesses on hand at the declaration of the war except the pursuing of the war. On the other hand, such was the state of Europe, so critical a stage had been reached in the Napoleonic conflagration, that Great Britain found herself unable to spare even secondary forces for the war in the West. Says the historian Alison:

"Three days after the declaration of war Wellington crossed the Aqueda to commence the Salamanca campaign. Six days after. Napoleon passed the Niemen on his way to Moscow at the head of 380,000 men."

All Europe was aflame. Bellona stood toe-a-tip, and flashed her naked sword across the world. The sweat ran from the brow of Britannia as she gathered her forces to grapple with the despot Napoleon. The struggle meant national life or death. Defeat could only be followed by destruction. It was at this moment that Madison, President of an English-speaking Republic, seated in the chair of authority so recently vacated by Washington, chose to strike a blow which, if successful, he knew must mean the destruction of liberty, the enthronement of despotism. That it did not succeed is to the lasting honour of the people of Canada.

Among the many strange and deplorable features of "the War of 1812," none were more remarkable than that Canada, a meagrely

OPERATIONS ON THE NIAGARA RIVER.

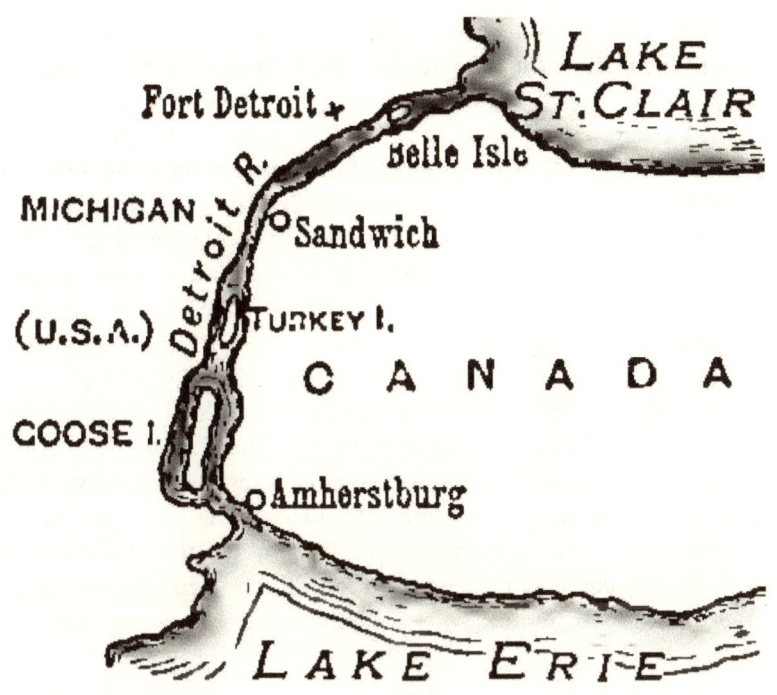

OPERATIONS ON THE DETROIT RIVER.

populated country, a poor country, and the people of which were no parties to the quarrel; a country having, in fact, everything to lose and nothing to gain, should have had thrust upon her the whole brunt of the war during the first years of its career. True, on the sea British and American frigates fought to a finish time and time again; and at the end of the war the Americans, good seamen and honourable, valiant fighters, were able to congratulate themselves on the stand they had made against the mistress of the sea. There was the crimson duel between the *Chesapeake* and the *Shannon*, a pounding match short and bloody, in which the *Shannon* captured the American. On the other hand, the Americans had their victories, and Perry's defeat of the British fleet on Lake Erie placed the great lakes under the control of the forces of the Republic. But the real struggle lay along the Canadian border, and its object was, on the part of the United States, the conquest of Canada, and on the part of Canada the determination not to be conquered by the invaders. In this the Canadians succeeded against well-nigh overwhelming numbers.

The United States declared war on Great Britain, June 18th, 1812.

Canada at once found herself on the defensive. Previous to the declaration of war, the United States had concentrated at the best strategical points large bodies of troops, and, as everything was ready, the moment the declaration of war was officially made known, these moved on Canada. On July 12th, General Hull withdrew his army from Fort Detroit, and, there being no opposition in that part of the country, bloodlessly established himself on Canadian soil by crossing the Detroit River with his army. The initial steps of what must have appeared to the American armies an easy task—the overrunning of Canada—had been successfully taken.

The dividing line between Canada and the United States is in every way worthy of so vast a continent as North America. The extent of it, as known during the years of "the War of 1812," is one succession of mighty rivers and mightier lakes. Beginning with the greatest lake in the world (Superior), the dividing line runs through the Ste. Marie River, with its foaming rapids, at the foot of which even to this day may be seen the Red Indian in his birch-bark canoe dipping his net and sweeping the struggling white fish from the waters. Through Lake Huron, down the St. Clair River, the imaginary line runs, cutting in two the great reed marshes that stretch farther than the eye can see, the home of wild goose, duck, muskrat, and black bass; on down the majestic River Detroit into Lake Erie, then through the turbulent Niagara, plunging the Falls famous the world over, and out upon the breast of the blue Ontario. Running for some distance down the St. Lawrence River, the dividing line leaves the waterways at last, and, striking off into the bush, makes for the shores of the Atlantic. A waterway this, a succession of lakes, rivers, thundering falls, and swirling whirlpools, unparalleled in all the world. But this stretch of 1,700 miles was far too great a frontier for the meagre population of Canada, with its 4,450 regulars, to defend with ease. Every war has its commanding figure, its hero, standing out clearly among the mass, towering head and shoulders above his brothers-in-arms, and he is imposing in proportion to the importance or number of the undertakings in which it has been his fortune to play a part. It may appear strange that the hero of "the War of 1812," from the Canadian standpoint at least, did not live to take more than a momentary part in any battle of the war—in fact, he was killed by one of the earliest volleys fired by the American soldiers in the first battle of the war. Yet it is a fact that of all those who took part in this war there is no one who is held in such kindly remembrance by the people of Canada, nor to whom so much honour has been paid, as Sir Isaac Brock, who fell early in the morning of the battle of Queenston Heights.

Brock was a Guernsey man by birth, born in the same year as Wellington and Napoleon. When but fifteen years of age he joined the British army, first serving in the West Indies, and, rising rapidly, he commanded the 49th Foot as senior colonel in the expedition to Holland. In 1801 he served under Lord Nelson in the attack upon Copenhagen. In 1802, he went with his regiment to Canada, and soon obtained command of all the troops in that country. He was among the very first to recognise the threatening attitude of the authorities across the border, the drilling and concentration of troops, and he at once set to work to put Canada into an efficient state to resist invasion. But in this he had an uphill fight, for the people of Canada were loath to believe that their neighbours to the south would wilfully bring about a collision.

Brock, himself seems to have recognised the pacific intentions of

the American people, but disbelieved altogether in the honour or good faith of the men who at that time governed the States.

In 1810 General Brock established his headquarters at Fort George—a small post on the Canadian bank of the Niagara River, and some miles from Queenston. From this centre he paid a visit to the frontier ports, spending some time at Fort Maiden and Sandwich. In 1811 the Lieutenant-Governor of Upper Canada (Francis Gore) returned to England on leave, and Brock succeeded him in his position. So it happened that when the war was declared Brock held both civic and military command in Upper Canada.

The general direction of the campaign for the conquest of Canada was entrusted by the Government of the United States to General Dearborn. This able soldier determined to invade Canada at three points simultaneously. General Hull, at the head of his well-equipped army of 2,500 troops, was, as has been told, stationed at Detroit, with only the broad blue river between him and Canadian soil. In all that part of Canada there were only some 300 troops, and these were stationed at Fort Maiden—a small post at a point where the Detroit River flows into Lake Erie. His part of the campaign was looked upon as a foregone conclusion. He was to subdue the western peninsula of Canada, and if necessary march its length to Niagara. Niagara was, of course, the second point of invasion. On the banks of this river, at the little village of Lewiston, General van Rensselaer assembled a force of some 4,000 or 5,000 soldiers, preparatory to crossing the river. When he finally took this step, it resulted in the Battle of Queenston Heights, the death of General Brock, and the slaughter or capture by the Canadians of the whole of the American troops who crossed the river.

The third army of invasion headed for Montreal and Lower Canada. This was under the command of General Dearborn himself, and he and his army made for Canada by way of that strange waterway, famous in the annals of the cruel wars between the English and French, to wit—Lakes George and Champlain. Every schoolboy is familiar with this historic waterway, with its Fort Frederick, its Crown Point, its Ticonderoga, for has not Fenimore Cooper told the tales of the forest and the streams, and re-peopled the rugged country with the red man, the light-hearted *voyageur* and sturdy pioneer? Along this route General Dearborn moved his forces. Canada found herself in sore distress. Three armies to withstand, armies divided by hundreds of miles of practically uninhabited country, and each one of them consisting of almost as many troops as Canada had at her disposal altogether!

When the bad news sped through the land there were many sinking hearts, and few indeed who believed that the invasion could be for long withstood. Nevertheless, at the call for volunteers, the farmers and townsmen, tradesmen and the followers of the professions, all shouldered their guns and made off for the front. They rallied in such numbers that it was found impossible to arm them all, and many were sent back to their homes to look after the tilling of the ground. Everyone feared that a long war lay ahead.

General Hull was the first to cross the frontier. Establishing his headquarters at Sandwich, he issued a fire-eating proclamation to the people of Canada, and did nothing. True, he made some ponderous movements against Fort Maiden, held by the 350 regulars—these, no doubt, supported by many volunteers from the south of Essex, a part of the country which had been settled by United Empire Loyalists, sturdy patriots who had given up their all and made their way to Canada when the United States gained their independence. But soon the invading General Hull received a severe reverse. He depended for his supplies on convoys from Ohio, and these had to make their way through a very wild tract of country. On the 4th of August, 1812, a convoy commanded by Major van Horne was suddenly confronted by Tecumseh, chief of the Shawnese Indians, and his followers. A wild fight took place in the woods, and in the end the great chief was victorious, scattering van Horne's command and capturing the stores. General Hull had but a short time before this heard of the fall of Michillimackinac, thus establishing a Canadian force at his rear. And now the news that General Brock was hurrying from Niagara to confront him caused the cautious Hull to take fright. He at once retreated across the river, and again established himself behind the strong defence of Fort Detroit.

When General Brock heard of Hull's invasion of Canada he lost not a moment. Gathering around him some 300 volunteers, and taking a handful of regulars, he marched to Long Point on Lake Erie, and there embarked for a two-hundred miles journey in open boats, in tempestuous weather, along a dangerous coast—the northern shore of Lake Erie. Night and day the little force continued its dangerous journey, tossed about by the waves of the great lake. Only the sound leadership, together with a cheerful determination on the part of officers and men alike, saved this expedition from disaster. On this remarkable journey not a man was lost.

Amherstburg was reached on the night of August 13th. The energetic Brock was struck with amazement when he heard of General Hull's retreat; but, as he had little time to spare from the more important strategical position—Niagara—he made up his mind to storm Fort Detroit without delay.

At Amherstburg Brock and Tecumseh—the two clear figures of "the War of 1812"—met, and together they planned the taking of Detroit.

Tecumseh was, without doubt, a warrior of valour and craft, a fit follower of Pontiac; and about him he had chiefs of sagacity and daring—the Wyandot Roundhead, Noonday, and Saginaw, to mention but three. These Indians, under the leadership of Tecumseh, rendered invaluable assistance to the Canadians in that part of the country. He generalled his warriors brilliantly on every occasion, and fell—cornered but still fighting furiously, as was his wont—at the Battle of the Thames.

On August 16th Brock summoned Hull to surrender Fort Detroit. Hull, having an army of 2,500 soldiers behind the breastworks, refused. That night Tecumseh led his warriors across the river and lay in the woods that surrounded the post, cutting off all communication between the fort and the outside world. Early the next morning Brock landed his force, consisting of 730 regulars and militia, safely on the American side at Springwells, and marching rapidly up the river bank appeared before the fort. General Hull took fright. When the war-whoops of the Indians struck on his ear and the glint of the bayonet flashed in the sunlight, and when a bold summons came from Brock, without striking a blow he surrendered fort, army, stores—everything. Brock found himself with 2,500 prisoners of war on his hands, and in possession of the key to all that part of the continent, besides thirty-three pieces of cannon and stores to a vast amount. What might have happened if the aged general had made a fight of it there is no telling. The fort was a stronghold, well equipped, well garrisoned, and the Canadian army was small in numbers. Brock must have found his hands full had the gates been shut in his face instead of being flung wide open. For this mad surrender General Hull was sentenced to be shot, but it is good to know that this sentence was not carried out. In his day he had served his country well.

Brock's triumph sent a thrill of joy and pride through Canada. Foreboding, and even despondency, quickly gave place to hope. Success nerved the people of Canada, and they prepared for a stubborn defence of their beautiful country.

Leaving Proctor in charge of the captured fort, Brock hastened back to Niagara to confront General van Rensselaer.

A grander setting for a battle could not well be found than Nature had prepared for the battle of Queenston Heights. This neat little town of Queenston, with its population of five hundred souls, was in the stirring days of 1812 a place of no small importance. Here were established the depots for all public stores brought from Lower Canada and bound for the West; here was the focus-point between the Upper and the Lower Canada—the outlet for the now rapidly-developing West. The two western forts—Erie at the juncture of Lake Erie and the Niagara River, and Maiden at the mouth of the Detroit River—were both dependent upon Queenston for their stores and supplies, as were also the great tracts of countries those two forts dominated.

In those days there centred at Queenston a picturesque gathering of queer, rough people: fur-traders, merchants, Indians, *voyageurs* from Lower Canada, pioneers, soldiers, hunters—indeed, a typical frontier throng. Here the civilised East touched elbows with the barbarous West. From the West came stores of rich furs; from the East many things—including rum. But trade is precarious: Nature alone is unchanging. The commercial glory has long since deserted the little town on the banks of the Niagara. The fur-ladened canoes have drifted down the streams of Time. The pioneer has shouldered his axe and marched into the past. But still, perched upon a ledge of the rock, Queenston looks down upon a river—deep, rapid, braided with currents, dimpled with eddies, and carrying on its bosom the bubbles born of the mammoth falls. Across this strait the banks of the American shore rise to a great height. Behind the quiet town the land heaves abruptly to a hill which commands a view of all the surrounding country. On top of this hill now stands the grandest shaft in Canada, to the memory of the general who fell in the fight below. In the distance can be seen the perpetual cloud of spray which is flung to heaven by the thundering waters of the Falls of Niagara, for these are only nine miles distant from Queenston.

The latter days of September and the opening days of October of the year 1812 were busy ones on either side of the Niagara River. Both Americans and Canadians were energetically preparing for the struggle that was inevitable. Van Rensselaer had chosen the village of Lewiston as his headquarters, and here he assembled a motley crew, almost as diversified in its atoms as were the Canadian ranks across the river. Among the American general's 4,000 men were many strange characters—frontiersmen, trappers, bushmen, Indian fighters, half-savage troops from the West and the South, together with New England farmers and sailors from the seaboard. These were more or less loosely knit together by the 1,500 regulars that were under the valiant general's command.

But, do what he might, the unruly troops failed to understand a number of things—for instance, why a flag of truce should be allowed to shelter its bearer, and many other niceties which go without saying when regulars confront one another on the field of battle. However, the men, unruly or no, proved themselves brave in battle, which in the

world of arms covers a multitude of sins. Those who chose to take part in the battle fought to the bitter end.

During the second week in October General van Rensselaer found himself in command of a sufficient force to warrant him in beginning operations without further delay. He chose the morning of the 11th for crossing the river. General Brock was uncertain as to which part of the river the Americans would pick upon for crossing, and had established himself in Fort George, leaving Queenston in charge of a small force under Captain Dennis. From some cause, the American general found it impracticable to cross on the 11th, as he had intended, and, unfortunately for him, was under the necessity of postponing the movement until the 13th.

Now it so happened that on the 12th of October General Brock,

desiring to effect an exchange of prisoners, despatched, for the purposes of negotiation, Colonel Evans across the river under the meagre protection of a flag of truce. When this British officer reached the American shore, he was met at the waterside by an American officer who forbade him to land, and, after a couple of hours' delay, he was told to return to his commander and tell him that "Everything would be satisfactorily arranged the day after tomorrow." This strange reply set the colonel a-thinking, and as he was turning the matter over in his mind, trying to make head or tail of such a message, his quick eye discovered boats slung in the fissures of the rocks and covered with bushes. At once he guessed that an attack was imminent. He hastened back to Queenston, and, without waiting to ride the seven miles to Fort George, he took matters in his own hands, and prepared the place for the threatened attack.

At this time the only regulars at Queenston—men of the 49th—were under arrest for mutiny. These Evans at once released, as he did so urging them to do their duty, and word was sent far and wide to the Canadian Militia, calling upon them to assemble at Queenston and Fort George. When these arrangements were completed, Colonel Evans, leaving Captain Dennis in charge, rode to inform General Brock of what he had heard, seen, and done. Brock agreed in his surmises of an attack, approved of his acts, but had his doubts as to whether the Americans would land at Queenston or no. That night the officers slept in their uniforms.

Sure enough, at two o'clock in the morning, the ominous boom of cannon awakened the garrison in Fort George. The attack on Queenston Heights had commenced.

The morning was black. The wind blew cold and raw, and a drenching rain—such as, in North America, usually follows the lovely days of the Indian summer—had for days been stripping the last remaining leaves from the trees, and beating them into the sodden ground, and hurrying the laggard bird to its winter home in the south. But neither the darkness and dampness of the morning, nor the dangers of the swirling river daunted the hearts of the American troops as they set out in silence to cross the water and to scale the heights of Queenston. Skilled navigators of the treacherous river had been pressed into service, and all things having been carefully arranged, great boats loaded with troops breasted the rapid river, and commenced to make a landing on a narrow ledge below the village of Queenston. The darkness and the silence seemed only to be increased by the lap of the swiftly flowing waters.

That night the Canadians kept a vigilant watch. Brock anticipating a crossing, and quite unable to guess at what point of the rocky shore the Americans would attempt to land, had seen to the throwing up of slight breastworks all along the river from Queenston to Fort George—a distance of seven miles; and behind each of these a handful of troops were posted and on the alert for any signs of an invasion. In the grey of the morning sharp eyes made out the boats upon the waters, and an alarm was at once sounded. Captain Dennis called to arms his two companies of the 40th, and these, together with a hundred militia, set out to oppose the landing of the forces. The troops under the charge of Colonel van Rensselaer—a relation of the commanding general's—first encountered the Canadian forces.

The Americans effected a landing on a woefully narrow strip of beach, and notwithstanding that the batteries on the American side of the river swept the heights above where stood the adventurous invaders, Captain Dennis managed to bring his little band within rifle shot, and to direct his hail of bullets so well that van Rensselaer and his men were driven to take shelter behind a steep bank, where, safe from the Canadian riflemen, they awaited reinforcements, firing as best they might up the steep cliffs. But soon the boats, industriously plying across the river, had landed more and more of their comrades at different points of the shore. Not without serious loss, however, for the Canadian volunteers were splendid marksmen. Captain Dennis and his small band found themselves sorely pressed. The Americans, crouching behind the rocks on the narrow strip of shore, began to cast about for a place to scale the cliffs. They were not long in finding one to their liking.

When General Brock, away at Fort George, heard the cannonading from the direction of Queenston, he called for his horse, and at once mounted. There seems to be little doubt that he thought the firing at Queenston a feint by the Americans, made in the hope that he would withdraw the garrison from Fort George, and that the invaders, when their expectations in this particular should be fulfilled, would land and take easy possession of the fort. Determined to find out the true state of affairs, and leaving General Sheaffe in command at headquarters, he set out, unattended, on the back of his favourite horse, Alfred, for Queenston. He rode hard. On his way he passed the Canadian volunteers hurrying on foot to the succour of their comrades at Queenston. Arriving at a favourable position for a survey of the field, a height where stood an 18-pound battery, he and his two *aides-de-camp*, who had now caught him up, dismounted.

Matters were going well with the defending forces. The Americans had been discovered much too early for the good of their project. Cap-

tain Dennis, with his handful of regulars and their backing of militia, doggedly confining the invaders to their original landing-place, and although lacking the necessary force to prevent a landing, still harassed the troops as they crossed the wide river. Brock swept the scene of action through his telescope. His officers and men were doing the best that could be done. That the movement on the part of van Rensselaer's troops was no feint, but a full-blooded action, was now quite apparent to Brock. That it was very unlikely to succeed should Dennis manage to hold the Americans to their strip of white sand by the margin of the swirling river until reinforcements, at that moment on the way, had time to arrive from Fort George, Chippewa, and the various breastworks on the river, must also have been the thoughts of the general who had planned, with the minutest care, the defences of the frontier. Although in van Rensselaer he had to deal with a general of a calibre altogether different from that of Hull, he could have had no more than the anxiety a good leader must always harbour as to the result of the conflict.

But a sad disappointment heralded a still more calamitous loss. At the very moment that General Brock had finished his survey of the field, and was lowering his telescope, the rattle of small-arms came down from the heights. This was immediately followed by a sweeping hail of bullets which cut into the ranks of the gallant defenders of Queenston Heights. Enemies in the rear! There was no time for mounting. General Brock and his aides, together with the men in charge of the battery, being hopelessly exposed to a fire they had no power to silence, rushed pell-mell to a place of safety.

The volley which had caused such a startling change in the aspect of affairs came from the crest of the heights.

Captain Wool, a young American officer, finding the position on the strip of sand a far from pleasant one, with men falling about him and no prospect of an immediate alteration in the state of affairs, and being of a daring turn of mind, asked for and obtained permission from his senior officers to attempt the scaling of the heights at a point which seemed to him to hold out hopes of success. Taking with him a strong detachment of regulars, he began to search the face of the cliff, and was not long in discovering a fisherman's path cut into the face of the rock. This had been looked upon by the Canadians as an impossible path. But Wool and his brave men quickly turned the impossible into a most successful possibility. Scaling the heights undetected by the Canadians, displaying in so doing singular agility, coolness, and sagacity for one so young and unused to war, he established his force in a commanding position before making his presence known to the Canadians by the most disastrous volley that whistled past the ears of General Brock. This bold movement put an entirely different complexion on the conflict. The Canadians were now between two fires. The salvation of the Canadian position demanded that he be driven from his dangerous hold.

General Brock saw that this must be done, and done at once. First despatching in hot haste a message to General Sheaffe, ordering him to bring on the troops from Fort George, Brock prepared to personally lead the attack on the young American's position. Placing himself at the head of Captain William's command of one hundred regulars, and with his own beloved York (Toronto) Volunteers supporting, he advanced towards the stronghold. After exchanging a heavy fire, he ordered a charge. But the Americans, tenaciously holding their ground, all the while poured down the hill a steady and well-directed fire.

General Brock standing as he did quite six feet two in height, dressed in the conspicuous uniform of a British officer, and in the very thickest of the fight, small wonder that the men of Captain Wool's command, good shots as were all frontiersmen, soon singled him out. At the very instant the brave general raised his hand toward the height and shouted, "Push on, the York Volunteers!" a bullet struck him on the right breast, and passed completely through his body. Brock sank to the earth. Many who saw him fall ran to give him the assistance that not one of them had in his power to give. As they raised his head he had only breath left to ask that the news of his death be kept from the soldiers, so that they might not be discouraged. Then he spoke some words of his sister; but his voice was weak, his breath failing, his heart's-blood gushed from him, and those about who strained an ear were quite unable to make out his request. As his body lay wrapped in his cloak at a small house in Queenston, the cannon of the Tower of London thundered, and the bells of London rang madly and merrily. The news of Brock's capture of Detroit had, that very hour, reached the people of England. The honours that were bestowed upon him fell upon a pale, dead face.

Here let it be told to the credit of mankind that when the body of the British general was on its way to its first burial-place the American general caused his men to fire minute guns, out of respect for the dead. "The War of 1812" was conducted with peculiar cruelty. Life and property were destroyed needlessly, wantonly. But it had its moments of conscience.

The death of the leader of the Canadian forces brought the battle to a momentary lull. The nerve-centre of the army had been struck. But when the first shock of the news passed, consternation changed to fury. With an angry shout the Canadians made for the heights. However, Wool and his men were not to be driven, and the Canadians quickly sustained a second shivering blow. In the charge Brock's Provincial *aide-de-camp*, Macdonell, who had assumed command of the York Volunteers, fell mortally wounded.

But the losses were not all Canada's. Wadsworth and Colonel van Rensselaer, the American leaders, had fallen badly wounded. In fact, about this time so many officers were down on both sides that there came a second cessation in the fighting. The Americans had much the better of the position at this stage of the game. Wool had been reinforced, and fresh boatloads of soldiers crossed the river.

But a change was now about to take place. General Sheaffe, on whom the command devolved, was on his way to the field of action when he heard of Brock's death. He proved to be the man for the emergency, acting with promptness and great determination. When, after a hard march, he arrived within sight of the field, matters looked black indeed for the defenders of Canada.

Sheaffe set about his task in soldier-like fashion. With the assistance of the two Indian chiefs Brant and Norton and their warriors, 200 volunteers from Chippewa, a post some miles above the Niagara Falls, and his own 300 regulars and two companies of militia, he formed, on the brow of the heights, a cordon around the whole field, the flanks of his forces resting on the river; and taking every advantage the ground offered him, he began to narrow the semicircle, firing volleys into the now exposed forces of the States. The Americans, in turn, now found themselves taken in the rear. The fighting had not long continued when Wool fell badly wounded, and Scott took his place. But the fatal tightening of the cordon continued, and General van Rensselaer saw that unless substantial reinforcements were brought forward at once his hardy men, who, at the cost of so much blood, had gained a firm footing on Canadian soil, would be swept into the river. He took boat across the Niagara to hurry over the necessary reinforcements. When he stepped ashore on his own side of the river he found a pretty how-d'ye-do. His troops refused to cross. They were Fencibles. They had not enlisted to serve out of their native land. The invaders refused to invade.

The truth of the affair seems to be that the sight of the dead and wounded brought back to camp from Queenston Heights had struck terror into the hearts of those who had remained behind, and that

when their general commanded them to cross the river they fell back upon their undoubted rights as Fencibles. But it was a pretty mess for an invading general to find himself in.

Van Rensselaer did all that he could under the circumstances to induce his troops to go to the assistance of their comrades now clinging for dear life to the precipitous cliffs of Queenston Heights. But no; they refused to quit their native land. Meanwhile the Canadian volunteers, now aware of the death of their leader, were fighting with the fury of maddened tigers. The cry ran along the lines "Avenge Brock!" and the Indians, who all looked upon Brock as a father, launched on the air their ominous war-whoops as they darted here and there like evil spirits, firing with unerring aim at the invaders, who in turn shouting "For the honour of America!" clung to the face of the heights like lichen.

In the core of that fatal circle the Americans fought grimly, and prayed for the reinforcements that never came. As time passed the Canadians tightened and tightened the circle. Soon the American officers were in difficulties; then the men slipped out of hand, and at last, with a rush and "Hurrah!" the Canadians were upon the invading forces. Nothing could withstand the downhill charge of Sheaffe's men. Wool and his men were spilt over the shoulder of the cliffs like water. Many a man with the bayonets and tomahawk behind him, leaped to his destruction, falling on the rocks below or into the ominous silent river; while the Indians, infuriated, hurled down the cliffs many that would have fain placed themselves as prisoners in the hands of the Canadians. The carnage was horrible. The cliffs dripped with red.

When at last Scott, bearing on his sword-point a fluttering white cravat, surrendered the American Army to Sheaffe, and when the Indians could be called from their slaughter—they had fought a winning fight with their wonted fury, for they hated the Americans ("Long Knives," as they called them) and were maddened by the death of Brock—General Sheaffe found himself in possession of a field slippery with blood and about 1,000 prisoners, including Major-General Wadsworth and many officers.

The number killed in this, the first great battle of "the War of 1812," will never be known. A great many men were seen to throw themselves into the river, preferring death by drowning than from the tomahawk of the red man or the bayonet of the white. One man was heard to cry significantly to a group of his fellows, "Come, men: it's better to be drowned than hanged;" for there were many British

renegades serving in the American army and navy during the years of this war. Although the Americans were severely defeated in their determined invasion, yet it is probable Canada lost more by the death of General Brock than she gained by the victory at Queenston Heights. For he was a man trained to war in the ablest school, and a leader who knew every mile of the frontier he was called upon to defend, and who was loved by his soldiers.

July 22, 1812

Salamanca

Major Arthur Griffiths

In after years the Duke of Wellington told a friend that he looked upon Salamanca, Vittoria, and Waterloo as his three best battles. He went on to say:

"Salamanca relieved the whole south of Spain, changed all the prospects of the war, and was felt even in Russia"

Where Napoleon was just then meeting his first great failure. Salamanca also showed Wellington at his best—it displayed the finest qualities of his generalship, his quick unerring eye, his prompt detection of his enemy's mistakes, his consummate skill in turning them to his own advantage. For it was the serious and unmistakable error made by Marshal Marmont, the French leader, that led to Wellington's victory. The duke said:

"He wished to cut me off, I saw that in attempting this he was spreading himself over more ground than he could defend; I resolved to attack him, and succeeded in my object very quickly. One of the French generals said I had beaten forty thousand men in forty minutes."

"*Mon cher Alava, Marmont est perdu,*" was his remark to the Spanish general of that name as he shut his telescope with stern contentment, and gave the orders that paved the way to victory.

Up to that moment, however, Wellington had been much disquieted. Matters had not gone well with him; he had been really outmanoeuvred, outgeneralled. Just when Marmont gave himself into his hands, he had been on the point of retreating, of escaping, indeed, while there was yet time. How Wellington felt that morning may be gathered from a story told at Strathfieldsaye years afterwards in the

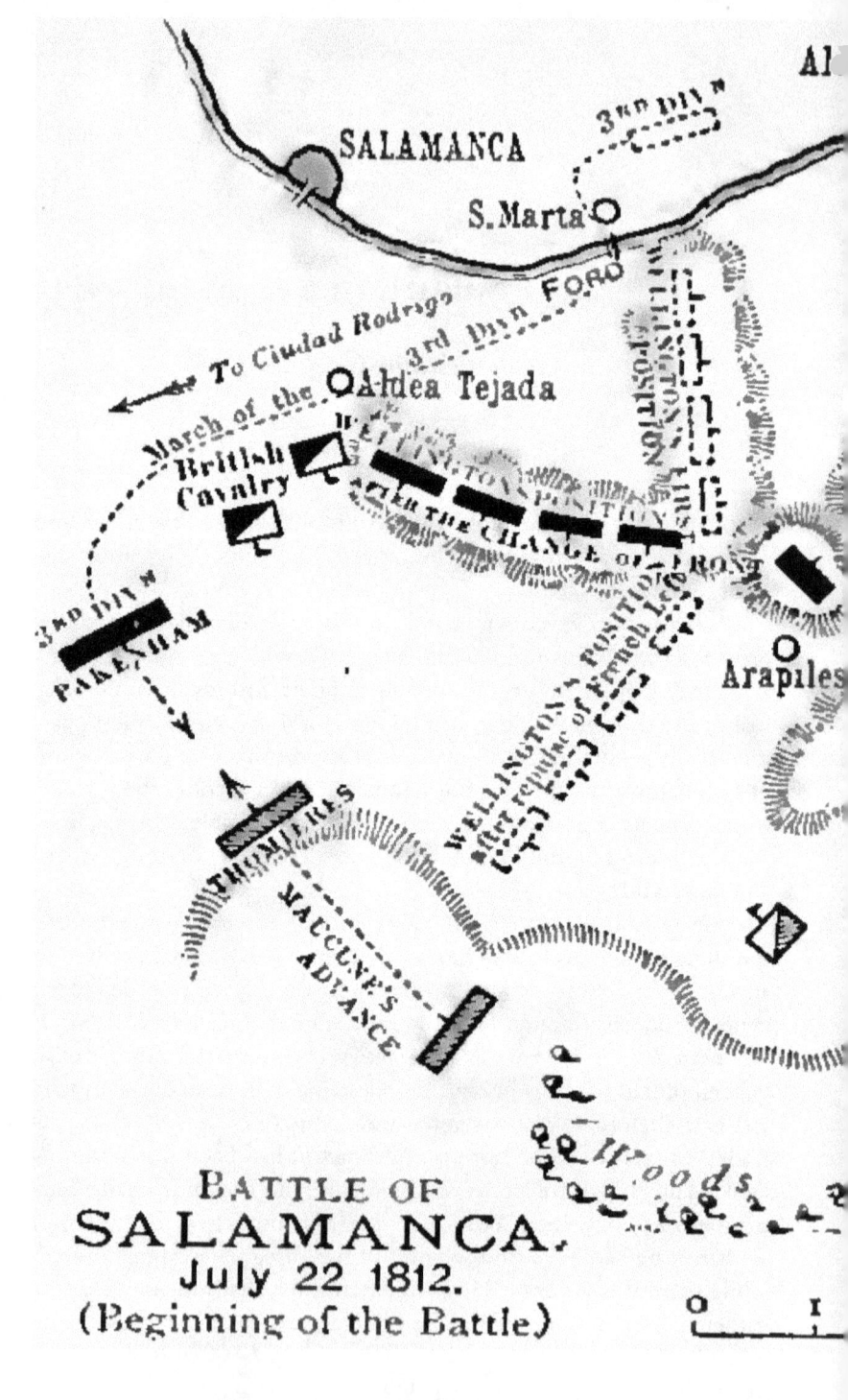

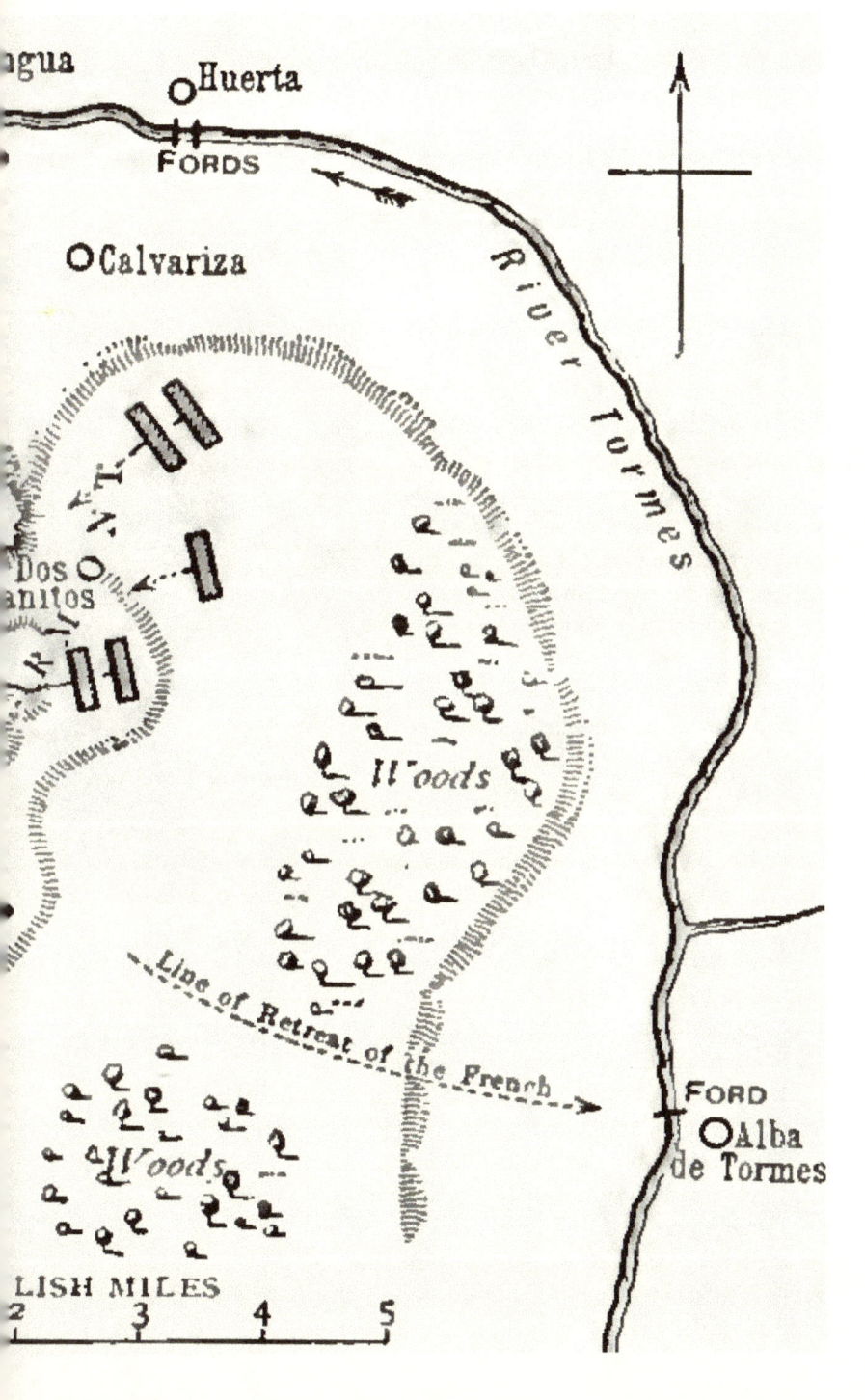

duke's presence by that very General Alava mentioned above. The duke had been too busy, so the story ran, probably too anxious, to think of breakfast on the morning of the battle. At length, about two o'clock in the afternoon, his famishing staff seized the opportunity of laying out a sort of picnic lunch in the courtyard of the farmhouse. Wellington rode into the enclosure, but refused to dismount like the rest, declined to eat anything, and desired the others to make haste. At last someone persuaded him to take a bite of bread and the leg of a roast fowl, when, suddenly, on the arrival of an *aide-de-camp* with certain news, he threw away the leg over his shoulder and galloped out of the yard, calling upon the rest to follow him at once.

The news brought him was no doubt that of the French flank movement which so jeopardised them, and was the prelude to the battle. Alava's comment on this episode was:

"I knew something serious was going to happen when anything so precious as the leg of a fowl was thrown away."

Food was scarce in those campaigning days. The duke, it may be added, sat by while the story was being told with a quiet smile on his face, but saying nothing. He was thinking, no doubt, that the narration was pleasanter than the reality had been.

But a true appreciation of the actual battle can only be had by considering first the long and intricate operations which preceded it.

The position of the English and French forces in the Peninsula during the early summer of 1812 was briefly as follows:—

Wellington was still in Portugal, although he had captured the two strongholds of Ciudad Rodrigo and Badajoz in Spain. These were to serve as advanced posts for his invasion of that country and the expulsion of the French, which, it must be remembered, was the main

object of the Peninsular War. But there were 300,000 Frenchmen in Spain distributed nearly all over it, in five different armies. That immediately opposed to Wellington was under Marshal Marmont; it was said to be nominally 70,000 strong, and further reinforcements were expected from France. Moreover, Marmont was in touch with three other armies, one to the north of him, one behind him at Madrid, a third to the South in Andalusia. Wellington had never more than 50,000, so it is obvious that while Marmont alone was quite equal to cope with him, he might be courting overwhelmingly superior concentration. Again, Marmont's army was a fine fighting force in excellent condition, stronger in artillery, although inferior in cavalry; an army, moreover, composed entirely of Frenchmen, of men animated with one spirit, obeying one supreme leader, the great emperor himself.

Wellington, on the other hand, commanded a mixed force: it was made up of four different nationalities—British, German, and Portuguese. His cavalry was superior, the very flower of British horsemen, but he had fewer guns; his men were ill-found, pay was in arrears, for ready- money was desperately scarce through the niggardliness of the British Government, and the want of it, the real sinews of war, was severely felt in his matter of supplies—which had to be paid for, cash down. Still, Wellington was nothing daunted. He hoped to achieve some signal success if only he moved against Marmont, taking him promptly, and before his supports could join him. There was at this time much friction between the French generals, and this was likely still further to delay concentration. Everything depended, therefore, upon immediate action.

Wellington advanced upon the 13th June. On that day he crossed the Agueda, and moving on towards the Tormes, laid siege to Salamanca. This city was defended by several forts and held by a French garrison. Marmont retired before Wellington, then returned to relieve Salamanca; Wellington took it, and Marmont again retired It was a sort of see-saw between the opposing generals. Wellington now pursued Marmont as far as the River Douro; Marmont crossed and stood firm on the farther bank. Then reinforcements joined the French, and Marmont once more advanced, determined to drive Wellington before him. He also was anxious to win a victory soon, because King Joseph was on his way from Madrid to supersede him. Moreover, he was a little disdainful of the English general's military capacity, which he had not yet tried in actual conflict.

It was now the month of July, and for the first fortnight the two generals were like skilful chess players engaged in a closely contested game. Each tried to take advantage of the other and bring on a checkmate. Marmont had, if anything, the best of it. The very direction of his advance jeopardised the safety of the English army, and Wellington's only hope was in rapid retreat. The French now all but forestalled them at Salamanca, and it was a race between them for the river Tormes, behind which lay the English line of communications with Portugal and the rear. As the two armies hurried forward, the spectacle is described by eye-witnesses as almost unparalleled in war. Napier, the historian of the war says:

"For there was seen the hostile columns of infantry at only half musket-shot from each other (not a hundred yards!) marching impetuously towards common goal, the officers on each side pointing forwards with their swords touching their hats fend waving their hands in courtesy, while the German cavalry, huge men on huge horses, rode between in a compact body as if to prevent a collision. At times the loud word of command to hasten the march was heard passing from the front to the rear, and now and then the rushing sound of bullets came sweeping over the column, whose violent pace was continuously accelerated."

This neck-and-neck contest went on for ten miles, and in themost perfect order. The same strange manoeuvre was repeated a couple of days later, and on a larger scale. In the end, Wellington reached Salamanca safely, but none too soon. The French had the command of the Tormes river, and still threatening the road to Ciudad Rodrigo, could still force the English to retire.

Fortune at this time seemed to frown on the English commander. He had had one chance of attacking Marmont, and had missed it. Now Marmont had the best of it, and could take him at a disadvantage if he persevered. Wellington realised that he must soon withdraw into Portugal, and he wrote to the Spanish general Castaños to this effect: a letter which fell into Marmont's hands. It was said after the victory that this letter was a lure to draw Marmont on; but it was a *bonâ fide* despatch conveying Wellington's real intention: the retreat was all but ordered, and it was to have commenced on the very night that the Battle of Salamanca was fought and won. In the meantime, Marmont, too eager to snatch a victory, had committed his fatal mistake.

At daybreak, on the 22nd July, the day of the battle, the positions of the two opposing armies were as follows:—

The English were on both sides of the River Tormes; the bulk certainly on the left or southern shore, but one division, the third, was still on the right bank, as Wellington did not feel certain by which side Marmont would move. The left flank of the army rested about Santa Marta in the low ground; the right extended eastwards towards the village of Arapiles and the hills of that name.

The French at daylight were advancing into position; they had crossed the river by the fords at Huerta, some had occupied the heights opposite the English from Calvariza Aniba to Nuestra Señora de la Pena, and others aimed at Seiziz, two isolated hills close to the English right, thus clearly indicating Marmont's design of forcing on the battle.

The possession of these two last-named hills now became of vital consequence to both armies. They were called the Arapiles hills—sometimes *los Dos Hermanitos*, the "two little brothers"—and they stood steep and rugged, rising like two small fortresses straight out of the plain. Had the French gained them both, Wellington would have been obliged to throw back his right, and fight with his back against the river—always a hazardous proceeding. But once more there was a race between the opponents, and the result may be called a dead-heat. Both sent off light troops living past to capture the hills, and each got the one nearest it. The twins were divided, and for the rest of the day one was known as the English Arapiles, or Hermanito, the other as the French.

This first small contest had an important bearing on coming events. It confirmed Wellington in his intention of retreating, but it obliged him to postpone his movement till after dark. For the French, in occupation of their Hermanito, could use it as a pivot around which to gather strongly and then swing a determined attack on Wellington's retrograding columns.

So menacing was their possession of this hill that Wellington was half disposed to attack and try to capture it. But he forebore, preferring to wait on events, and knowing something of Marmont's impetuous character, hoping still that the Frenchman might commit himself to a general attack on the English position.

This was precisely what happened. Marmont was seized with a sudden fear that the English were about to escape him. He saw great columns of dust rising from the Ciudad Rodrigo road, and rashly concluded that the enemy was already in full retreat. He was altogether wrong, as we shall see. The English were no doubt on the move, but not as yet to the rear. They were only taking up the new positions which Wellington found necessary since the French general had so unmistakably shown his wish to fight, and to fight upon the left bank of the river. These new dispositions amounted to a complete change of front. Till now the English line had faced north from the river at Santa Marta to the Arapiles hill; hereafter it faced south and east from Aldea Tejada on the right to the Arapiles village and hill, which became the left. This left was held by the fourth division; the sixth and seventh divisions were in a hollow compact behind and below the Arapiles hill; the third division was now definitely brought across the river, and being posted at Aldea Tejada, became the right of the line. It was the march of this last-named division, with its trains and commissariat waggons all pointing towards Ciudad Rodrigo, that betrayed Marmont and precipitated the battle to his own immediate defeat.

Inspired by this quite groundless fear, he suddenly directed General Maucune, with two divisions of infantry and fifty guns, supported by the light cavalry, to reach out and intercept the English in their supposed retreat. They were to menace the Ciudad Rodrigo road, while he him- self, if the English showed fight, would fall upon them with all his remaining force at about the Arapiles village and hills. Maucune's movement was the fatal mistake. It was an error, a tactical error

of the very worst kind. By this hasty and too adventurous march the French advance—their left—was entirely separated from their centre and their right; both the latter were still in the woods to the rear or crossing the river, and altogether disconnected with—entirely unable to support or act with—Maucune. Marmont had, in fact, as the duke put it, spread himself out too far. He was like a man who has lunged out in striking, and, unable to recover himself, is exposed to a counter-stroke from an opponent who has held himself compact and collected, ready to return a much more vigorous blow.

It must have been the report of Maucune's movement that was brought Wellington in the farmyard, and led to the sacrifice of the drumstick of a fowl. Napier says that the duke was resting when the news reached him; but whether he was throwing away an untasted lunch or sleeping, he certainly rode straight to the English Arapiles hill, and from that high vantage ground fully realised what Marmont had done. It was then, no doubt, he told Alava that it was all over with Marmont For Wellington no sooner saw the situation than he grasped it with the full and complete appreciation that marks true genius in war. His orders were few and precise; their object was to fall upon Marmont's advance, and crush it before it could be reinforced. He formed his troops in three lines: the first consisted of his 4th and 5th divisions, with some Portuguese on their right, and beyond them the heavy cavalry; in the second line were the 6th and 7th divisions, with the light cavalry on their right; and in reserve the third line, made up of the 1st and 8th divisions, the rest of the Portuguese and more cavalry. The right of the second line was closed by the 3rd division, under General Pakenham, and to him was entrusted the honour of opening the ball. For as soon as the above-mentioned changes of position were completed, Pakenham was ordered to come up in four columns with twelve guns on his left or inner flank and cross the enemy's line of march. This meant "taking them in flank," as it is called, or at their weakest point. As soon as Pakenham attacked, the first line was also to advance and second his endeavour. Then, on the English left, which would thus become uncovered, an assault was to be made on the French Hermanito hill.

And here, at this the most critical juncture, on the very eve of joining issue with a determined enemy in a great and momentous struggle, Wellington gave a fresh proof of his iron nerve and strong character. Troops march slowly: three miles an hour is the average rate of infantry. There must therefore be a considerable interval of time before the orders first issued could take effect; the French divisions on the march under Maucune had a couple of miles or more to cover, and would hardly get within vulnerable distance under an hour. Wellington was tired; he had been at full stretch, mentally and physically, since daybreak, and it was now past three in the afternoon. "I am going to take a little sleep," he said to Lord Fitzroy Somerset, his military' secretary, and the most favoured and confidential member of his staff. "Watch with your glass. Do you see that copse where there is a gap in the hills? When the French reach it call me: do you understand?" Then wrapping himself in his cloak, he lay down behind a bush and was soon sound asleep. Wellington had the faculty, like Napoleon and other great leaders, of sleeping at will, and he rose refreshed when Lord Fitzroy roused him presently with the information he needed. The time for action had arrived. *Aides-de-camp* and gallopers were despatched with last orders, while Wellington himself rode to the third division, where Pakenham was waiting impatiently for the signal to commence the fight.

What passed between the two generals (they were brothers-in-law) is historical. "Do you see those fellows on the hill, Pakenham?" said the duke, pointing to the French columns as they straggled along unconscious of the impending attack. "Throw your division into columns; at them directly and drive them to the devil."

Pakenham saluted, and then, as he passed on to the attack, stopped short to say, "Give me a hold of that conquering hand."

His admiration for his chief was repaid by Wellington's warm approval, for as the 3rd division went forward in grand order, a perfectly arrayed military body, the duke, turning to his staff, observed: "Did you ever see a man who understands so clearly what he has to do?"

One who was present says:

"Lord Wellington was right. The attack of the 3rd division was not only the most spirited, but the most perfect thing of its kind that modern times have witnessed."

Meanwhile, Marmont had fully realised his terrible error. The rapid movements of the English told him, too, that the mistake was patent to his enemy. He saw the country beneath him alive with their troops moving in combined and well-concerted strength, while his own army was scattered, and in the midst of a difficult and half-completed manoeuvre. But still he had no knowledge of Pakenham's intended attack, for the third division was invisible, and he did not yet despair.

He hoped he might yet reunite his army before the moment of collision; and with this object he despatched messengers in hot haste in all directions, one way to hurry up the centre and rear columns, the other to check Maucune in his overreaching advance. At the same time some of the troops in hand opened a fierce fire upon the central part of the battlefield, and others made a bold attack upon the Arapiles village and English hill of that name.

It was now, when hoping almost against hope, that Marmont caught sight of Pakenham and his division " shooting like a meteor across Maucune's path." Marmont, in utter dismay, was hastening to the spot most threatened, when he was severely wounded by a bursting shell, and had to be carried off the field. General Bonnet, who succeeded him, was also disabled before he could take any steps to restore the fight, and the command devolved upon General Clausel, an excellent soldier, who, in Napier's words, was "of a capacity equal to the crisis." But much delay ensued, many conflicting orders were issued before the French troops again benefited by their commander-general's controlling hand.

It had fared badly with General Thomières, who led the first of Maucune's two divisions. Pakenham had come on, supported by cavalry and guns, and, while the artillery took the French in flank, the infantry formed line and charged furiously. The French guns at first essayed to answer, but were silenced and driven off the field; then the French formed a poor, disconnected line of battle upon two fronts, one to face Pakenham, the other opposed to the 5th division and the Portuguese. At this time, too, the 4th division had come into action, and had beaten back the attack made upon the Arapiles village and hill. Already within one short half-hour serious discomfiture had overtaken the French. It is true that General Clausel's own division, part of the centre, had come up through the wood, and had regained touch with Maucune. The latter now rallied a little, and made a gallant stand along the southern and eastern hills, but his line was loose and broken, without much coherence or formation, while the westering sun shone full in the eyes of the soldiers, joining with the dense dust to half choke and blind and deprive them of the full power of defence.

Their complete overthrow was now near at hand, and it was accomplished by the masterly tactics of Wellington, who appeared as usual at the critical point at the critical time. Under his orders a great cavalry charge put the finishing touch to Maucune's discomfiture. This charge, made by Le Marchant's heavy and Anson's light cavalry brigades, was one of the most brilliant feats performed by British cavalry. Napier gives the story in Homeric language, telling how "a whirling cloud of dust moved swiftly forward, carrying within it the trampling sound of a charging multitude;" how the horsemen rode down the French infantry:

" . . . with a terrible clamour and disturbance. Bewildered and blinded, they cast away their arms, and crowded through the intervals of the squadrons, stooping and crying out for quarter, while the dragoons, big men on big horses, rode onwards, smiting with their long, glittering swords in uncontrollable power."

Le Marchant was killed, but others were there to lead his cavalry on. Pakenham, with his infantry, followed close, and, after a bitter struggle, which laid many low, the French were completely defeated. Guns and standards were captured and 2,000 prisoners: "the divisions under Maucune no longer existed as a military body." These

were the memorable forty minutes which sufficed to conquer the French left. At the end of this short space of time, the 3rd and 4th divisions, with D'Urban's fresh cavalry, formed an unbroken line across the basin or plain, a mile in advance of where Pakenham had so nobly begun the fight.

But the victory had been gained in only one part of the field. The French in the centre still maintained the contest with stubborn courage. Clausel had rallied his forces with surprising energy, and, for this purpose, skilfully used those that were still fresh and unbroken. His whole line of defence was now connected and stretched from where Maucune had been so severely handled to the western side of the Arapiles, where General Foy was firing on the reserves. He held the divisions of Bonnet, Ferey, drawn nearer to him, those of Sarrut and Brennier and the whole of his cavalry together covering his line of retreat to Alba de Tormes, and they were all firm and full of fight. Upon these the shattered remnant of Maucune's corps re-formed, and the hopes of the French were now revived by two serious failures on the English side—Pack with his Portuguese had assaulted the French Hermanito, and gallantly ascended to a few feet from the summit, when he came unexpectedly upon the French reserves strongly posted among the rocks. Their attitude was so determined, their fire so fierce, that the Portuguese recoiled, and were driven down the hill defeated and with great slaughter. Another disaster at this moment overtook the 4th division, which, just when it had won with much toil the higher slopes of the southern heights, encountered a large body of French on the far side. The latter being fresh, charged the breathless and somewhat disordered assailants, and forced them to give way. The French here were quite victorious, and would have pursued but for the stout resistance of two English regiments drawn up in line below.

Clausel was not slow to follow up these successes. He now pressed the left flank and rear of the discomfited 4th division, his cavalry came up at a trot and charged, the English were outflanked, overmatched, and lost ground; so that the fight rolled back into the basin, where several of the English generals were struck down—Cole, Leith, and Beresford—and the French Horse, having free scope, did great execution. For a moment the issue seemed doubtful. This was the final crisis in the battle; victory was to be secured by the general who had the strongest reserves at hand.

Wellington was in this position, and his opportune presence, as usual when most wanted, decided the day. He had fortunately still disengaged and untouched his 1st and 6th divisions, and part of his 5th. They were close to the centre, at the point most menaced, and ready to second their leader's prompt initiative. The 6th division now came up charging with great vehemence, but meeting a sturdy resistance and a murderous fire. But, undeterred by severe losses, they held bravely on, and presently regained the southern heights. The tide of battle again turned, and, although the French still showed a bold front, it was all to no purpose. Pakenham and the 3rd division constantly outflanked and hammered their left; the other divisions continued the frontal attack. Then the 1st division was employed to cut off the French right, under Foy, from the main body. But Clausel, who although wounded had not left the field, employed these unbroken troops, flanked by cavalry, to show a front while he drew off his shattered forces. General Foy bravely and skilfully withstood the last charges of the now conquering English. He had to face the light division and a part of the 4th, with the 6th and the Spaniards in reserve. Maucune also, to whom fresh troops had been entrusted, "maintained a noble battle," holding his own for a time against the ever-impetuous Pakenham. Behind the shelter thus unhesitatingly afforded, and greatly aided by the darkness, for night had now fallen, the beaten French retreated across the Tormes by the ford at Alba de Tormes, and by a happy accident escaped utter disaster.

Wellington to the last thought the Castle of Alba was held by the Spaniards. But he had been deceived wilfully; the Spanish general, Carlos d'España, had not only withdrawn the garrison, but he had made no mention of the fact. Accordingly Wellington was in complete ignorance of the fact that Marmont had reoccupied it the previous day. So the English general, thinking retreat by Alba barred, had turned all his attention to the only remaining ford, that of Huerta, where he counted upon finding the entire French army huddled together in dire confusion. But, while he strengthened his left wing to intercept their retreat by Huerta, the French drew off unmolested by Alba, and when the fact was discovered it was too late and too dark to continue the pursuit.

But for this bitter disappointment the whole French army would have been compelled to lay down its arms. As it was, Wellington captured 11 guns, 2 eagles, and 7,000 prisoners. Other results, direct and indirect, followed from this great victory. One of the first was the occupation of the capital of Madrid, which King Joseph immediately left to join and strengthen the defeated and retreating Clausal. Of the indirect results the greatest was the clearance of Southern Spain, for Soult was now obliged to abandon Andalusia, and, moving round by a circuitous route through the south-east, to regain touch with the road from France.

Wellington's reputation, already high, was greatly enhanced by this brilliant feat of arms. It was his magnificent generalship that secured the victory. Not a fault was to be found with his conduct; from first to last, from the moment he caught his enemy tripping through all the changing fortunes of the hard-fought day, until he smote him hip and thigh, true genius was displayed. "Napier says:

I saw him late in the evening of that great day, when the advancing flashes of cannon and musketry, stretching as far as the eye could command, showed in the darkness how well the field was worn; he was alone, the flush of victory was on his brow, and his eyes were eager and watchful, but his voice was calm and even gentle. More than the rival of Marlborough, since he defeated greater generals than Marlborough ever encountered, with a prescient pride he seemed only to accept this glory as an earnest of greater things."

OCTOBER, 1813
The Battles Round Leipzig
D. H. Parry

The well-worn old simile of the Phoenix rising from her ashes may be applied with truth to the French army on its return from Moscow; for, before its wounds were healed, almost before its actual losses could be counted, another mighty force was called into existence, and Napoleon, once more humming "*Malbrook s'en va-t-en guerre,*" set forth from Paris to lead it to fresh glories and terrible defeat.

Lützen, Wurschen, Bautzen. Dresden, were victories dearly won at the expense of enormous slaughter; but Culm, Katzbach, and Gros Beeren came as heavy blows, and Napoleon's projects seemed threatened with tragic failure.

Whilst *his* men dwindled, and the German roads were thronged with his wounded *cuirassiers* in wheelbarrows, or his troopers riding on lean cows, the allied armies, on the contrary, seemed to increase. Disaffection followed. The Saxons were deserting him *en masse*. Austria and Bavaria declared against him. As the enemy drew closer round him from all points, he hazarded everything on one cast of the die, chose a bad position, suffered a crushing reverse, and fled under circumstances of almost unparalleled horror.

Leipzig was at that time a small city girdled by a crumbling wall with four large and three smaller gates, a wet ditch where mulberry trees grew plentifully, and was separated from the extensive suburbs by a fine walk or *boulevard* planted with lindens which had grown to giant size. It was a great centre of learning and commerce: Fichte, Goethe, and a host of famous men had studied or taught at its university; its three annual fairs were attended by booksellers from all parts of Europe; and before

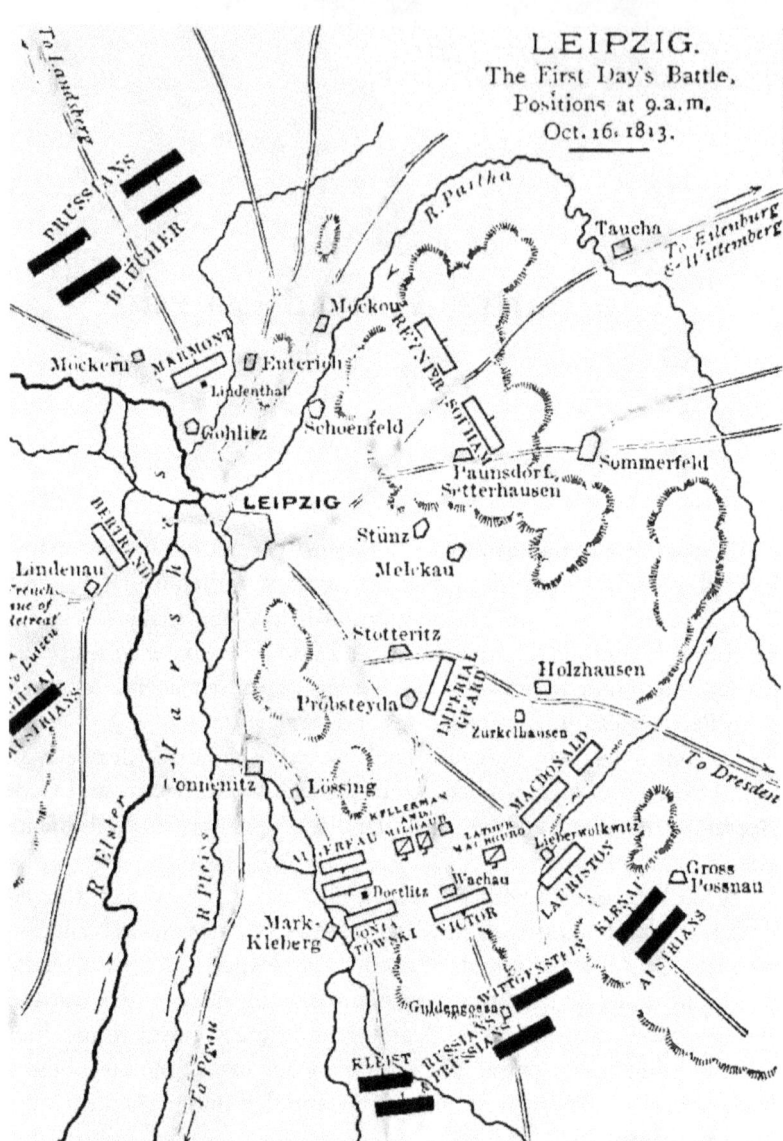

Napoleon's Continental system crippled trade it had lucrative industries in gold and silver, leather, silk, wool, yarn, and Prussian blue. Had you mounted to the summit of one of its many towers, as hundreds did during the events I am about to describe, you would have seen beneath you the narrow streets of the quaint city, and farther out the gardens, public and private, for which Leipzig was justly famed, with the villas of the wealthy merchants peeping out of groves and orchards.

Far as the eye could reach stretched a gently rolling plain, wooded here and there, in other places barren where the harvest had been gathered and the stubble fields were brown; the whole expanse dotted with villages innumerable, each with its pointed spire; the plain intersected by great highroads and winding byways.

West of the city lay a marshy tract, where the rivers Pleiss and Elster flowed sluggishly in narrow channels, and joined the Partha, which came round the northern side. This tract was a mass of tiny streams and dykes, crossed by a narrow causeway leading to Lindenau, and so to the road by Weissenfels, Erfurt, and Frankfort to the Rhine.

From the Rhine Napoleon had allowed himself to be cut off, by staying at Dresden when every hour was of the utmost consequence. There seem to have come to him towards the close of his marvellous career strange attacks of indecision which no one has satisfactorily explained, and the lingering at Dresden while the allies had drawn nearer and nearer until they had him in a net, from which he escaped but with difficulty and at great sacrifices, was one of these.

At last his various corps were ordered on Magdeburg, and on the 7th October, at seven in the morning, the emperor himself left Dresden, and quitting the Leipzig road beyond Wurzen, eventually reached the little moated castle of Düben on the 10th, where he stayed three days in further indecision, until he suddenly commanded a countermarch of his troops upon Leipzig, stopping himself to breakfast in a field by the roadside, at a point some fifteen miles from the city.

While there, the distant booming of cannon told him that Murat

was engaged to the south of Leipzig, and at the same moment the King of Saxony came up with his queen and a strong escort. Napoleon had desired them to accompany him, and advancing to the carriage door, he reassured the frightened lady, who went on after a short halt with her unfortunate husband, destined to pay so dearly for his loyalty to the French cause.

It was the anniversary of Iéna, and by a strange coincidence Napoleon was using the identical copy of Petri's atlas which he had consulted for the campaign that had laid Prussia at his feet in two short weeks. Now the tables were turned, and Prussia was about to have a terrible revenge.

The day was grey and lowering, and Murat had had several smart cavalry affairs near Borna. in one of which he narrowly escaped with his life. Returning with a single trooper, he had been hotly pursued by Lieutenant De Lippe of the 1st Neumark Dragoons, who repeatedly shouted "Stop, King!" "Stop, King!" After a galloping fight the pursuer was killed by Murat's attendant, to whom Napoleon gave the Legion of Honour, and who rode the dead man's horse next day in his capacity of equerry to the King of Naples.

Meanwhile, the columns were tramping in and taking up their positions; outside the house of Herr Vetter at Reudnitz, a picturesque village two miles from Leipzig, a *chasseur* of the Guard with loaded carbine showed where Napoleon had fixed his quarters. Waggons, carriages, escort, and orderly officers thronged the streets; every hour witnessed the arrival of a grenadier regiment, a corps of *tirailleurs*, or a rumbling battery of guns, whose grey-coated drivers forced a passage through the crowd with almost as little ceremony as the emperor's suite itself. The citizens had experienced a foretaste of French usage since Marmont's corps came among them at the beginning of the month, but that was going to prove as nothing to the misery of the next six days.

Early on the morning of the 15th, Murat clattered up to the door of the *quartier général*, and swinging off his horse went in to hold long counsel with his brother-in-law; after which, about noon, they both rode away into the stubble and the sheep pastures to reconnoitre around Lieberwolkwitz on a hill to the French left, and Wachau village with its orchard in a hollow, which formed the French centre five miles or so from the city, paying Poniatowski's corps a visit among the gardens of Dolitz, and finally returning to Liebervolkwitz, where one of those dramatic Napoleonic ceremonies took place usual upon the presentation of the cherished Eagle to corps that had not previously possessed it.

Three regiments of light infantry clustered round their emperor, and, turning to one with the standard brandished in his hand, he exclaimed in a piercing voice:

"Soldiers of the 26th Léger, I intrust you with the French Eagle: it will be your rallying point. You swear never to abandon it but with life; you swear never to suffer an insult to France; you swear to prefer death to dishonour: you swear!"

"We swear!" came the answer; "*Vive l'Empereur!*" And each regiment took the oath, and meant it.

The columns had filed down to their posts in the position chosen by Murat and sanctioned

by Napoleon, and the line of battle stretched in a huge semicircle south of Leipzig, three miles and a half from end to end; Victor in the centre behind Wachau with the 2nd Corps; Prince Poniatowski on the right with the 8th, on the banks of the narrow Pleiss at Mark-Kleberg and Doetlitz; Lauriston on the left, on the hill of Lieberwolkwitz with the 5th Corps; while farther away still, beyond Lauriston, was gallant Macdonald, on the Dresden road, keeping a sharp lookout for Beningsen or the Hetman Platof

In rear of Poniatowski were Marshal Augereau's men; between Poniatowski and Victor, the cavalry of Kellerman and Milhaud; between Victor and Lauriston the cavalry of Latour-Maubourg; and, finally, when they arrived, the Imperial Guard was stationed near the village of Probsteyda, behind Victor, and in front of the ruined windmill and tobacco factory where Napoleon took his stand when the fighting had once begun.

To the west, across the causeway previously mentioned, General Bertrand held Lindenau with the 4th Corps, and covered the road to Erfurt destined to form the French line of retreat; Marshal Marmont, with the 6th Corps, lay round Lindenthal, and protected Leipzig to northward; while Ney and Reynier, with the 3rd and 7th Corps, were in full march from Eilenburg, either to support Marmont or operate to eastward of the city—in all, 182,000 men to sustain the advance and attack of more than 300,000—namely, the Allied Grand Army, or Army of Bohemia, 90,000; the Army of Silesia, under Blücher, 70,000; the Army of the North, commanded by Bernadotte, 72,000; and about 15,000 partisans, Cossacks, and light horse.

There had been heavy rains for several days preceding the 14th, the night of which was miserable; but the weather cleared on the 15th, and everything was quiet, except the continued march of troops and the loopholing of the Leipzig walls.

Suddenly, about eight in the evening, three brilliant white rockets rose into the starlit sky from the allies' headquarters at Pegau on the Elster, and these were answered a minute later by four red ones that trailed up beyond Halle—a signal which put the French on the *qui vive*. That night Colonel Marbot, of the 23rd Chasseurs-à-cheval, lost an opportunity of changing the whole face of the campaign through no fault of his own, for, being in observation at the foot of a hill called the Kolmberg, or Swedish Redoubt, he saw several figures on the summit, outlined against the sky, and heard a conversation in French that made the blood tingle in his veins.

Stealthily drawing his regiment forward in the darkness, while the 24th crept round the other flank of the hill, a few minutes more would have sufficed to enclose the Kolmberg and capture the speakers, but one of his men accidentally fired his carbine. There was "mounting in hot haste." The figures vanished at full speed towards the allied position, and Marbot had a sharp brush with an escort of cavalry, learning afterwards, to his intense chagrin, that the Emperor of Russia and the King of Prussia were in the group that had escaped him!

Early in the foggy dawn of the 16th October Napoleon left his quarters, attended by his orderly officers and the escort of the Guard, and riding on to the hill of Lieberwolkwitz again, he was joined by Murat, the pair gazing long through their glasses towards the enemy's lines, where, when the fog melted into the drizzle of a cold and gloomy day, they saw several columns forming for the attack.

Huge riding-cloaks were then the fashion, and as the cavalcade left the hill muffled to the ears three signal-guns crashed out about 9 o'clock, sending their balls over the heads of the staff into the Guard and the *cuirassiers* beyond, doing some damage, and commencing what is known as the battle of Wachau.

Kleist, with a mixed force of Russians and Prussians, advanced on the French right wing in the marshes of the Pleiss and took the village of Mark-Kleberg; Wittgenstein, commanding two columns, also of Russians and Prussians, was partially successful in the Wachau hollow; and the Austrian general Klenau flung his men at the hill of Lieberwolkwitz, which Napoleon regarded as the key of his position.

Ordering forward half the young Guard under Marshal Mortier, and sending for a part of Macdonald's corps, the emperor repulsed

the Austrians with great loss, captured a portion of the wood of the university, and having separated Klenau from the rest of the allied army, turned his attention on his centre at Wachau, bringing up two divisions of the Guard under Oudinot to support Victor, placing his reserve artillery on the heights behind the village, and moving Milhaud's and Kellerman's cavalry to attack the Russian left.

All this while the most furious cannonade was in progress along the whole line, until, as one who was present has declared, "the earth literally trembled."

As the French horsemen gained the plain, affairs became serious for the allied centre, which was bayoneted out of Wachau by a superior force, and retired slowly, fighting all the way, leaving a thousand men dead in the stubble fields before it reached its reserves at the farm of Auenhayn; but, fortunately for Prince Eugene of Würtemberg, who commanded the retreating column, Nostitz arrived with a host of white-coated Austrian cavalry, which, after some dashing charges, drove Milhaud's and Kellerman's back, and saved the allied centre from a similar separation on the left wing to that which had already happened on the right.

Still, the allies had gained nothing but the village of Mark-Kleberg. Six desperate attacks had been repulsed by the French; and at Napoleon's command the bells of Leipzig were rung during the afternoon to celebrate a victory and a band played gaily in the market square, where the Saxon grenadiers stood under arms for the protection of their king. Away beyond the rivers at Lindenau, Bertrand had stood his ground against General Giulai while the great fight waged to the south; but north of Leipzig Marshal Marmont had been less fortunate at the Battle of Möckern, where Blücher took 2,000 prisoners, three guns, and forty ship's-cannon, which Marmont could not remove for want of horses.

The marshal fought hard though, in spite of the odds of three to one against him; and although he had to retire at nightfall on to the Halle suburb, he retained Gohlitz and Möckern as advanced posts, and kept possession of Euterich. Ney had drawn up in Marmont's rear early in the morning; but hearing the cannonade at Lieberwolkwitz before Marmont was attacked, the Duc d'Elchingen marched off towards the firing until Blücher's guns recalled him, and he is said to have lost both combats in consequence.

Returning once more to the south, one little incident deserves to be recounted, which had happened when the Kolmberg was stormed.

Napoleon, seeing the necessity of a strong charge, turned to a regiment drawn up motionless spectators, and asked which it was.

"The 22nd Light, sire."

"Impossible!" he cried. "The 22nd Light would never stand with its arms folded in presence of the enemy!"

Instantly the drums rolled the *pas de charge*, the colours were waved, and, supported by Marbot's *chasseurs*, they rushed forward. The sides of the Swedish redoubt became alive with blue figures and white cross belts, and the hill was taken under the eye of that leader who knew so well how to flatter the vanity of his followers, and who probably got more out of flesh and blood by a few artful sentences than any commander who ever existed, "charmed he never so wisely."

Between three o'clock and four, when the allied centre had been driven back, leaving its right exposed, Murat detected that weakness and prepared to swoop down with Latour-Maubourg's cavalry into the plain. Alexander, whose station was behind the village of Gossa, tried to get his reserves up in time, but by some mischance they were jumbled together in some broken ground, leaving two regiments, the lancers and dragoons of the Guard, to face the rush of fifty-squadrons, thundering down from the heights, the sun full on them as they came.

They were the 5th Cavalry Corps, with Murat, Latour-Maubourg, and Pajol leading—five thousand horsemen, mostly dragoons, green coated, grey breeched, high booted; white cloaks rolled *en banderole* across the square *revers*. which showed scarlet and crimson and rose, and bright yellow and dull orange; brass helmet, with the whisk of horsehair about them; bearskins of the *Compagnies d'élite* bedraggled with the rain: one of those furious waves that in the early days of the empire were wont to annihilate everything in their course, and which now tore, heedless of a storm of cannon shot, capturing twenty-six guns in the twinkling of an eye, and hustling the Russian dragoons over a brook in their rear.

A few causeways crossed the rivulet and the ground was swampy; the cavalry were splashed with mud from crest to spur, and the horses hock-deep in many cases.

The Russian lancers fell back and formed to the left, without crossing the brook; and checked in the moment of victory by the marsh into which they had floundered, the French squadrons became confused and unmanageable.

Guns were brought to bear upon them; the hussars of the Russian Guard charged in on their right rear, and they scrambled out in great disorder which degenerated into a panic and a hasty retreat, seeing which, the Emperor Alexander sent his personal escort of Cossacks under Count Orloff Denissof to take the mass on the other flank.

Back streamed the broken dragoons, nor did they halt until they reached their infantry, for they had been sent at the enemy without any supports into ground where a *voltigeur* would have hesitated.

Latour-Maubourg had his leg taken off at the thigh by a ball, and brave Pajol met with a terrible experience.

A shell entered the breast of his horse, burst inside, and flung the general many feet in the air, breaking his left arm and several ribs as he fell, to be rescued with great difficulty by his *aide-de-camp*, Lieutenant-Colonel Biot, and some staff officers.

Murat had a narrow escape; twenty-four of the guns were retaken by the Russians, and a grand opportunity was lost, while Gossa later in the day became the scene of a fierce encounter with the light troops of the Russian Guard, who forced the French to retire, and held that place as the allied right; their centre being then at Auenhayn, their left at Mark-Kleberg.

At Connenitz, between Doetlitz and Leipzig. Count Meerfeldt had crossed the Pleiss unexpectedly, but Curial, with the *Chasseurs-*

à-pied of the Guard, came upon him, routed his battalion, and being unhorsed and wounded, the Austrian general gave up his sword to Captain Pleineselve.

Darkness fell, and as the clocks chimed six the guns ceased firing, the rattle of small-arms died away, and the French remained practically in the same position, while the front of the allies had been considerably narrowed.

Nevertheless, Napoleon had gained no real advantage: it was of little consequence that he had maintained his ground. Many men had fallen on both sides, but the allies could afford to lose them, and the French could not.

He was hard pressed by Blücher on the north; to southward the enemy were being strongly reinforced, and a hideous stream of wounded crawled back to the city to show how severely the Grand Army had suffered.

The corn magazine, capable of holding 2,500 men, was crammed full to overflowing, the rest lay about the streets untended, and reflected the greatest discredit on the ambulance arrangements, never adequate to the needs of any of those gory campaigns; while out beyond the city a circle of fires and blazing villages showed where the armies bivouacked among the dead.

Sunday came, the 17th October, dark and stormy with gusts of rain; and the allies, hearing that Beningsen and Collorado would not be up before evening, postponed the attack until the following day. But Napoleon, finding that Wintzingerode, with the advance-guard of Bernadotte's army, had worked round to the east of Leipzig and appeared at Taucha on the Partha's banks, and that the net was closing tighter, spent the hours in anxious meditation, and made fresh plans to concentrate his forces closer round the city.

He pitched his five blue and white-striped tents in a dry fish-pond near Probsteyda that night, with the Old Guard encamped about him, and waited in vain for a reply to his negotiations, having sent General Meerfeldt, on his parole, to the allied sovereigns with certain proposals. He had said to that officer:

"They are deceived in respect to me. I demand nothing better than to repose myself in the shade of peace, and ensure the happiness of France, as I have ensured her glory."

But the sovereigns were no longer to be hoodwinked by specious words: with time had come experience.

*****

Down a long *vista* of eighty years we can now look back calmly, if with wonder, at this stirring period; feeling almost a reverence for the little figure on the white horse, as we marvel at his mighty genius, and gaze with admiration at the faded flag he kissed at Fontainebleau, or the moth-eaten *chapeau* he wore at Eylau; but set the clock back, and picture how he looked in 1813.

Napoleon had become a public nuisance in Europe: no king was safe on his throne, no people within his reach knew at what hour the tap of the drum might not sound on the high-road and a locust scourge spread over their fields and homesteads.

******

During the night Napoleon knew no sleep; Nansouty and various generals were called up to be questioned, and at 3 o'clock in the morning the four lamps of the emperor's carriage flashed outside Ney's quarters at Reudnitz—the same that Napoleon had occupied on his arrival.

After an hour of close consultation the emperor left in the rain, and walking with Murat along the swollen dykes for half an hour, again sought his tent, much absorbed.

It is also said they rode along the causeway as far as the Kuhthurm, or Cow Tower, towards Lindenau, to give Bertrand instructions to occupy Weissenfels and keep the road clear.

An alteration in the French position had been effected in the night and early morning, and now Connenitz formed the right wing under Prince Poniatowski, raised to the dignity of marshal for his gallantry the day before.

Victor had fallen back to Probsteyda; Lauriston, between that village and Stötteritz, upon which latter place Macdonald had retired; General Reynier with a brigade of Saxons occupied Mockou, and also Paunsdorf, on the Wurtzen-Dresden road; Ney was in force near Setterhausen, not far from Reudnitz, and at Schoenfeld on the Partha; while the northern suburbs of Leipzig were defended by Marmont as before. Thus, with Bertrand on the west, the city was completely surrounded, the position having one great fault, as Napoleon well knew—namely, in case of defeat all these scattered corps, miniature armies in themselves, would be forced to get away by the narrow causeway across the Pleiss and Elster.

South of Leipzig Murat was in command; east and north, Marshal

Ney; the emperor himself remaining the greater part of the time on a hill behind Probsteyda, near the ruined windmill and tobacco factory, that gave him a panoramic view of the field, and round about which his guard was waiting.

By eight o'clock on the 18th, Napoleon was on the windmill hill, and a little later the allied troops were again descried on the march to attack him.

The weather had cleared and the sun was shining; the Prussians began to sing "Hail to thee in victory crowned," their bands joining in; and, from their quarters at the dismantled *château* of Rotha, some ten miles away, the Emperor Alexander and his suite rode into the plains at Glossa, joined by Frederick William of Prussia, who had slept at Borna, to witness the commencement of a conflict so fierce that it has been called the "Battle of the Giants" by some, and by others the "Battle of the Nations." Three columns were in motion:

1st, Beningsen, with Bubna, Klenau, and the Prussians under Zeithen—35,000 in all, or thereabouts—was to advance by Holzhausen on Plural's left—helped, it was expected, by Bernadotte's army; 2nd, Barclay de Tolly, with Kleist's Prussians, Wittgenstein's men, and the Russian reserves—estimated at 45,060 in all—who was to aim for Wachau and the centre; and, 3rd, the Prince of Hesse-Homburg was to lead 25,000 Austrians down the marshy Pleiss against Dösen and Doetlitz, while Meerfeld's Corps, under General Lederer, went down the left bank of the same stream to renew the attempts against Connenitz which the Old Guard had baffled the day before.

At first the columns found little to oppose them: Beningsen cleared the French advanced posts out of Engelsdorf and stayed there, as Bernadotte was not

yet in evidence; Zeithen carried Zurkelhausen with much spirit and took some guns, while Klenau drove Macdonald's rearguard from Holzhausen village; but the near presence of Ney and the non-arrival of the Army of the North crippled the action of the 1st column for a time.

The 3rd column flung its white battalions on Dösen and Doetlitz, and had a hard fight among the bushes and garden walls.

Napoleon stayed for an hour on his right flank to watch the opening struggle; Hesse-Homburg was wounded, and Bianchi took command; Kellerman's Horse and old Augereau's men supported Poniatowski with some success, but the Austrians eventually took Connenitz, and there they stayed, unable to do more, and held in check by the firm front of brave Poniatowski, backed by Oudinot with some of the Guard.

All day they kept up an incessant skirmishing, and the brown batteries of Austrian artillery on the one side, and the blue batteries of the French on the other, continued to thunder and boom almost without intermission until darkness fell.

Somewhere about ten o'clock, or an hour after the battle began. Napoleon left the right flank and galloped away to Probsteyda, a circular village surrounded by villas and gardens, strongly occupied by Victor; and there he found the 2nd column of the enemy, which had passed through Wachau unmolested, preparing for the attack.

Probsteyda, and Stötteritz a mile off to the left, were the keys of the French centre, and massing Lauriston's men between the two, rather in the rear, with the bulk of the Imperial Guard on the windmill hill behind Probsteyda, Napoleon turned all his attention to that portion of the field, viewing the conflict from the ruined windmill itself.

A furious artillery duel began on both sides—a duel which was, perhaps, the most prominent feature of the Leipzig battles, for, from morn till eve the whole plain resounded with the roar of cannon, and the smoke of 1,600 pieces hung round the city, through which the watchers on the ramparts and steeples could catch hasty glimpses of surging cavalry or the progress of infantry columns rushing to engage.

Under cover of the guns three Prussian brigades flung themselves on Probsteyda, met by the fire of Victor's troops, who lined the walls and fired from the attics and windows.

Many forgotten scrimmages took place in alleys and pretty gardens; the hedges hid long lines of dead and dying who had fought with desperation in attack and defence; the people in Leipzig questioned the wounded who staggered in through the gates, "How is it going?" and it was always the same reply, "Badly enough; the enemy is very strong!"

By two o'clock Prince Augustus and General Pirch had taken half the village, but reprisal was at hand, and the emperor descended at the head of his Guard and led it with loud shouts of victory down the hill, where the bearskins thronged into the streets and hurled the Prussians out again.

French horsemen in a dense body rode round the end of the village soon after, but Grand Duke Constantine—he of the lowering brow—moved *his* troopers forward with a strong support of foot and held them in check, while smoke and flames rolled over Probsteyda, and the horsemen did not charge. Shot and shell tore backwards and forwards, until it seemed little short of miraculous that men could live; battery after battery swept the plain: the officer riding with a vital order, the drummer beating to advance or retire, the surgeon dressing a limb in the shelter of a burning farmhouse—all were hit, death was in the very air itself; yet Murat, in sable-trimmed pelisse, galloped hither and thither unhurt, and the emperor himself tore heedlessly through

his troops after his usual manner; his suite sometimes riding down an unlucky *fantassin* or two who did not get out of the way fast enough.

All day they fought at Connenitz, at Probsteyda, and round about Stötteritz, without making any headway on either side; but to north and east clouds were rolling up in spite of every effort of the heroic Ney to ward them off.

After hot skirmishing all morning on the banks of the Partha, Langeron's Russian corps crossed that river at Mockou; and about two o'clock Wintzingerode's cavalry passed it higher up and came into touch with Beningsen, whom we left waiting at Engelsdorf.

Ney accordingly concentrated his forces between Schoenfeld and Setterhausen to oppose the approach of the Army of the North, which began to appear at Taucha.

Reynier, who was under Ney, had been fighting hard for several hours with Bubna, and his difficulties were increased by the presence of the Hetman Platoff, with 6,000 roving Cossacks.

Poor Reynier was destined to meet with severe reverses on that day, and also to experience a novelty in warfare, for there trotted up about the same time a little body of horsemen clad in smart blue jackets braided with yellow, with large semicircular crests of black bearskin on their leather helmets. English horse artillery they might have seemed from a distance but for the long bundles of what appeared to be lance-shafts which they carried in buckets by their sides.

English they were—Captain Bogue's troop of the Experimental

Rocket Brigade attached to the Swedish army; and soon there came fiery serpents into Reynier's ranks, whizzing and burning and causing great disorder. Bogue was killed by a ball in the head, and Lieutenant Strangways took command—the same man who, as General Strangways, said gently, "Will someone kindly lift me from my horse?" when a cannon shot tore off his leg at Inkerman in 1854.

Often enough those rockets went the wrong way, and caused consternation among the troop itself; but it is certain that they astonished the French tremendously, and not long after eleven Saxon battalions, three squadrons of cavalry, and three batteries of guns stalked over from Mockou in the heat of action, and deliberately joined Bubna, leaving Reynier to his fate.

The French *cuirassiers* understanding too late what was happening, charged after them, but the traitorous artillery slewed round and fired on their late comrades, the rest of the Saxon brigade marching into bivouac a league behind the allies.

This serious defection caused Napoleon to send a strong force to Reynier's assistance; but all it could do was to rescue the remnant of that general's corps, and the desertion remains a standing disgrace to Saxon honour for all time.

Twice during the morning had Ney sent to Reudnitz for a fresh horse, and again for a third in the afternoon. Several times did Langeron assault Schoenfeld without success, but at last he took it; and Bülow carrying Paunsdorf later in the evening, Ney fell back on his quarters at Reudnitz, wounded by a ball in the shoulder, Sacken having pressed Marshal Marmont hotly in the suburbs of Leipzig itself, and Blücher having been driven out of Reudnitz by Napoleon in person. Darkness was approaching, and with it came the rain.

The guns continued after that, and, as on the previous night, a circle of conflagration once more surrounded the city, thirteen villages and farms being in a blaze, and a multitude of bivouacs glowing wherever the eye rested.

A fire was kindled by the ruined mill, and Napoleon dismounted beside it with a heavy heart.

It was 6 o'clock, and the result of the battle was practically against him, for, though his position had been retained, the carnage had been frightful, and the allies were in perfect touch with each other along his whole front from Connenitz to Schoenfeld. He was not in a condition to renew the combat next day, and there only remained a retreat under cover of the night, for which he gave orders to Berthier, and then

threw himself on a bench they had brought from a neighbouring cottage, and slept in the open air by the fire for a quarter of an hour with his arms folded, the staff standing round him silent and sorrowing.

Waking, he received a report from Generals Sorbier and Dulauloy, of the artillery, to the effect that since the actions began the French had expended no less than 250,000 cannon balls, and, including the reserve, there only remained 16,000 more, or enough for two hours' firing.

The Austrian return for the 16th and 18th is 56,000 from 320 guns alone. That of the whole allied army must have been something stupendous!

Order upon order did the baffled emperor give, directing his troops to retreat by the causeway on Lindenau, which was still held by Bertrand; and somewhere about 8 o'clock Napoleon rode away to Leipzig, where, finding the Thunberg crowded with wounded, he put up at the "Prussian Arms," or, as some have it, the "*Hotel de Prusse*," in the horse-market, leaving his windmill at the same time that Excelmann's division startled for Lindenau, which they did not reach until 4 a.m.

The night was intensely and unusually dark. The plain was thronged with the retreating army, and so great was the confusion inside the city that whole corps had passed through before the inhabitants realised that the French were leaving them.

The baggage entered by four gates, and tried to get out through one, and that so narrow that a single carriage alone could pass it at a time. Farther on, again, the Cow Tower was only the same width, and nowhere was the road more than thirty feet from side to side, crossing three English miles of marshy meadows and five unfordable streams by small bridges until it reached Lindenau, where a larger bridge finally conveyed it to firm ground.

No sleep had Napoleon that night, nor indeed had anyone in Leipzig save those utterly worn out by the protracted struggle, for the city rang with tumult as the troops struggled through the narrow streets, often in single file where the way was blocked with waggons and guns. Mounted Grenadiers of the Old Guard, Cuirassiers muffled against the rain in white cloaks, conscripts crying from very weariness—all streaming onward, many under the windows of the hostelry itself where Napoleon, in his dressing gown and with head tied in a handkerchief, sometimes looked out on the defeated mob, which had no "*Vive l'Empereur!*" then.

For once the Grand Army—or, rather, its remnants—showed a provident spirit, making great efforts to guide large herds of lowing cattle through the press, in which they were not altogether successful, and only added to the confusion thereby, as we read that numbers of oxen were browsing quietly in the town ditch when the allies stormed the suburbs next day.

Officers had pleaded for the construction of other bridges over the Pleiss and the marshes, and one had been made, though by whom is not clear; but it broke down as the first battalion crossed it, and was not replaced, Berthier afterwards making his usual excuse, "The emperor had given no orders."

Napoleon's horse was waiting at 2 o'clock in the morning, but it was 9 ere he got into the saddle, and for half an hour before that the enemy's cannon had been heard beyond the Grimma suburb.

To the house where the King of Saxony was staying the emperor rode at a quick pace, and for twenty minutes he was alone with his faithful ally and the distressed queen, the king ultimately attending him to the head of the staircase when he took his departure.

Apparently irresolute wine course to pursue, he threaded the crowd with some difficulty, and finally dashed by St. Thomas's Church to the gate of St. Peter, where he paused in obvious indecision.

His proposal to the allies that he should evacuate the city, and declare all the Saxon troops neutral, on condition that he should be allowed to convey his artillery and baggage to a specified point, was insulting to the intelligence of those to whom he had addressed it, and the guns he heard thundering on several sides made fitting reply. Still, he seemed loath to go, and finally rode as far as the Civic School in the direction of his quarters.

There he came under fire, and is said to have had an interview with Prince Joseph Poniatowski, nephew of the last king of Poland, and as brave a man as any in that brave age. So hotly had the prince been engaged in the various battles about Leipzig, that fifteen officers of his personal staff had been killed or wounded; he himself had been hit on the 14th and again on the 16th, and he was destined to receive two further wounds before the wafers of the Elster closed over him forever.

To him Napoleon entrusted the defence of the Borna suburb with a handful of 2,000 Polish troops, and Poniatowski's last words to the man who had made him a Marshal of France two days before were: "We are all ready to die for your Majesty!"

Lauriston, Macdonald, and Reynier likewise remained in Leipzig, and abandoning an idea he had entertained of firing the suburbs

to check the enemy. Napoleon gave orders to protract the resistance from house to house, and rode away with a small suite through St. Peter's Gate, calm and inscrutable of face, but as eve-witnesses tell us, in a profuse perspiration

"*Place pour Sa Majesté!*" secured no passage; the chaos of the Beresina was in progress, without the snow, though the Cossacks were close at hand; and compelled to leave the highway, the fugitive emperor plunged into a labyrinth of lanes, and had proceeded some distance *towards the enemy* before the mistake was discovered, when, after questioning some natives closely as to whether any byway to Borna and Altenburg existed, and being answered in the negative, he at last rode through Richter's garden, and so gained the crowded causeway by the outer Ranstadt Gate.

After he had gone, the King of Saxony sent a flag of truce to the allied sovereigns, who occupied the same hill from which Napoleon had directed the battle of the 18th, entreating them to spare the city, the answer being "as far as possible," on the condition that no French should be harboured or concealed; General Toll, one of Alexander's *aides-de-camp*, riding back with the messenger to see the King himself.

Against the city on the south the three great divisions of the allied army began the attack in pretty much the same order as on the preceding days, the Austrians marching along the road from Connenitz, Barclay de Tolly on their right, Beningsen still farther to the right again; at last the Army of the North came into absolute action, and stormed the eastern suburbs, while Sacken's corps bombarded the city from the north across the Partha.

Poor Bernadotte has been abundantly reviled for taking part against the French; but it must be remembered that it was forced upon him, in the first instance, by Napoleon's arbitrary conduct, and that he gave strong proof of his reluctance to shed the blood of his own countrymen in arriving so late; for had he wished otherwise, the Army of the North could well have joined the rest of the allies several days before.

As a Marshal of France Bernadotte had won his spurs worthily, in spite of the jealousies of some of his comrades-in-arms and the dislike of Napoleon himself; when he had it in his power to be revenged against his old enemy, he refrained as long as honour allowed it to be possible, which cannot be said of some who owed more to the emperor than ever Bernadotte had done: that his character has stood the test of time Swedish annals show.

A nominal rear-guard of 6,000 men had been left in the city, but it is asserted by many present that there were quite 30,000 about the walls and suburbs, to say nothing of sick and wounded; for the remains of Reynier's corps were still in the place, with a host of others more or less disorganised, and under such leaders as Macdonald, Poniatowski, and Lauriston. the fiercest resistance was made, every house being loopholed in some quarters, and barricades constructed of furniture and felled trees.

The attack was in full swing at eleven, and the fighting desperate; shot crashed in from the north and east, and a few shells dropped into the streets from the direction of Halle. The Pfaffendorf farm hospital was burnt, with most of the wounded, when the *Jägers* got there; but in spite of their overwhelming numbers, the allies only took the city inch by inch, and the final catastrophe was even then hastened by a terrible and unforeseen accident.

When Napoleon had traversed the causeway and crossed the Elster, he ordered General Dulauloy to have the bridge undermined, and then galloping on to Lindenau mounted to the first storey of a windmill, while his officers attempted to infuse some order into the fugitives by directing them to certain paints where they would find their regiments.

Dulauloy entrusted Colonel Montfort of the engineers to form *fougasses* beneath the bridge, which were to be fired instantly on the approach of the enemy; Montfort handed over the charge of the mines to a corporal and four sappers, and everything being ready, they listened to the uproar growing louder and louder in Leipzig, and watched the stream of retreating humanity which still poured towards them over the marshes.

The bulk of the Guard and the best part of the baggage had already passed through Lindenau; regiments, squadrons, batteries, and stragglers had been going by for many hours, and but for the crash of musketry in the distance, it seemed as though the crowd then on the causeway must be the last of the Grand Army to leave the city.

Sacken, Bülow, and Bernadotte's Swedes gained a foothold about the same time; the Young Guard stood at bay in the cemetery of Grimma, sallied out, were repulsed, and died almost to a man among the graves, fighting to the bitter end—neither the first time, nor the last, that French valour has showed itself at its best in "God's acre."

The Russians carried the outer Peter's Gate, and fell with tremendous violence on the rear-guard in Reichel's garden; the Baden *Jägers* bolted from the inner gate without firing a shot, and afterwards turned their weapons on the defeated French.

The wild burden of the "*Stürm*" march rang through the streets with loud huzzas and shouts of "Long live Frederick William" as the

Prussians entered the Grimma Gate; the Halle suburb and the northern side of the city were in the enemy's hands, in spite of Reynier and his men; but still the French maintained an heroic resistance.

The houses of Leipzig were tall, with many landings, and some of those landings have their legends even now!

But while they were fighting with a fierceness that increased as they felt the superior weight of numbers was surely if slowly overpowering them, a loud explosion boomed in their rear towards the marshes and the causeway, and a whisper followed it: "We are cut off; the bridge has been destroyed!"

The whisper became a cry—a wave of panic followed it; the gallant bands left the streets and yards and gateways, and rushing to the head of the causeway, found the rumour true!

Under the walls of the city the Elster approached very close to the Fleiss, and ran roughly parallel with it until the two rivers joined; across the Pleiss and the first narrow strip of swamp the horrified rearguard could pass, but no farther: a gulf yawned between them and the continuation of the causeway, isolating every soul in Leipzig from their more fortunate comrades at Lindenau.

Alarmed by the low *shackoes* of Sacken's light infantry, who had got into the Rosenthal island close to the bridge, the corporal had fired his train and shattered the only means of escape. A panic followed, and the enemy were not slow to take advantage of the circumstance, which in a moment had transformed a resolute foe into a mob of frantic fugitives.

Napoleon sent the 23rd and 24th Chasseurs full trot towards Leipzig, where they rescued about 2,000 men, who managed to scramble through the Elster, among them Marshal Macdonald, who arrived stark-naked, and who was hastily rigged out and mounted by Colonel Marbot on his own led horse. Lauriston, returned drowned in the bulletin was taken prisoner in full uniform, over which he had thrown an old drab great-coat; and, including those captured in the battles, 30,000 men, 22,000 sick and wounded, 250 guns, and upwards of 1,000 waggons fell into the hands of the allies.

Poniatowski's heroic end is well known. When everything was lost he drew his sabre, and with his left arm in a sling, for he had been wounded again during the morning, he exclaimed to the little band of officers and mounted men that still surrounded him: "Gentlemen, it is better to fall with honour than to surrender!" and straightway dashed into a column that interposed between him and the river.

A bullet struck him, strangely enough, through the Cross of the Legion of Honour on the breast of his gala uniform of the Polish lancers, but he cleared the column, and leaped down the steep boarded banks into the Pleiss, where he lost his charger, and was helped out on the other side thoroughly exhausted.

Somebody gave him a trooper's horse, and on it he managed to cross the intervening marsh and plunge into the Elster, but the animal had no strength to mount the farther bank; the mud was deep, its hind legs became entangled, and falling backwards on to the weary man, steed and rider disappeared!

Five days after, a fisherman recovered the body, still wearing the diamond-studded epaulettes, and rings on many fingers, and it was embalmed and ultimately buried in the cathedral of Warsaw, a monument being erected on the banks of the Elster by M. Reichembach, the banker, from whose garden the unfortunate prince sprang into the river, the actual spot being now, covered by a handsome quay.

Colonel Montfort and the corporal were tried by court-martial, the result of which has never been made public; but the report afterwards circulated that Napoleon had ordered the premature explosion to cover his own retreat is without foundation. Charles Lever has woven a pathetic romance round it, but all the evidence goes to prove that the corporal was alone answerable, and that no *blame* in reality attached to him, as his orders were explicit, and the enemy had appeared a few yards off when he fired the mines.

*****

The exact moment when the allies came into possession of the city is difficult to discover: the bridge was blown up shortly after eleven. Cathcart says he rode in with the sovereigns about twelve, but other accounts from eyewitnesses say the entry was at half-past one. If the time is uncertain, however, the attendant circumstances are clear: Alexander and the King of Prussia marched into Leipzig at the head of a brilliant column of Guard cavalry, passed the Saxon monarch on the steps of his house without notice, and eventually took up their station in the great square, where they were joined by Bernadotte, Blücher, Beningsen, Platoff, and later by Napoleon's father-in-law, the Emperor of Austria.

Every effort was made to prevent excesses: if the allies afterwards made loyal allegiance to Napoleon an excuse for robbing Frederick Augustus of an immense portion of his territory, they certainly took

steps to ensure the safety of the citizens, and that is to their credit, whatever may be thought of their subsequent treatment of an unfortunate king whose memory is still revered in the land where he once held sway.

Leipzig had suffered terribly, and its inhabitants were starving.

At the Ranstadt Gate piles of corpses met the gaze, and the milldam was full of them; in Löhr's garden on the Gohlitz side, where dark groves once sheltered the nightingale, and Grecian statues stood among the greenery, the French gunners and artillery horses lay scattered about in death. In Richter's garden, through whose iron railings Napoleon had escaped, the *cuirassiers* had been engaged: their steel breastplates littered the walks, and arms and feet protruded above the water.

Seventeen generals are said to have been taken, and among those slain on the 18th was General Frederichs, the handsomest man in the French army. Pursuit abated a league from the city. The French retired to Markränstadt, nine miles off, and thence continued their way towards the Rhine, severely handling the Bavarians who tried to oppose them at Hanau.

A solemn *Te Deum* was sung in the great square at Leipzig, all the sovereigns and their officers attending. Alexander reviewed the Swedish force and the English rocket troop, and preparations were made to follow on the track of the Grand Army; a march which, in spite of the campaign of 1814, greatest of all Napoleon's efforts, may be said to have never stopped until the allies entered Paris and drove the emperor to Elba.

JUNE 1, 1813
Fight Between the "Chesapeake" and the "Shannon"

Herbert Russell

The whole volume of British naval history has no more glorious and inspiriting page to offer than that which bears the record of the memorable conflict between the *Chesapeake* and the *Shannon*. It may lack the lurid splendour that throws Trafalgar out bright and strong in the story of nations; but one would hesitate to declare that it was not as proud an achievement in its way as Nelson's dying victory. One needs, indeed, to understand the philosophy of the maritime annals of that period to appreciate how much deeper than the actual defeat of the Yankee frigate went the moral effect of that ocean triumph. Our war with the Americans was an unpopular one from the very beginning. We had taken up arms against them, not in that spirit of hearty animosity which characterised the Napoleonic struggle, but in a half-reluctant manner, as though influenced by the feeling that no honour was to be gained by fighting the young colonies across the Atlantic. The lesson which our soldiers and sailors received very early in the conflict was a staggering revelation. John Bull soon realised that if he meant to cope with his antagonist, he must cease to treat him as a mere sparring infant; but gird his loins, tighten his belt, and go at him as a man to be reckoned with.

If the British army chafed under the reverses it met with upon American soil, the British Navy was tenfold more chagrined by the humiliations put upon its flag on the high seas. Our sailors were flushed by the triumphs of long ocean campaigns. They had learnt to think of themselves as irresistible. Their domination of the deep

had come at length to a habit of thought not for one moment to be questioned. When, therefore, news began to come in of the discomfiture of our ships by Yankee vessels, the effect was likely to prove correspondingly demoralising. The higher the see-saw of pride soars, the greater the depression when the descent begins. Time has taught us to look back dispassionately upon that period of our naval history. We were not fighting the Spaniard, or the Frenchman, but our own flesh and blood. Now that the dwarf Prejudice has long been crushed under the heel of the giant Time, what true-born Englishman but must honour and admire the pluck of the unfledged Yankee bantam sparring up at its old mother with such effect that the little creature's victorious crowing resounded from the Land's End to Massachusetts?

The British sailor was burning with a desire to prove whether, man to man, he was not a match for the American. Unequal contests were no test. If a ten-gun brig were captured by a Yankee cor-

204

vette of treble her size and weight of metal, the achievement could scarcely be held to prove Brother Jonathan the better man. Captain Broke, of the British frigate *Shannon*, sailed from Halifax, bound upon a cruise in Boston Bay, on the 21st of March, 1813, and he had but one end in mind: that of engaging an American frigate of his own calibre. So resolute was he in this desire that, according to James's *Naval History*, he sacrificed no fewer than twenty-five prizes on his voyage down, in order not to weaken his complement by putting prize-crews on board.

On the 1st of June, the *Shannon* having been for some weeks hovering off the port of Boston, inside the shelter of which the eager British tars could descry the lofty spars of the famous American frigate *Chesapeake*, Captain Broke sent a direct challenge to Captain Lawrence to bring his vessel out and try the fortune of war. The letter in which this challenge was conveyed is one of the most manly, chivalrous, and gallant pieces of literature ever addressed by a British officer to a foe. It begins:

"As the *Chesapeake* appears now ready for sea I request you will do me the favour to meet the *Shannon* with her, ship to ship, to try the fortune of our respective flags. The *Shannon* mounts twenty-four guns upon her broadside, and one light boat-gun, 18-pounders upon her main-deck, and 32-pound carronades upon her quarter-deck and forecastle, and is manned with a complement of 300 men and boys (a large proportion of the latter), besides thirty seamen, boys, and passengers who were taken out of recaptured vessels lately I entreat you, sir, not to imagine that I am urged by mere personal vanity to the wish of meeting the *Chesapeake*; or that I depend only upon your personal ambition for your acceding to this invitation. We have both nobler motives. You will feel it as a compliment if I say that the result of our meeting may be the most grateful service I can render to my country; and I doubt not that you, equally confident of success, will feel convinced that it is only by repeated triumphs in even combats that your little navy can now hope to console your country for the loss of that trade it can no longer protect. Favour me with a speedy reply. We are short of provisions and water, and cannot stay long here."

The armament and crew of the *Shannon* is stated in this letter. The *Chesapeake* was sixty tons larger, carried heavier guns, and seventy more men. Although Captain Lawrence landed four 32-pound carronades and one long 18-pounder at Boston, so as to reduce his broadside to the same numerical strength as that of the British frigate, the weight of his vessel's metal exceeded by one-tenth that of the *Shannon*. Therefore the advantage of superiority was considerably on the side of the American.

Captain Broke sent his memorable challenge by a Yankee prisoner, one Captain Slocum, whom he released along with his own boat on the condition that he should deliver the missive. The British frigate, with colours flying, then stood in close to Boston lighthouse, and there lay-to until it was seen whether Captain Lawrence would accept his opponent's invitation. The *Chesapeake* was plain to their view, moored in President Roads, with royal-yards crossed, and apparently in readiness to come out. It was a fine morning, with a light breeze blowing from the west and north, and the blue waters of Boston Bay were flashful with the high sunshine. The British officers had little doubt that the Yankee intended going to sea, for her three topsails were hoisted: but would she come up to the scratch, or try and give them the slip? No, no; the thing was

not to be thought of, after such illustrations of Yankee pluck as had already made the Stripes and Stars a flag to be honoured and dreaded. If the *Chesapeake* got under weigh, there was pretty sure to be a fight, and hearts beat high on board the *Shannon*, whilst speculation ran into wild desire.

At about half-past twelve, whilst the British men-of-warsmen were below at dinner, Captain Broke, with a telescope slung over his shoulder, himself went to the masthead, and there beheld the *Chesapeake* fire a gun and almost simultaneously break into a cloud of canvas. He likewise perceived that Captain Slocum's boat had not yet reached the shore. Therefore Captain Lawrence had not received the challenge, but was coming out in response to the verbal invitations that the English commander had frequently sent to him. It was a brave sight to watch the stately American ship slipping nimbly through the smooth water of the Roads, heeling gently over to the breeze which filled her swelling sails, and surrounded by a great concourse of small boats coming out to watch the famous ocean duel from a safe distance. A few minutes later Captain Broke was again on deck, and the yards of the *Shannon* were swung, whilst the roll of the drum rattled fore and aft the vessel, summoning the hands to quarters.

If needs no very powerful effort of imagination to conjure up before the mind's eye the spectacle of Boston Bay as it appeared on the 1st of June, 1813. At one o'clock, the naval historian tells us, the *Chesapeake*, under all sail, rounded the Boston lighthouse. A right gallant show she must have made, with her long black hull slightly leaning to the impulse of her wide gleaming wings, her three ensigns streaming from various parts of the rigging, and a great white flag topping the fore-royal yard, and bearing a motto which must now sound strange to the Protectionist Yankee—"Free Trade and Sailors' Rights." For above a couple of leagues the two frigates held on in grim silence, standing directly out towards the open sea. The *Shannon* was repeatedly brought to the wind, in order to shiver her canvas, that the American might overhaul her. Meanwhile the *Chesapeake* was busy in reefing topsails, hauling up courses, taking in the lighter sails, and getting into war trim—like some veteran stripping ere he steps forth into the ring to try his prowess.

The *Chesapeake*, firing another gun, whose sullen boom was intended as a note of defiance, came bearing down upon her enemy, watched with a thrill of pride from the land and the numer-

ous boats hovering about out of cannon-shot. There could be no possible doubt in the minds of the spectators as to the issue of the contest. Flushed by a brief but marvellously triumphant record, the Yankees stood waiting with impatience to cheer their pet frigate—commanded by one of their most gallant officers—as she towed her prize in. On board of *her*, it is said, the Union Jack had been spread upon the table in the cabin for the English officers to dine off when they should be prisoners below.

At half-past five in the afternoon of that eventful day the action began, and before half-past six the pall-like clouds of smoke had settled away to leeward; the crimson dye gushing from the scuppers of both vessels had become diffused, and vanished upon the clear waves; the groans of the wounded were muffled down in the depths of the cockpit; and all was over. Never before, in all maritime annals, was such a sharp and decisive engagement; never, in the history of nations, was a more staggering issue than the result of the fight to the confident spectators who watched it from their native shore.

At the hour named—half past five—the two ships were close together, so close that the crews could distinguish one another quite plainly. Among those waiting and resolute crews—all speaking one tongue, and sharing, at heart, in the same sympathies—were doubtless many who had relations in common. It was blood fighting kindred blood, and the struggle was likely to prove the deadlier for this. Captain Broke, watching the Yankee frigate as a cat watches a mouse, perceived her intention to pass under the stern of his ship. Anticipating a soul-subduing raking as the *Chesapeake* brought her broadside to bear, the English commander gave the word for his men to lie flat down upon the deck. But the gallant Captain Lawrence held his fire, waiving the deadly opportunity that presented itself, and luffed his vessel up sharp within pistol-shot of the *Shannon's* starboard quarter. And then the tremendous fight began.

In reading the accounts of the conflict, one cannot fail to be struck with the rapid and complete demoralisation of the Yankees. That they could not have been wanting in courage, one may safely affirm; but they seem to have been "struck all of a heap." The battle speedily furnished the British sailor with his pet chance —the boarding-pike; and when once it came to *that*, with anything like equality of numbers to contend against, there could never be any question as to what the issue must prove. Captain Broke, in his account of the engagement wrote:

"The enemy made a desperate but disorderly resistance. The firing continued at all the gangways and between the tops, but in two minutes' time the enemy was driven, sword in hand, from every post, the American flag was hauled down, and the proud old British Union floated triumphant over it. In another minute they ceased firing from below, and called for quarter. The whole of this service was achieved in fifteen minutes from the commencement of the action."

A lurid and life-long memory must the sight of that brief, but incredibly fierce, struggle between the two frigates have been to those who stood gazing at it from the land, or crouched, pale and startled, in their boats nearer at hand. The belligerents would be scarcely visible for the white, wool-like clouds which hovered over them, full of darting crimson tongues of flame. The very ocean must have been stagnated for a league around by the reverberating thunder booming over its surface. How was the fight going? None could tell for the first seven minutes. Then the pealing of the artillery ceased, the smoke rolled slowly away in great bodies of vapour, and the two vessels were seen locked abreast. Expectation and anxiety were at fever pitch. It was a hand-to-hand struggle now; the watching crowds knew that the cry of "Boarders, away!" had gone, and that upon the decks of one or the other of those vessels, dwarfed by distance to the dimensions of mere toys, a frightfully bloody conflict must be waging.

In very truth so it was. The *Chesapeake* had missed stays while endeavouring to fore-reach upon the British frigate, and before any further manoeuvre could be executed on board of her she drove down stern first alongside the Shannon, her quarter grinding the latter vessel's side just forward of her starboard main chains. Captain Broke had intended delaying boarding until he reckoned that the guns of his ship had done more execution amongst a crew supposed to be at least one-fourth superior to his own in number; but when the Yankee collided with his ship he ran forward, and perceiving that the *Chesapeake's* quarter-deck gunners were deserting their posts, he ordered the two frigates to be lashed side to side, the great guns to cease fire, and the main-deck and quarter-deck boarders to make a rush for it. The veteran boatswain of the *Shannon*, who was a survivor from Rodney's famous action, had his arm hacked off, and was mortally wounded by musketry, whilst securing the two ships together. The wild confusion, the clashing of steel, the savage cries and curses of men, the groaning and shrieking of the wounded, the whole uproar of that deadly conflict, must have formed a hideous nightmare-like memory to those who lived to look back upon it.

Captain Broke, followed by about twenty men, sprang from the *Shannon's* gangway-rail and gained the *Chesapeake's* quarter-deck. Here not an officer or man was to be seen. In the gangways about thirty of the crew made a small show of resistance, but were driven helter-skelter towards the forecastle, through the hatch of which they endeavoured to escape below, but in their eagerness prevented one another, and several actually jumped overboard into the sea. The Americans seemed to be completely bewildered by the turn the battle had taken. The *Shannon's* crew came pouring in, but they found almost a clear deck, fore and aft. Aloft the topmen were keeping up a destructive fire of musketry. But this was presently stopped by a midshipman named William Smith and his topmen, five in number. The exploit of this little band is one of the most gallant incidents of that truly gallant action. Smith, followed by his handful of sailors, deliberately crawled along the *Shannon's* fore-yard and gained the main-yard of the Yankee, with which the former spar was interlocked. Thence he reached the main-top, stormed it, and silenced the fire that was harassing our men.

Captain Broke had been wounded in the head by a blow from the butt-end of a musket, and whilst a sailor named Mindham was binding a handkerchief round his brow, he paused and cried out: "There, sir!—there goes up the old ensign over the Yankee colours!" A melancholy incident marked the hoisting of these flags. Lieutenant Watt, the first lieutenant of the *Shannon*, who had been wounded in boarding, raised himself upon his legs, and, calling for a British ensign, hauled down the Stripes and Stars and bent the flag on above it. But the signal-halliards being foul, the officer hoisted the colours so that the American flag was uppermost. Perceiving this, the *Shannon's* gunners immediately reopened fire, and killed their own first lieutenant and five of their comrades before they discovered their blunder. A straggling fire was kept up through the hatchways by the seamen who had been driven below. But it would not do. The *Chesapeake* had been captured in an incredibly brief struggle, and the resistance of a handful of men here and there was not likely to check the tide of victory. In a few moments the Americans surrendered, and the triumph was complete.

The old sea-story, has been often told, and who would think of again repeating it were it not that any record of the battles of the century would be signally incomplete without it? The moral influence of that victory was prodigious in its invigorating effect upon our sailors. It seemed at once to restore to them all that prestige which they had been slowly losing since the first gun of the war was fired. Yet, for the Yankees, it was a duel which they can well afford to look back upon with pride. The fact of the death or disablement of one hundred and seventy of the *Chesapeake's* crew is sternly significant of the fierce, res-

olute manner in which they maintained the short, desperate struggle; whilst the memory of the manner in which the vessel came out to boldly meet the enemy cannot but be a proud recollection. Britain made much of her triumph; and if the Americans desire atonement that the laurels did not happen to fall to their lot, they should find it in remembering the words of Captain Broke's letter, which is the highest admission of splendid qualities that one foe ever made to another.

November 11, 1813
Chrystler's Farm
C. Stein

After the successful issue of their struggle for independence, the United States of America increased in wealth and importance with greater rapidity than any other nation of the time. The long continuance of war had caused much distress in Europe, and many emigrants of all nationalities, carrying with them their arts and experience, had betaken themselves to the great new Republic, which offered countless openings for energy and ability. Besides the numerical force and political weight which were thus gained, the circumstances of the time threw a vast amount of neutral commerce into American hands, bringing profitable employment to ship-owners and seamen and an increasing revenue to the Republic. This condition of affairs in itself caused considerable jealousy in Great Britain, and the fact that France was deriving great benefit from the carriage of its seaborne commerce in American ships forced the British Government to adopt defensive measures. England also asserted her right of searching neutral merchant vessels on the high seas and of impressing English subjects found in them for service in the navy, as it was denied that the nationality of such men could be cancelled by easily obtained American acts of naturalisation and certificates of citizenship. The United States, with more or less justification, then declared war on the 18th June, 1812.

The Dominion of Canada was the only British possession open to the invasion of the American land forces, and, though its long frontier line from Lake Superior to the Bay of Fundy gave many points against which enterprises might be undertaken, the settlements and strongholds were so far apart, separated from each other by stretches of wilderness and impassable natural features, that such enterprises could, for the most part, only be isolated blows, and could have no great strategical effect. The most important feature of the frontier was the series of lakes, or vast inland seas, connected by mighty rivers, and no movements of troops could be made un- assisted by armed vessels and boats. Both sides, therefore, in the coming campaign relied for success quite as much on their navies on the lakes and rivers as on the land troops which they could put into the field.

The theatre of war was little adapted for the exercise of the best qualities of the English army of the day. As has been said, the settlements, small and few as they were, were separated by great tracts of virgin forest and wilderness. Soldiers had to be conveyed by water from one held of action to another, and when they were landed they had seldom an opportunity of executing such manoeuvres as would have been possible in almost any part of Europe, but they were called upon to fight in districts broken by woods, precipices, creeks, and morasses, where their discipline and stiff, steady training were useless and their courage and determination were more likely to lead them into an ambush or to entangle them among insurmountable obstacles than to ensure their victory. They were opposed to an enemy to whom the character of the country was familiar, men who from their youth had been accustomed to the use of the rifle in the pursuit of game, who were initiated into all the expedients of life in the backwoods, and were hardened by hunting toils into the handiest and most enduring of soldiers for irregular campaigns. Small wonder if the English regular battalions often found themselves at a disadvantage from the very excellence of their military training, and were unable in the wild regions of America to show proofs of the high value at which they were appraised on the battlefields of Europe. It was fortunate for the defence of Canada that it was possible among the loyal inhabitants of the Dominion to enrol a considerable force of militia, which, composed to a great extent of settlers or their sons, possessed a knowledge of the country's features, enabling them to act efficiently when regular troops might be at a loss. There were also some tribes of friendly Indians who could be utilised as light troops and scouts, and of whose chiefs some, and especially the famous Tecumseh, were warriors of the highest merit, combining gallantry in the field with the utmost loyalty to the English flag and great ability in the operations of war.

During 1812 and the greater part of 1813 the war was carried on by Americans and British with varying success, but, as has been seen, it was impossible for either side to attempt any great strategical operations. Detached raids were made by each Power upon more or less isolated positions of its enemy, but no crushing blow was struck which could have a decisive effect on the ultimate issue of the struggle, the Americans had, however, been so far successful that they had for the time secured complete command of Lake Erie. It was therefore possible for them to devote all their resources to operations on Lake Ontario, and their War Department conceived the idea of making a combined movement on Montreal by two armies, one starting from Lake Ontario and one from a post on the Chateauguay River near the boundary line of Lower Canada. The first was to consist of 7,000 men under General Wilkinson, and the second, of 8,000 men under General Hampton. If these two forces could unite on the lower St. Lawrence, it was believed that they would be sufficiently strong to overcome any probable resistance, and that they would be able to take up their winter quarters in Montreal. This scheme promised well, and the whole energies of the Republic were devoted to carrying it out.

On the 21st October General Hampton commenced his march along both banks of the Chateauguay river, and, after some preliminary skirmishes, was encountered on the 25th by a weak force of Canadian militia under Lieutenant-Colonel de Saluberry, which, covered by breastworks formed of felled trees, was able to receive with a well-sustained and deadly fire the American attack, and finally to succeed in checking it and driving it back. General Hampton, believing that he was opposed by greatly superior numbers, though in fact his repulse was accomplished by not more than 800 men, fell back to his original starting-point, and had not the resolution again to cross the frontier.

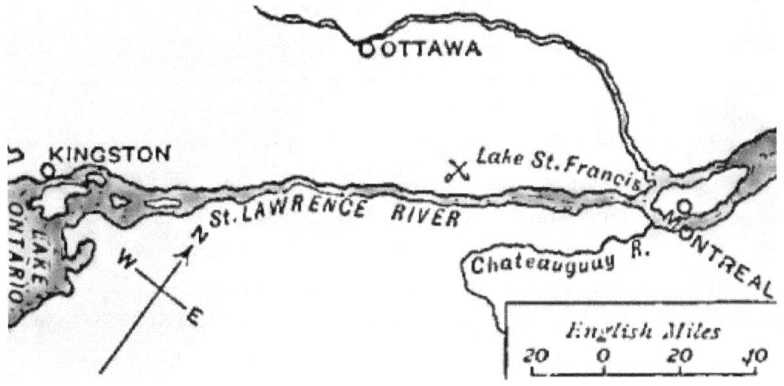

Meantime-General Wilkinson had concentrated his force at Grenadier Island, on Lake Ontario, near the St. Lawrence, and was preparing to move down the river towards the point of proposed junction with General Hampton. In making his dispositions he allowed it to be supposed that his object might be an attack upon Kingston, to which place all the troops which had occupied the Niagara peninsula had been moved; but he made no actual demonstration in that direction. As a matter of fact, the English and American fleets neutralised each other on Lake Ontario, and no successful attack could have been made upon Kingston while the English armed vessels were still unsubdued. In Kingston also were almost all the regular troops available for the defence of Lower Canada, and it was very obviously a more feasible operation to move on weakly protected Montreal than to make an attack on a town strongly guarded by land and on the lake.

The transport of General Wilkinson's force down the current of the St. Lawrence could not be made in the comparatively large vessels which navigated Lake Ontario, and he caused a number of small craft, scows and boats, to be prepared, sufficient for its accommodation. On the 25th October all was ready, the men were embarked and the flotilla dropped down the river to a point on the southern bank called French Creek. The American armed vessels, under Commodore Chauncey, covered the movement, and watched the English fleet in Kingston Harbour; but in spite of their vigilance, some English brigs, schooners, and gunboats managed to slip past them unperceived, and took up a position off the creek, from which they were able to fire on Wilkinson's army, and to do it some damage. The Americans had erected a battery of 18-pounders on shore, but these were able to do little or no harm to the English ships, which maintained their position until Commodore Chauncey's fleet, which they had evaded, suddenly made its appearance, and forced them to retire to Kingston.

On the 5th November the camp at French Creek was broken up, and. General Wilkinson re-embarking his men, the flotilla continued its voyage till midnight, when it again anchored after passing over forty miles of the river's course. Six miles lower down the St. Lawrence its channel was commanded by the guns of Fort Wellington on the Canadian bank, and it was a matter of anxiety to General Wilkinson how his flotilla should pass this fort unscathed. He met the difficulty by disembarking his ammunition and placing it in waggons. Every man who was not required to navigate the boats was also landed, and the whole marched along the American bank by

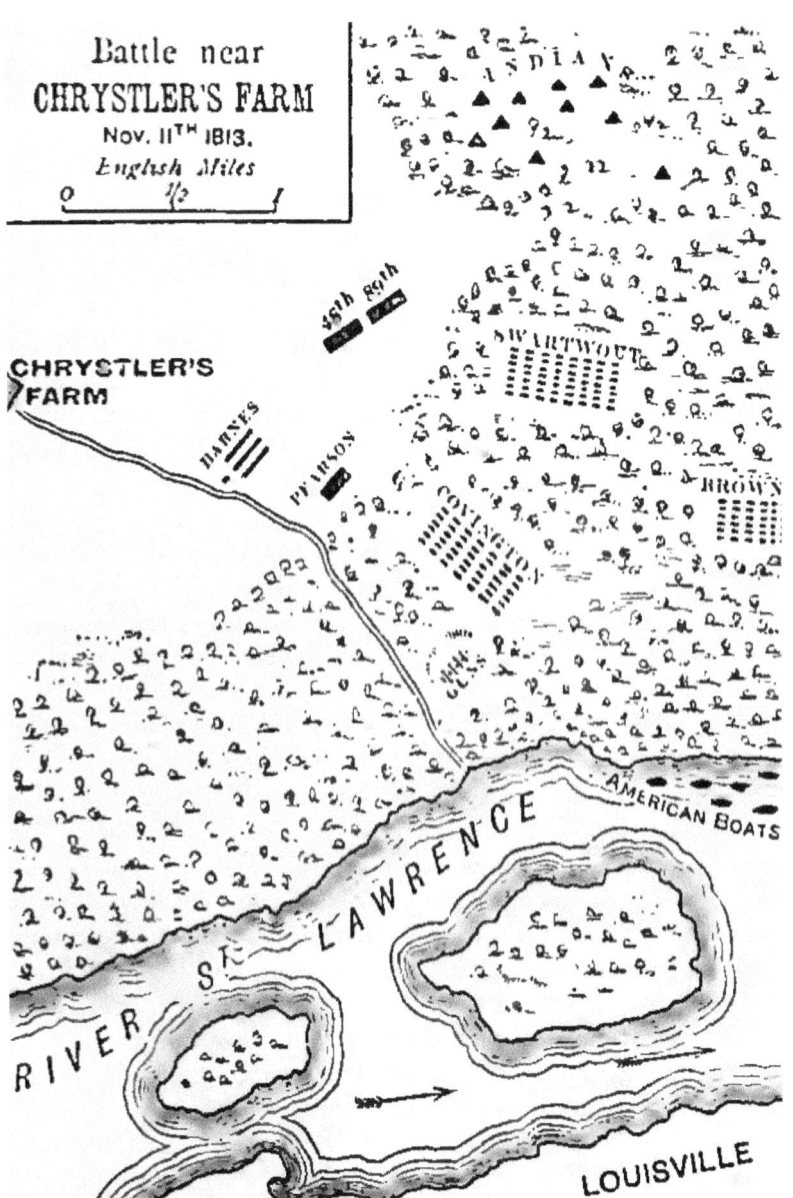

night to a point two miles beyond the threatening fort. The flotilla itself was placed in charge of General Brown, who took every precaution to enable it to move undiscovered by muffling the oars and causing the boats to keep as close as possible to the bank. General Wilkinson himself in a light gig reconnoitred the river and piloted the leading boats. Fortunately for him a heavy fog spread over the river's channel, and under its cover the greater part of the flotilla dropped silently downstream unobserved. A sudden shift of wind, however, caused the fog to lift, and the garrison of Fort Wellington detected the boats and the marching column on the American bank. Fire was opened by the English guns, but too late to check the success of General Wilkinson, who effected his movement with little loss. Pressing orders were now sent to General Hampton, whose repulse on the Chateauguay was yet unknown, directing him to make every effort to effect the proposed junction of the two armies.

Major-General de Rottenberg, who was commanding at Kingston, quite alive to the object of Wilkinson's expedition, had directed a force under Lieutenant-Colonel Morrison to follow and watch it on the St. Lawrence. Little could apparently be done in direct opposition to it. Only about 1,500 men were at Kingston, and it was unadvisable to leave that place wholly unprotected. It was expected that a militia army might be gathered to cover Montreal, but the best that could now be hoped for was to harass Wilkinson's march, and to watch for opportunities of causing loss to his army. Morrison could only take with him eight very weak companies of the 49th Regiment, and nine equally weak companies of the 89th, with a small detachment of artillery and artillery drivers, having in charge two 6-pounder field-pieces, the whole amounting to about 560 rank and file. This little band embarked on some gunboats and small craft manned by men of the Ontario fleet commanded by Captain Mulcaster of the Royal Navy, who had the audacity to stand out of Kingston Harbour in view of Commodore Chauncey's blockading squadron, and the skilfulness to evade his enemy by slipping down the north channel, which, as presenting great difficulties of navigation, had fortunately been left unguarded. On the 8th November Lieutenant-Colonel Morrison was joined by Lieutenant-Colonel Pearson, the commander of Fort Wellington, with all his available men, consisting of the two flank companies of the 49th, some detachments of Canadian militia, a few artillerymen with a field-piece, about half-a-dozen provincial dragoons, and thirty Indians under Lieutenant Anderson. Morrison's whole force now numbered 800 men all told, and with it he followed in the wake of the American flotilla as far as Fort Iroquois on the north bank of the St. Lawrence, where he left the boats and prepared for land operations. Wilkinson's army had been delayed by the necessity of landing in order to pass Fort Wellington, and its commander was now informed that difficulties might be expected at every point

where the channel of the river narrowed, as the Canadian bank was occupied by militia and artillery. The reports which came to him were greatly exaggerated, however, and there was really no force then in the field which could have offered any effectual opposition to his passage. On the forenoon of the 7th he had landed 1,200 men under Colonel McCombe to clear away any possible resistance, and to cover the flank of his flotilla, which, thus secured, pursued its way down the river. On the 8th, General Brown with his brigade was sent by Wilkinson to reinforce McCombe, and the 2nd Dragoons, part of the army's cavalry, which had been marching along the American bank, were ferried over to the Canadian side. On the afternoon of the 8th the American flotilla arrived at Williamsburg, near to Chrystler's Farm, and a further force of 400 men was sent on shore *en reconnaissance*. General Brown was now ordered to take command of the whole of the landed forces, and to make good the possession of the bank as far as the head of the "*Longue Saut*," a long rapid a short distance down the river. On the 10th November, General Brown on shore and the heavily laden boats on the river had both arrived at the "*Longue Saut*." General Wilkinson now judged it advisable, with the view of holding the Canadian shore, and also to lighten all the boats as much as possible before undertaking the passage of the rapid, to land every man capable of bearing arms, and a considerable proportion of his artillery.

The American commander-in-chief had been for some days ill, and was now completely incapacitated. General Lewis, the second in command, was also ill; so the direction of the troops devolved upon General Boyd, who, besides other senior officers, had with him Generals Covington. Brown, and Swartwout. The Americans commenced their march on the morning of the 10th, and near the village of Cornwall the advanced guard was opposed by about 300 of the Glengarry Militia under Captain Dennis of the 49th, who, by breaking down a bridge over a creek in his front and distributing his men in concealment round a wide semicircle, was able by their fire to delay General Brown for three hours, and finally to withdraw with little loss, carrying away also all the stores which were in his charge. But Lieutenant-Colonel Morrison's small force was now in touch with and harassing the American rear, and some skirmishing had taken place in which the advantages were evenly balanced. The English gunboats also were so threatening the flotilla that it was unable to leave the shelter of the bank, where a strong battery had been erected for its protection. General Boyd therefore resolved to turn upon and attack Morrison, and, his force being so superior in numbers, he believed that he could have no difficulty in crushing his audacious foe. A belt of forest surrounded the ground occupied by the English and hid from the Americans their strength and disposition; and General Boyd, thinking that he had only to show his strength to ensure complete success, formed his men in three columns, each commanded by one of his generals, with a reserve under Colonel Upham. One of the battalions of General Swartwout's brigade, the 21st American Regiment, was sent forward as an advanced guard to cover the movement and bring the English to action. This advanced guard, moving in open order through the forest, emerged upon Morrison's leading troops, the 49th flank companies, some Canadian militia, and one field-piece under Lieutenant-Colonel Pearson. The 21st Americans were accompanied by four guns, which took up a position from which it was hoped that they would be able to enfilade the right of the British line of battle.

Let us examine the ground occupied by Lieutenant-Colonel Morrison, and see how he marshalled his men to meet the overwhelming numbers which were about to be brought against them. Chrystler's Farm was a large clearing in the forest surrounding the log-built homestead, from which a rude track led down to the bank of the St. Lawrence. In November the crops were all off the ground, which was thus quite open to the movement of troops, though it was cut up by occasional drains and fences, and the soil, from long-continued rain, was a mass of deep adhesive mud. Such as it was, however, it was better adapted to the steady manoeuvres of English infantry than many of the previous scenes of combat during the war. We have seen that the little English army was only about 800 strong, including regular infantry, artillery, and Canadian militia, and that it had with it thirty Indians. Its artillery consisted of three field-pieces, and its cavalry of half-a-dozen dragoons, who acted as orderlies. Its advanced guard under Lieutenant-Colonel Pearson was posted *à cheval* of the road near the belt of forest which intervened between the clearing and the river. Behind it, echeloned in support on its right rear, were three companies of the 89th with a field-piece under Captain Barnes, while on its left rear the remainder of the 49th and 89th with a field-piece were both main body and reserve. The woods on the left of the position were occupied by the Indians and the Canadian militia. Every fighting-man was in the place which best suited his peculiar capabilities. Everywhere the handfuls of infantry were formed in line so as to give the fullest effect to their fire and the utmost freedom to their powers of tactical movement. Grimly determined, they awaited the advance of General Boyd's army, for they felt that on them depended the safety of Lower Canada. The three American columns followed their advanced guard through the forest, General Covington being directed against the right of the English position, General Swartwout against its left, while General Brown was still some distance in the rear.

The action commenced at 2 p.m. by the attack of the 21st Americans, over 600 strong, on Lieutenant-Colonel Pearson's advanced

post. The power of the swarm of men was too much for Pearson, who fell back, steadily fighting and disputing every inch of ground, until his assailants were checked by the supporting fire of the 49th and 89th. The four American guns failed to give to the 21st all the support which was expected from them, as they had taken up a position too far behind the fighting line, from which, ill served and ill laid, their action was little effective. At half-past two General Swartwout's brigade had pushed forward, and tried to turn the British left; but, weary from being under arms all the previous night under an incessant rain and from their march to the attack almost knee-deep in mud, the men lacked vigour and determination. The fire of the In-

dians and militia, whom Swartwout had neglected to drive out of the wood on his right, made itself felt with fatal effect, and when the 89th, wheeling to their left, presented a stern, unbroken front, the Americans, deficient in training and discipline, paused, staggered, and gave way. The 49th and 89th, re-forming their proud line and with colours uncased, followed them with confident step, firing volleys by platoons and effectually prevented them from making an attempt to rally their disordered ranks. Meanwhile General Covington had led an assault against the English right, and, forcing Captain Barnes with his three companies of the 89th to fall back, nearly made good his way to the farmhouse; but Morrison, seeing his right thus in peril, moved to the help of their comrades the main body of the 49th and 89th, flushed with their success against General Swartwout. These gallant soldiers then gave a brilliant example of that power of cool manoeuvre in battle which in so many wars has been displayed by England's infantry. They halted in their victorious pursuit of their first antagonists, and, crossing the field from left to right in *échelon* of companies, re-formed their line in front of Covington, and, recommencing their crushing fire by platoons, struck confusion into his brigade. General Covington, who, sword in hand, was leading his men with a courage and determination worthy of the young Republic's army, was struck down mortally wounded and carried from the field, and on the right of the British position, as on the left, the Americans were driven back discomfited. The American battery of four guns was still in position, covering the movements of their infantry, and the 49th prepared to capture it with a bayonet charge. Ere they were in motion, however, Morrison's wary eye had marked the movement of mounted men behind the disorganised crowd that was falling back before him. It was the 2nd American Dragoons, who, hitherto impeded by the belt of forest near the river, were now able to form in the clearing, and, under the command of the Adjutant-General, Walbach, were about to make an attempt to retrieve the fortunes of the day. Fortunately for Morrison's force the intersecting ditches and deep mud of the battlefield prevented the charge from being delivered with the impetus and cohesion which give three-fourths of their power to attacking cavalry, and Captain Barnes had time to form his three companies and to receive the dragoons with calculated volleys. Like Swartwout's and Covington's brigades, Walbach's men failed to make good their purpose, and turned rein. The last serious danger to the English army was past. General Brown's third column and Colonel Upham's reserve did little more than show themselves, and took no part in the fight. Their comrades were defeated, discouraged, and in retreat, and all that could be done was to shield them from complete demoralisation.

Morrison had hitherto fought the action of the day with conspicuous completeness and success. His men had stood the brunt of a struggle with a greatly superior force, and in cool courage, disciplined manoeuvre, and ready response to his initiative, had failed their commander at no moment in the trying hours of that November afternoon. Now, however, he was unable to reap the full advantage of his victory for want of that cavalry which might have swept down upon his foe's retreat, and added crushing disaster to their disheartening

failure. But, if cavalry were wanting, the sturdy British infantry, which had held its own so long and so stoutly and adapted its tactical formation to every mood of battle, now dashed forward eager to do what in it lay to secure trophies of mastery. Captain Barnes's companies, with levelled bayonets, charged upon the four guns which so long had been in position before them. Captain Armstrong, who commanded the American battery, did his best to withdraw his pieces; but, impeded by the tumultuous retreat of the infantry, and by the deep mud in which the wheels were sunk, he only succeeded in saving three. The fourth was captured, Lieutenant Smith, the subaltern in charge, lying dead at the post of duty. Lieutenant-Colonel Pearson, who, with the flank companies, had at the beginning of the action formed the English advanced post till he was driven back by the American 21st, now again pressed forward and fell on the enemy's light infantry, which was covering their retreat. Victorious in his turn, his advance was irresistible and opposition melted away before him. The line of the 49th and 89th followed Barnes and Pearson. The shrill war-whoop of the Indians rang through the forest, the artillery was hurried forward to hurl some last shots into the woods, in whose shelter General Boyd's columns were received, and the whole English force stood triumphant on the edge of the clearing where they had given such proofs of valour. But Morrison could do no more. Night was falling, and disparity of numbers forbade further pursuit of the Americans, who, falling back to their boats on the St. Lawrence, had the means of reinforcing themselves to such an extent as would give them a dominant superiority, which it would have been folly to encounter.

The Americans hurriedly re-embarked and formed their camp about four miles lower down the river on its southern bank. Here the tidings of Hampton's defeat on the Chateauguay reached them, and they learnt of that commander's resolution to make no further attempt to effect the proposed junction of the two armies. There was nothing for it but to consider the advance against Montreal at an end. De Saluberry on the Chateauguay and Morrison at Chrystler's Farm had broken the force of the two American columns of invasion and had saved Lower Canada for the British Crown. The American losses in the action of the 11th November were 102 killed and 237 wounded, besides a field-gun and more than 100 prisoners. In proportion to their numbers the casualties among the English force were nearly equally severe, amounting to 21 killed and 182 wounded. The opposing forces met in open champaign, where the incomparable discipline of trained English infantry gave to them signal advantage. The Americans were defeated not by superior valour, but, though fourfold superior in numbers, they fell before prompt and regular tactical movements executed by professional soldiers who were handled by a commander of consummate ability.

August 26-27, 1813
Dresden
C. Stein

After the Battle of Lützen, on the left bank of the Elbe, in the beginning of May, 1813, the allied Russo-Prussian forces, retiring before Napoleon, were obliged to recross that river, to evacuate Dresden, and to fall back into Silesia. They were again defeated with heavy loss at Bautzen and Wurschen on the 20th and 21st May, thus losing the line of the Oder. In one month the young and hastily-organised French army had been victorious in three great battles, besides several minor engagements of advanced guards. At the same time Marshal Davout had retaken Hamburg and Lübeck, and on the 29th May the French eagles were seen everywhere triumphant from Hamburg to Breslau. The honour and prestige of French arms, which had suffered so grievously in the Russian campaign, were completely re-established, and the coalition of European Powers which menaced the French Empire was paralysed, the monarchs in flight, their armies in disorder. But the legions of Napoleon were themselves worn out with constant effort, and required repose to give them time again to consolidate. The position of the Crown Prince of Sweden, Bernadotte, the renegade French marshal, was threatening in Pomerania; the death of his old and trusted comrade, Duroc, had saddened the emperor; and at the instance of Austria, till then neutral, Napoleon consented to an armistice, which was signed on the 4th June.

But the policy of Austria was opposed to Napoleon. Confident in her strong armaments and her position on the French right flank, she felt that, if she cast her sword into the scale, she must be the

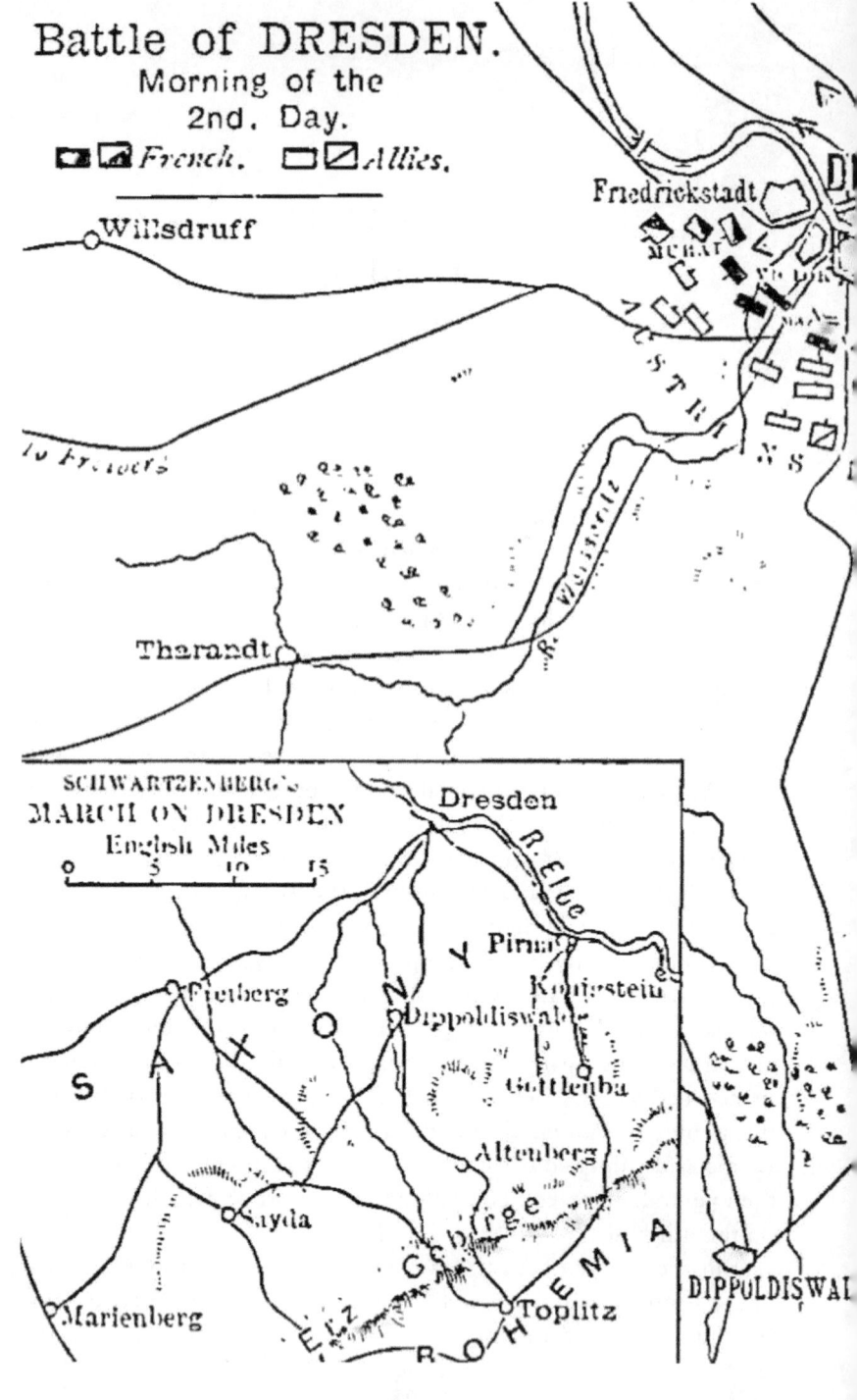

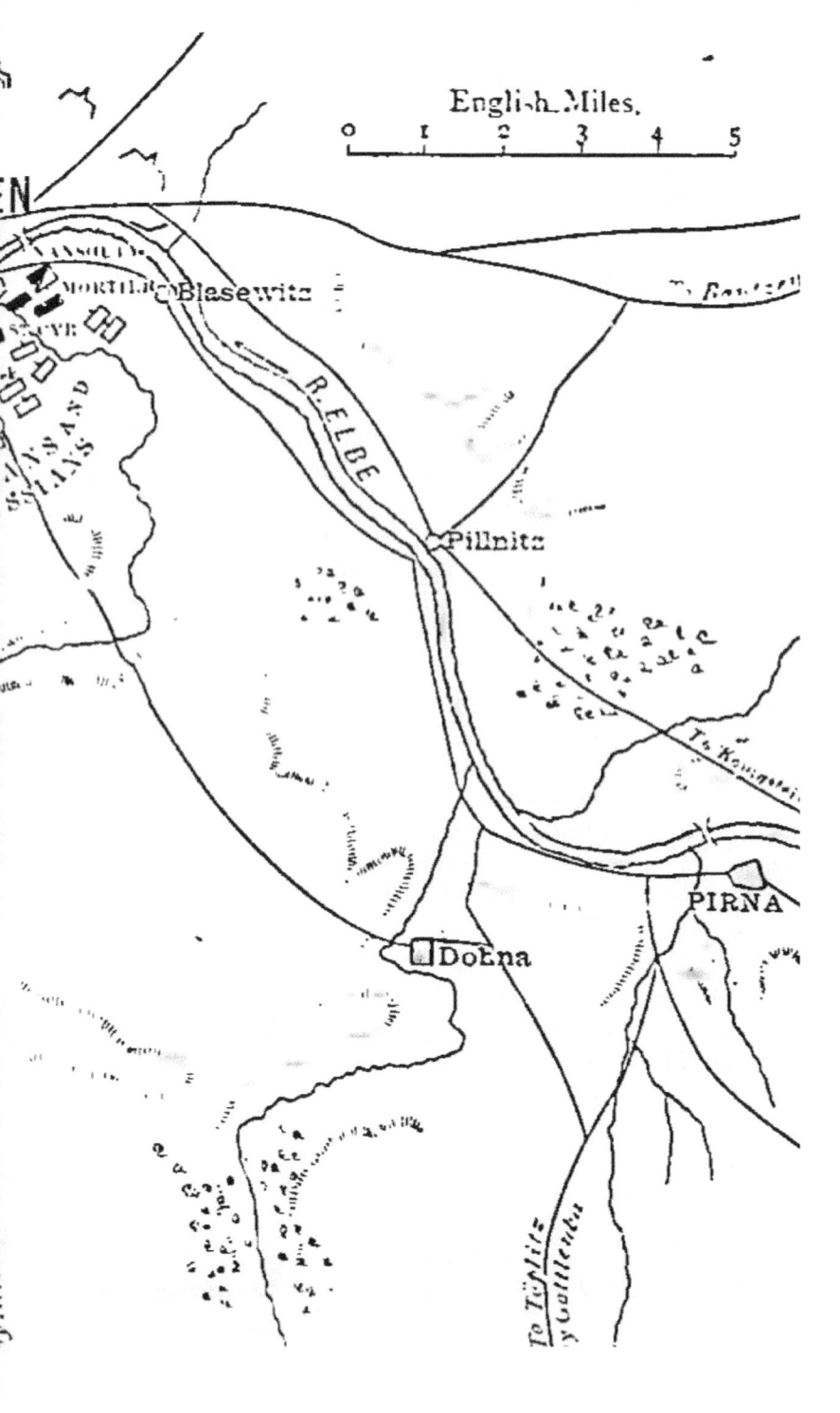

arbiter of future events. The Russo-Prussian coalition had failed because it had been surprised, before its complete development, by Napoleon's inconceivable rapidity of action. Even now the number of combatants which it could put into the field was nearly equal to that of the French armies. With the additional forces that could be raised during an armistice and with 130,000 men which Austria could dispose of, the numerical odds against the French emperor would be almost overwhelming. Fully alive to these facts, the diplomatists of Austria, in arranging an armistice and in providing that during its continuance a congress should be assembled at Prague to consider conditions of peace, resolved to insist upon such cessions by Napoleon as would bring the sway of France within normal limits and restore to other European nations the influence of which they had so long been deprived. Austria, in fact, let it be known that her neutrality was at an end, that it was for her to decide on the future of Europe, and that she would make common cause with Russia and Prussia unless the terms formulated by the congress at Prague were accepted by the French emperor. Hard these terms were, including demands for the cession of Illyria and the greater part of Italy, the return of the Pope to Rome, the yielding up of Poland to Russia, the evacuation of Spain, Holland, and Belgium and the re-establishment of the Confederation of the Rhine; but it is certain that even the proud spirit of Napoleon hesitated for a time whether he should not accept them. On one hand he had an immense army with his own unequalled genius to direct it: on the other he saw the advantages and indeed the necessity of peace to France worn out by long years of war. One of his ministers, whose name is unknown, struck the note which gave a key to his final decision, saying, "Ah, sire, and your glory!" How could he, who had distributed so many sceptres, descend to the level of the crowd of kings, conquered or created by himself? The die was cast. The 10th August, the day when the armistice expired, passed without his acceptance of the proposals made to him, and Austria, with Russia and Prussia, forthwith declared war.

In the presence of enemies so formidable, whose united forces numbered nearly 500,000, Napoleon found it necessary to remain on the defensive. His own army, including the Imperial Guard as a reserve, did not much exceed 300,000 combatants, and was distributed from the frontier of Bohemia, following the course of the Katzbach, to the Oder. The time of the armistice had been employed on both sides in preparing for war, in completing, organising, and instructing the troops, and both the French and their allied enemies were fresh and ready to enter on a new campaign.

The army of Austria was the factor of the future which Napoleon had principally to consider. If it marched on Dresden, it would temporarily be checked by the 1st and 14th Corps under Vandamme and Gouvion St. Cyr until the emperor could rush to their assistance. If it moved into Silesia, the whole French army would be gathered to meet it at Goerlitz or Buntzlau. In any case, Dresden was the base of Napoleon's system, as the bridges at Meissen and at Königstein enabled the French to manoeuvre on both sides of the Elbe. The town was therefore put into a defensible condition, and made secure against a *coup-de-main*. The old fortifications were repaired, the *faubourgs* were fortified and covered by advanced works, field fortifications were constructed between the Hopfgarten, the public park, and the Elbe, and the park itself was made available for the occupation of several battalions.

Shortly before this time the French army had suffered a severe loss, which not only deprived it of the services of a singularly able and experienced officer, but also shook its *moral* as showing that entire confidence could no longer be placed in soldiers of foreign extraction, even though they wore the uniform of a French general. General Jomini, a Swiss by birth, the chief of Marshal Ney's staff, deserted to the allies, taking with him the field states of the French army and complete notes of the intended plan of campaign. Jomini owed everything to Marshal Ney, who had raised him from a very humble employment to the high position which he occupied. Basely did this man betray the trust reposed in him, and it was to the astonishment of everyone that the Emperor Alexander of Russia rewarded his treason by making him his *aide-de-camp*. Even the Emperor of Austria was so shocked by seeing Jomini present at a dinner given by Alexander that he exclaimed:

"I know that sovereigns are sometimes obliged to make use of deserters, but I cannot conceive how such a one can be received into their personal staff or found at their table."

Having thus transferred his services, and, as said before, bringing with him Napoleon's orders for the movement of his several army corps, . Jomini urged the allied sovereigns to commence hostilities two days earlier than had been their intention, so that time should not be given to the French emperor to alter his plans. He is also credited with having given them the sage advice always to fall upon the French armies wherever their great commander was not. With

what fatal effect that advice was followed in the ensuing campaign history may tell. It no doubt inspired the allied movements in the campaign's commencement, though for that time these movements were not crowned with success.

The first blow was struck by the impatient and fiery Blücher, who hurled himself upon the French army under Marshal Macdonald in Silesia. His intention was to draw Napoleon himself to that part of his line of defence and to retreat before him, while the main Austro-Russian-Prussian army of 200,000 men, under Prince Schwartzenberg, which had been concentrated at Prague, would then be able to attack Dresden opposed only by the great warrior's lieutenants.

The plan was only partially successful. The emperor, indeed, met Blücher and drove him back, but he had divined the intended movement of Prince Schwartzenberg upon Dresden and prepared to return to the defence of that town by forced marches, at the head of the 2nd and 6th corps of infantry and the whole of his guard, together

with the 1st corps of cavalry and the Polish cavalry. Vandamme was also directed to march with the first corps of infantry upon Königstein, and, restoring the bridge there, to threaten the enemy's flank.

The great allied army crossed the chain of the Erz Gebirge on the 22nd August, and debouched by Gottleuba, Altenberg, Sayda, and Marienberg. The only French troops then in front of them were the 14th corps, 20,000 strong, commanded by Marshal St. Cyr, which occupied the environs of Pirna, about eighteen miles from Dresden. Weak as this force was, it was in the hands of one of the most able captains who had been produced by the many previous years of war. Gouvion St. Cyr, of tall and dignified figure, sparing of speech, but when he spoke clear, concise, and trenchant, had a calm and methodical mind. War was for him an art to be loved, and, constantly studying it, he aimed to carry it on purely by rule. He calculated military issues not only by the place, the circumstances, and the numbers engaged, but by the character of the enemy opposed to him and that of the chiefs and soldiers whom he commanded. He knew always how to gain the confidence of his subordinates, to mould them to his purpose, to inspire them with pride in themselves, and, in the midst of the greatest perils and privations, to raise their courage to the level of his own. He sought glory, but it must be gained by following principles, otherwise for him it lost its value. He preferred to succeed by prudently-calculated and wisely-combined manoeuvres, leaving as little as possible to chance; and he was often known, by able strategy, to turn a stubborn and prolonged defensive into an offensive, unforeseen and victorious. This great soldier had the fault that he did not show all his value except in a position of separate command. Independent by elevation of character as well as by pride in his own abilities, he ill brooked an equal and still less a superior. Caring not to share his glory with anyone, he but coldly seconded his chiefs, and gave to his equals the smallest measure of support.

Such as he was, no better man could have been found to carry out the task which now fell to him. He knew that the emperor would hasten to secure Dresden, but that time was above all things necessary. With a weak corps of 20,000 men he had to check the overwhelming masses of the allies till an adequate force could be present to give them battle. No finer tactical display could be possible than his gradual withdrawal to the defences of Dresden, inflicting heavy loss on his enemy during three days of fighting, and then placing his troops behind the works which had been already prepared. Admirable as his dispositions were, however, and brilliant as was his leadership, he owed much of his success to the delay's of Prince Schwartzenberg, who, proverbially slow and cautious in the field, would not risk, even against a feeble enemy, a bold attack on Dresden till the corps of General Klenau had come into line. If the Austrian commander-in-chief had nerved himself to use fully the crushing forces already under his hand, he might have cut the French line of communication and secured the passage of the Elbe before Napoleon appeared on the scene with the men drawn from Silesia. On the morning of the 26th August the situation was this—Marshal St. Cyr with his corps was holding the field-works which protected Dresden, while the great allied army, still hesitating to make a determined attack, occupied in strength the heights of Zschernitz and Strehlen to the south of the town, while at the same time spreading themselves out towards both flanks.

Napoleon was hastening towards the threatened town at the head of the troops which were to secure its defence. Even then an attack in force by the allies would have been successful, and in the race for the possession of the important position they might have outstripped the succours which were toiling breathlessly to the critical point. But still Schwartzenberg delayed to grasp the prey which was really in his power; still the columns of his army stood inactive. The opportunity slipped away, not again to return. At nine in the morning the French emperor arrived on the outskirts of Dresden. He paused for a moment to inspect the battery which had been placed on the right bank of the Elbe to flank the left of the French position, and ordered that it was to be strengthened by the first pieces of artillery which should arrive. Then he pressed on to the front of St. Cyr's line, and by twelve o'clock he had mastered all the details of the situation. His presence produced a magical effect upon the sorely harassed 14th corps, and everywhere shouts of "*Vive l'Empereur*" gave voice to the renewed confidence of the soldiers, who felt that they were no longer called upon to struggle against hopeless odds.

An hour or two after mid-day Prince Schwartzenberg at last resolved that he would no longer wait for the arrival of General Klenau's corps, but would move forward to the attack. Three cannon shots gave the signal, and at once six columns, each covered by the fire of fifty guns, threw themselves against the entrenchments of Dresden. The combined discharge from such a formidable artillery was crushing in its effect, and, making the outworks untenable, gave for a time an easy success to the infantry columns. General Colloredo carried the main redoubt in the centre of the French line; General Kleist obliged the troops who had occupied the park to fall back upon the *faubourg*; and the corps of General Wittgenstein debouched near the Elbe, threatening to turn the left of the French position. The whole of the reserves of the 14th corps were now engaged, and the shot and shell of the attack were falling in the streets of Dresden. A few short hours earlier such an assault so delivered must have driven St. Cyr into hopeless retreat, but now it was too late. Even while the allied armies were making their effort, unknown to them masses of French soldiers were entering the town and forming for battle. The Old and Young Guard were both there, the infantry division of General Teste, the cavalry of Latour-Maubourg had moved to the extreme right, and a numerous artillery was ready to come into action.

Napoleon, who had been watching the progress of events, judged that the time had come to show the hidden strength upon which the allies had unwittingly closed. The French centre was secured by the old fortifications of the town, so he was at liberty to disregard that point and operate against the flanks of the enemy. Two divisions of the Guard, under Marshal Ney, were sent to the right, while two others, under Marshal Mortier, were directed to the left, where also were Teste's division and Latour-Maubourg's cavalry. The allies were surging up to the old walls, driving the 14th corps, still sternly fighting, before them. No thought had they but to sweep victorious over the frail battlements into Dresden, and, shouting "To Paris!" as their war-cry, their order was relaxed in the expectation that no further resistance would be met. Suddenly the gates opened and the stately battalions of the Guard appeared in battle array. It was like the appa-

rition of Medusa's head. Startled into sudden discomfiture, the allies fell back before the charge of the sorties, which now issued from every gate of the city. They were driven out of the redoubts which they had taken earlier in the day, and in their retreat to the heights which they had occupied on the past night they suffered heavy loss from the charging squadrons of Latour-Maubourg. In the fighting of that one day Prince Schwartzenberg, while gaining no foot of ground, had lost 5,000 men killed and wounded, and nearly 3,000 prisoners. Thus ended a glorious day for France, but one whose glory for a time hung only on a thread, for, as has been seen. Marshal St. Cyr and his corps had made their last effort and fired their last cartridge before the Imperial Guard came to their assistance.

During the night the light infantry of General Metsko, forming the advanced guard of Klenau's corps, joined Schwartzenberg, and prolonged to the left the vast semi-circle occupied by his army. His tight rested on the Elbe above Dresden, and he intended Klenau's corps to fill the gap between his left and the Elbe below the town. But Klenau's march was still delayed by the state of the roads; the position which he should have occupied was insufficiently held by Metsko, and the left of the allies was practically *en l'air*. The French also received a great accession of strength, for the corps of Marshals Marmont and Victor, with Nansouty's cavalry, had followed the Imperial Guard, and were now at Napoleon's disposition. The night of the 26th was most trying to both armies. The rain tell in torrents, and both French and allies bivouacked in mud and water. A portion of the former were certainly able to find some shelter in the city, but the greater part of them had no such resource. How often has it happened that, on the eve of a great conflict, the soldiers who are to take part in it, and whose endurance and courage are to be tried to the uttermost, have been exposed to every hardship which can reduce their stamina and depress their spirits! In studying the great deeds recorded in history, how much our admiration of the heroes who performed them is increased by the knowledge of the surrounding conditions, to whose evil influence they rose superior!

The morning of the 27th broke dull and overcast. No single gleam of sunshine cheered or warmed the chilled and famished soldiery who rose from their flooded resting-places. The allied army occupied a strong position on the heights surrounding Dresden, while the French occupied the plain immediately outside the town. So completely were the troops of Napoleon exposed to view, that Schwartzenberg could not fail to know how great was the advantage in numbers which the allies still possessed. Thus were the French marshalled: on the extreme left were two divisions of the Young Guard under Mortier, supported by Nansouty's cavalry; next to them was the 14th corps under St. Cyr; in the centre was the emperor with the infantry' and cavalry of the Old Guard, two divisions of the Young Guard under Ney. and the 6th corps under Marmont; towards the right was Victor with the 2nd corps; and on the open ground on the extreme right was massed all the remaining cavalry under Murat, the King of Naples. Murat had only joined the army on the 17th August. For some months after he had suddenly given up the command of the shattered Grand Army during the retreat from Russia, he had been in disgrace with his great brother-in-law, and had even gone so far as to enter into negotiations with the English with the view of saving his crown of Naples if Napoleon's star had for ever set in the Russian snows. When the new French army was, however, organised and about to take the field. Napoleon sent Murat a message of forgiveness and a pressing invitation again to serve as a soldier of France. Whether the emperor did this in order to withdraw the King of Naples from the intrigues into which he had so unfortunately entered, or in order to give to his cavalry a chief worthy to lead them in battle, can never be known. Probably both motives influenced the invitation, which Murat accepted, again to prove himself the leading paladin of French chivalry, the most formidable cavalry officer who ever sat in a saddle.

The allied army was deployed, as we have seen, in a great semicircle, having its centre on the heights of Zschernitz and Strehlen, with its right under Wittgenstein resting on the Elbe. Its left was, however, not complete, and only a part of General Ginlay's corps, with the divisions of Lichtenstein and Metsko, was pushed across the deep ravine formed by the river Weisseritz. If Klenau's corps had arrived, the left would have rested on the Elbe, and there would have been no want of natural strength in any part of the position. In the general arrangement the Russo-Prussian armies were on the right and the Austrians on the left.

At six o'clock in the morning of the 27th, Napoleon was himself at the outposts of his army reconnoitring the dispositions of Schwartzenberg. His keen glance soon detected the weakness of his enemy's left, and, anxious that the Austrian general should not have time to repair the fault which had been committed, he gave the order for the skirmishers and the artillery to commence the action all along the line. He resolved that he would seize the advantage of being the attacker—an advantage which, besides being so congenial to the spirit of a French army, gave him the initiative in selecting the scenes of bitterest combat. As on the previous day his most important movements were against the allied flanks. Marshal Mortier, with his divisions of

the Young Guard, was directed against Wittgenstein, while Murat and his cavalry, with the assistance of Marshal Victor's corps, were to fall upon and roll up the Austrians on their weakly-held left. He himself, in the centre, intended to maintain a heavy fire from his artillery and light troops so as to engage the enemy's attention and cause them to anticipate other attacks from new directions.

One of the first shots fired in the morning inflicted a serious loss on the allies, shattering both legs of General Moreau, who was riding near the Emperor Alexander of Russia. Moreau, who had been one of the most illustrious generals of France, had been in exile for some years, having fled from his native land, suspected of complicity in schemes against Napoleon's power. Within the last few days he had taken service with the enemies of his country, and was now aiding them with his great military talents. It is yet uncertain how far Moreau was deservedly an exile, but there can be no doubt that the victor of Hohenlinden threw a dark cloud over the end of his life, whose beginning had been so glorious, by appearing in arms against France and advising her foes how best they might conquer her sons. He was removed from the field in a litter, and both his legs were amputated. Four days later he died in the house of a Saxon cure, cursing himself for his conduct and saying:

"To think that I—I, Moreau—should die in the midst of the enemies of France, struck down by a shot from a French cannon!"

A curious story, told of the manner in which the death of this celebrated man became known to Napoleon's army, may be mentioned here. On the evening of the 27th a French hussar found, after the battle, a magnificent Danish hound which seemed to be searching for a lost master. On the hound's neck was a collar with the inscription "I belong to General Moreau." This led to inquiries being made, when it was ascertained from people who had seen the event that Moreau had indeed been mortally wounded. A stone now marks the place, bearing the legend "*Hier fiel der held Moreau*" (Here fell the hero Moreau).

To return to the battle, it was never intended by Napoleon that the combat in which Mortier engaged should have more importance than attached to the object of keeping the enemy employed and uneasy. That marshal therefore did no more than take one village and, during the early part of the day, dispute the possession of another with the Russians. The real effort was to be made on the French right by Murat and Victor, who were to crush the allied left and, if possible, cut off Schwartzenberg's line of retreat by the Freyberg road, throwing him back on the almost impassable mountain tracks which lead to Töplitz by Dippoldiswalde and Altenberg. This manoeuvre would be seconded by Vandamme with the 1st corps, who, having been two days previously ordered to pass the Elbe at Königstein, was now pushing before him General Ostermann, the guardian of the bridges.

Murat and Victor, unlike some of the great French leaders on other occasions, acted without jealousy of each other, and gave that mutual support which doubles the tactical value of masses of infantry and cavalry. While Murat, with Latour-Maubourg's horsemen, made a long detour to gain the flank of the Austrians, Victor made a direct attack on their front and secured the Weisseritz ravine, thus cutting them off from the main body of their army. Then were the Austrian squares victims to the brilliant cavalry leader. Murat led the charges which he commanded with all the impetuosity and determination which had marked him in so many battles in so many lands. Never had he directed more effectively his "whirlwinds of cavalry." The cuirassiers, familiarly known in the French army as "*les gros frères*," reaped most of the day's honours, and scattered the most solid formations in their path. Lichtenstein's division was driven back into the ravine by the squadrons of Bourdesoulle; the Austrian cavalry, which bravely strove to support Metsko's division, was overthrown by the dragoons of Doumerc, and Murat himself, charging Metsko's division, forced it to lay down its arms. All these movements lasted from ten in the morning till two. Rarely has cavalry ever produced such an effect on a battlefield. Rarely have cavalry and infantry worked together with greater unison for a common end. As Murat said in his report to the emperor:

"The cavalry covered itself with glory, rending sword in hand the masses of troops opposed to it, in spite of a most stubborn resistance. The infantry charged the enemy with the bayonet, and the generals well directed in these difficult attacks the inexperienced bravery of their young troops."

In these early hours of the day Murat took 6,000 prisoners and thirty pieces of artillery, besides inflicting on the enemy a loss of 4,000 or 5,000 killed and wounded. There was one circumstance which undoubtedly gave a considerable advantage to cavalry in the battle of Dresden. At that period all soldiers were armed with flintlock muskets, which it was almost impossible to discharge if the powder in the pan became at all damp. As we have seen, there had been a continuous downpour of rain on the night previous to the battle, and, on the 27th

August itself, the driving storm never ceased. The firearms of the Austrian infantry were, therefore, nearly useless, and the cavalry had nothing to fear from them in charging up to their formation. With reference to this an incident of the day is recorded. A body of *cuirassiers*, commanded by General Bourdesoulle, found itself in front of a brigade of Austrian infantry formed in square, and summoned them to surrender. The enemy's general having scornfully refused, Bourdesoulle rode to the front, and called out that he knew that none of the muskets could be fired. The Austrian replied that his men would defend themselves with the bayonet and that with the greater advantage because the French cavalry, whose horses were struggling up to their hocks in mud, could not possibly deliver a charge with sufficient pace to make it effective.

"I will destroy your square with my artillery."

"But you have not any, for it is stuck in the mud."

"Well, if I show you the guns, now in rear of my leading squadrons, will you surrender?"

"Of course I must, for I will then have no means of defence left to me."

Bourdesoulle ordered the advance of a battery of six guns to a distance of thirty paces from the square. When the Austrian general saw the guns each with an artilleryman standing by it, portfire in hand, ready for action, he, perforce, surrendered at discretion.

Artillery, indeed, took a principal *rôle* on both sides during the whole of the 27th, and more markedly the French batteries, which were at all times able to accompany the other troops and to come into position wherever required. The foresight of Napoleon had specially

provided for the difficulty to be expected in crossing ground soaked and heavy with wet, by doubling all the gun-teams, and for this purpose he had made use of the horses belonging to the transport waggons, which were for the time in safety within the walls of Dresden.

Learning the complete success of Marat's action on his right and that Mortier was surely, if slowly, thrusting back Wittgenstein on his left. Napoleon began to press the centre of the allies. Columns of attack were formed by the 14th corps, the cavalry of the Guard were pushed forward in threatening manoeuvre, and the heavy cannonade from every available gun was redoubled. Ney, with the whole of the Guard, strengthened Mortier's forward movement. Above all, the emperor threw himself with his Guard into the battle, exciting every soldier by his personal presence and stimulating their valour by the electric vigour of his purpose. Superior as the allies still were in numbers to the French army they were everywhere worsted. Schwartzenberg saw his left crushed, his centre demoralised and barely holding its ground, his right rapidly giving way. Murat had cut his line of retreat by the Freiberg road, and Vandamme, with the 1st corps, was on the route by Pirna. Napoleon's strategy had been completely successful, and there were no roads open to the allied army but those through the mountains towards Töplitz. At four in the afternoon the Austrian general began his retiring movement, and soon Napoleon saw the great host which had threatened so much, melting away before him defeated and disheartened.

After his successes before two o'clock, Murat, still supported by Victor, had followed them up by pressing in pursuit of those who had escaped from his first blows, and now the whole French army was directed to complete its victory, of which the first results were the enemy's loss of 20,000 killed and wounded, 10,000 prisoners with 200 pieces of artillery, and caissons and several standards. Schwartzenberg was retiring on Töplitz by all the tracks and footpaths through the Bohemian mountains, and thither the defeated army was to be followed, there the last annihilating blow was to be struck. Vandamme, from his position near Pirna, was now to lead the pursuit. Ney, Mortier, the whole of the Guard were, on the morning of the 28th, marching to support him, while St. Cyr and Marmont were to join him by other routes. The fortune of the campaign, even the final event of the war, the empire of Europe, were to be decided at Töplitz. Nothing was wanting but to press forward and, having united the various corps, to strike one last blow. At mid-day on the 28th all were in movement. Immediately afterwards there was a general halt. Vandamme alone, who was acting independently, continued his march, alas! now unsupported. At this decisive moment, when all depended on his personal supervision and impulse, the health of the emperor broke down. Whether it was the long exposure to rain and storm, the anxieties of the. closing days of the armistice, or the strain of war which at last took effect, cannot be known; but certain it is that the cord snapped, the physical and mental powers of Napoleon altogether gave way, the great strategy which he alone could have directed collapsed, and the pursuing movements of his army ceased. Vandamme marched on unsupported to be defeated and taken prisoner at Kulm, the first of the

great series of misfortunes which now fell upon the French armies, leading to the invasion of France and the abdication of her ruler at Fontainebleau. The Battle of Dresden was the last of Napoleon's great victories. Some transient gleams of success did afterwards from time to time fall upon his arms, but never again did he appear as an invincible conqueror. Never did French soldiers gain by their conduct more glory than on the 26th and 27th August. Never were such great deeds followed by sequel more disastrous.

May 2, 1813

Lutzen

C. Stein

The disastrous Russian campaign of 1812 had shown that the great Napoleon was not invincible, that his combinations were not always superior to the influences which sway human affairs, and that he could no longer calculate on the assistance in arms of conquered countries which had been forced to give him unwilling allegiance. The "Grand Army" had ceased to exist. Famine, the slaughter of many battlefields, and, above all, the horrors of the winter retreat had destroyed it. A few scattered remnants, principally gathered from those *corps d'armée* which had been the last to enter upon the fatal campaign and had not undergone all its trials, were retreating through Prussia, under the command of the devoted and chivalrous Eugène de Beauharnais, who had taken up the burden after it had been suddenly relinquished by Murat in his anxiety to return to his kingdom of Naples, and his selfish desire to be relieved from a task in which there was much difficulty and little glory. The spirit of the superior officers in the army of France was now no longer what it had been in previous years. In spite of the adventurous career which they led, many of them had married and established homes, and, though they still were on occasions capable of the most brilliant actions and the noblest self-devotion, they were no longer the hard and fiery warriors who thought little of the past and recked not of the future, who entered lightly on the most arduous enterprises, who carried all their property with them into the field, having no interests beyond the fires of their bivouacs. But the great emperor was himself still indomitable, his energy unabated, his capacity as stupendous as ever. Undismayed by the terrible blows dealt

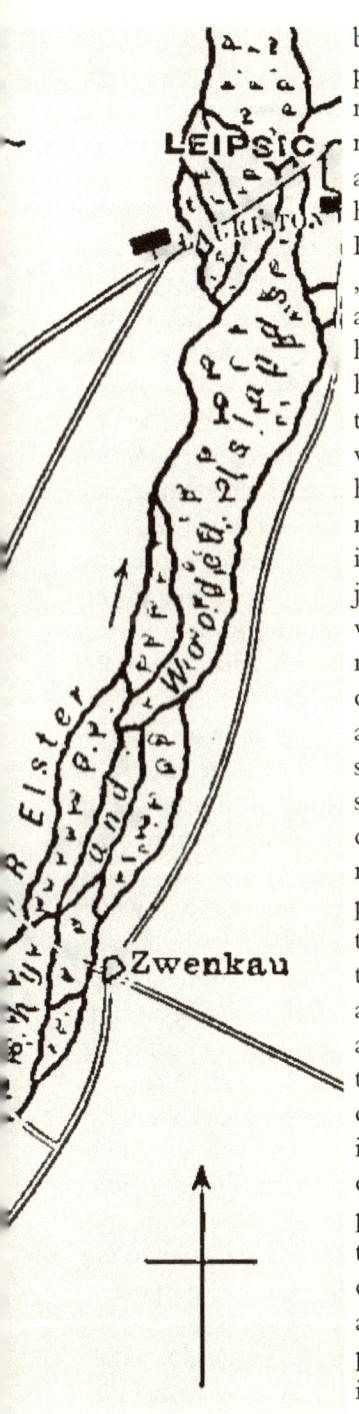

by fortune, he had set himself to work to repair the losses of the past, to provide for the necessities of the future, and astonished Europe saw fresh armies spring into existence at his bidding, and the power of France in his hands still loom great and unconquered. He arrived in Paris from Russia on the 18th, December, 1812, and the moment he was again at the centre of the vast system which he had created, he had made it vibrate to his war cry from end to end. From Rome to Brest, from Perpignan to Hamburg, the whole empire rose in arms at once; while he, master of the wide extent, with consummate knowledge of every detail in its organism, was able to direct all its resources with a judgment so clear, with a hand so firm, and with calculation so unerring, that in three months the *materiel* and *personnel* of an army of 300,000 men had been created, enrolled, and organised; and this enormous mass of soldiers, clothed, armed and equipped, was set in motion, and was about to find itself concentrated within reach of the enemy, ready for battle. Of all the administrative feats performed by Napoleon during his reign this was one of the most marvellous. Infantry, artillery, a proportion of cavalry, supplies, ammunition, transport, all were provided, and, both in forming these masses and in the smallest details of their equipment and organisation, nothing was neglected, nothing forgotten. It is said that at any moment of the day or night, whatever had been his preoccupation, the emperor was able to tell the numbers, composition, and actual value of each of the numberless detachments of all arms which he had put in motion in every part of his. empire, the quality of their clothing and armament, the number of stages in the line of march of each, and the day, even the hour, when each should arrive at its destination.

It has been said that Prince Eugène was retreating slowly through Prussia. He was pressed upon, but not hurried, in his still defiant march, by the overwhelming numbers of the following Russian army. For three months he had been able to dispute the possession of Poland, Saxony, and Prussia. At last his retreat, bringing his feeble force within reach of support, came to an end at Magdeburg. On his right and left, however, his enemy still poured forward their legions. They crossed the Elbe—Hamburg was passed by them. They occupied Dresden and Leipsic, and the empire of France itself was threatened. Prussia, so long cowed by Napoleon and forced to furnish a contingent to his armies, had roused herself in national revolt against his iron domination, and had declared war against him, putting into the field 95,000 men, and with them the veteran Blücher, who within the next three years was destined to reap so great a harvest of glory. But the onward movement of the enemies of France was now no longer to have before it only the *débris* of the hosts which had retreated from Russia, but its way was barred by the newly-raised army under the immediate command of the greatest warrior of the time. Napoleon had left Paris on the 15th April, and, rushing to the centre of the long line now held by his lieutenants, he was prepared to carry out his strategic scheme of surprising and turning the Russo-Prussian right, and thus rolling up and hurling back the forces of the allies who had dared to think that his power had been irretrievably shattered.

On the west of Leipsic lies the great plain in the centre of which is Lutzen. Here was the scene of the last and most famous of the victories gained by Gustavus Adolphus. Here the great Swedish monarch fell, and here his tomb marked the spot of his glorious death, the limit set by fate to his Protestant championship. To this plain as a gathering place had been directed the masses of troops with which Napoleon intended to operate as his field army. Hither came, under the command of the renowned generals of France, the numerous columns which had been formed in so many different countries—from the east of Europe, from the centre of Spain, from Italy, from the north, west and south of the threatened empire, all concentrated and fell into line with the utmost precision, with the most perfect unity of purpose.

On the night of the 1st of May, Napoleon was at Lutzen. Already, at Weissenfels, the young conscripts who filled the ranks had had their first encounter with the enemy, and, led by the heroic Marshal Ney, had borne themselves with the steadiness and valour of old soldiers. So brilliant had been their conduct, so decisive the success which they had obtained, that they filled their leaders with pride and confidence. The army of France seemed about to enter upon a fresh career of triumph. But there fell one dark cloud upon the success which had so far been achieved. Marshal Bessières, Duke of Istria, one of the emperor's oldest and most devoted adherents, who commanded the cavalry of the guard, was suddenly struck down by a stray cannon shot while reconnoitring not far from his master's side. As his body was borne from the field wrapped in a cloak, the fate of his old comrade painfully impressed Napoleon, who said, "Death is coming very close to us all."

On the 2nd May the emperor rose at three o'clock in the morning to give his orders and dictate his correspondence. The reports of spies, more explicit than any which he had yet received, led him to believe that the united Russo-Prussian army was moving from Leipsic, sheltered by the Elster, towards Zwenkau and Pegau. It seemed that they had not realised that the French were directly in their front, and that their commander, Wittgenstein, was looking for his enemy nearer to the southward mountains. Cavalry was the one arm which Napoleon had been unable to extemporise in sufficient numbers, and, in default of the more perfect knowledge to be gained by widely scouting squadrons, he made his arrangements for a forward movement with a prudence and caution which would enable him to retrieve an error if unhappily he should make one. He was only four leagues from Leipsic, and he resolved to push boldly on and to secure the passage of the Elster at that town. If he could carry out his plan, he believed that he would be on the flank of the enemy and cut their line of communications, after which he could give battle with every advantage in his favour. Prince Eugène was ordered to lead the advance with the corps of Lauriston and Marshal Macdonald, supported by the cavalry division of Latour-Maubourg and a strong reserve of artillery. Lauriston was to seize Leipsic, and Macdonald was to move on Zwenkau, at which point it was probable that the advanced troops of the enemy would be encountered. The emperor himself, with his guard, would follow in support of Prince Eugène. Meantime, in case, as was possible, the enemy should throw themselves against the French right. Marshal Ney was to establish himself with his *corps d'armée* in the neighbourhood of Lutzen; and a group of five villages was pointed out to him as a strong defensive position which would form a pivot for all the operations of the French army. There remained the corps of Marmont,

Bertrand, and Oudinot, which were still more distant from Leipsic. They were ordered to move forward and to form on the right of Ney if the enemy made an attack on that marshal's position. If no such attack was attempted, the whole was to press on to the passages of the Elster between Zwenkau and Pegau.

The whole French army was in motion. Prince Eugène's columns were on the march towards Leipsic and the Elster. The Old and Young Guard were following in the same direction. Ney's corps was taking up a defensive position in the villages south of Lutzen. Marmont, Bertrand, and Oudinot were all pressing forward to take part in the great struggle which was evidently imminent, though its exact locality was still uncertain. At ten o'clock the emperor himself mounted, and, followed by the crowd of war-worn leaders of men who formed his staff, galloped towards Leipsic. As he passed alongside the masses of his soldiers that were toiling over the plain, repeated cries of "*Vive l'Empereur,*" greeted his appearance. Nothing in the history of the time is more striking than the manner in which military ardour and veneration for the person of their emperor mastered the conscripts as soon as they found themselves in the ranks of the army; with what enthusiasm they followed the man, who had been the author of so many wars in which the blood of Frenchmen had been poured out like water, the man who had come to be detested by their countrymen for the sacrifices which he demanded, and who had only lately torn themselves from their peaceful homes to fight his battles.

As the Imperial cavalcade approached Leipsic the attack on the town by Maison's division of Lauriston's corps was being vigorously carried out. Great were the natural obstacles and stern the defence which the French had to encounter. The town was covered by a wide belt of marshy and wooded land, traversed by several arms of the Elster, and the only passage across this belt was by a road following a long series of bridges. General Kleist, who commanded the garrison, had filled the clumps of wood with light infantry, and had covered the entrance to the bridges by a strong battery of artillery, supported by heavy Prussian columns. The gallant Maison, having driven in the enemy's light troops and brought up some artillery and infantry to reply to the Prussian fire, detached a battalion, which, fording one of the branches of the Elster, threatened Kleist's flank. He then formed a column of attack, and, placing himself at its head, carried the first bridge with a bayonet charge. The Prussians stood their ground stubbornly, but were swept away by the fierce rush, and Napoleon saw his soldiers entering Leipsic pell-mell with their flying foe. The town was at his mercy, and the first portion of his plan of operations was apparently carried out with complete success.

It was eleven o'clock. Napoleon no longer thought there was any fighting to be done, except in his immediate front. There he believed that he had found the main force of the enemy which he wished to crush, and there he had struck a first successful blow. Suddenly the roar of many pieces of artillery struck his ear, resounding from his right rear apparently in the direction of the villages which he had left to the guardianship of Ney's corps. As we have seen, the chance of an

attack on his flank had been foseen and provided for, and he was neither surprised nor disconcerted. After listening for a few moments to the cannonade, which, increasing in volume, became more and more terrible, he said calmly, "While we have been trying to outflank them, they have been turning us. However, there is no harm done, and they will find us everywhere prepared to meet them."

Marshal Ney had accompanied him to Leipsic. Him he sent back at once, at a gallop, to rejoin his corps, impressing upon him that he must hold his position like a rock, which he should be well able to do, as he had 48,000 men at his disposal, and he would after a time receive the support of other troops on his right, on his left, and in rear. Then, with the composure of a mind prepared for any emergency, he issued orders for all his advanced troops to reverse their order of march, the most delicate of operations to execute with precision, especially in the case where enormous masses have to be handled. Lauriston was ordered to maintain his hold on Leipsic with one division, while the other two divisions of his corps were to move towards the left of Ney's position. Macdonald's corps was to fall back from Zwenkau also towards the left of Ney. Prince Eugène, with his reserve artillery and the cavalry of Latour-Maubourg, was to support Macdonald. So much for the strengthening of Ney's left. On his right, Marmont, who was now on the march north of Lutzen, was ordered to hurry into position; while Bertrand, still distant, was to connect with Marmont and make every effort to appear on the enemy's left and rear. Finally, as a support to the centre of the new battle-line, the whole of the Guard was to retrace its steps and form behind the group of villages held by Ney. No conscripts were these, but a mass of 18,000 war-hardened old soldiers who could be relied upon to maintain the prestige of French arms under any circumstances. His orders given, and having seen the wide and complicated manoeuvre well commenced, the emperor betook himself to the point where Ney's corps was sustaining the first onset of the allied army, and where long hours must be passed in strenuous resistance before the much-needed succours could make themselves felt.

The Emperor of Russia and the King of Prussia were present with the allied armies, which had entered on the campaign under the command of the veteran Kutusof. Kutusof was dead, however, though this was not publicly made known for fear of the influence the fact might have on the superstitious minds of the Russian soldiery. It was given out that he was absent, and the supreme command was placed in the hands of Count Wittgenstein, who had as chief of the staff General Diebitch, afterwards so well known in the Turkish war of 1828. The allied generals, well served in reconnaissance by their numerous cavalry, were aware of all the movements of the French army, and had detected Napoleon's scheme of attacking Leipsic. They had conceived the apparently very feasible plan of falling on the flank of the long-drawn-out French columns as they passed over the great Lutzen plain. Knowing their immense superiority in cavalry, they considered that they would easily break up a newly-raised infantry which had with it hardly enough squadrons to perform ordinary scouting duties. If they could succeed in penetrating the French line of march, they considered that Napoleon must inevitably suffer a shattering disaster. It was therefore arranged that, on the night of the 1st May, the Russo-Prussian forces should cross the Elster at Zwenkau and Pegau, and should be directed on the group of villages south of Lutzen, the very villages near which the French emperor had placed Ney's corps. Excellent as their plan was, however, it failed in one of the data on which it was founded. It was supposed that no great force would oppose them in the villages, as only a few bivouac fires, such as those of ordinary outposts, had been seen in their neighbourhood, and, till the crash of battle came, it was unknown that five strong divisions were lying hidden behind them, formed and ready for action.

Let us examine the position held by Marshal Ney, on the maintenance of which in French hands depended the chance of victory for the French army. Flowing northward through the plain towards Lutzen are two streams—the Flossgraben and the Rippach. Between them, south of Lutzen, are the five villages—Gross-Gorschen, the most southerly; Rahna and Klein-Gorschen, a little farther to the north; Starsiedel, towards the west; and Kaya, towards the north-east near the course of the Flossgraben. The three first named lie in a slight depression of ground, cut up by streamlets bordered with trees, which form here and there pools for watering cattle and eventually discharge their waters into the Flossgraben. Starsiedel and Kaya both stand on rising ground.

The allied forces which were about to pour themselves on this position were 24,000 men, under Count Wittgenstein in person and General d'York, who had commanded the Prussian contingent of Napoleon's army in the advance against Russia, and had been the first to desert the emperor when misfortune overtook him. After crossing the Elster, these leaders joined Blücher, who had with him 25,000 men. In support were 18,000 of reserves, and the Russian Imperial Guard. Some 12,000 or 13,000 cavalry, under Wintzingerode, had covered the movement of the infantry and artillery, and were now prepared to complete the success which seemed to await the decisive action of the combined army. Besides these, another corps of 12,000 men, under Miloradovich, was operating farther to the south, and might be expected to come into line in time for the coming battle.

The Russo-Prussian army rested its right flank on the Flossgraben and its left on the ravine through which the Rippach flows, and, as it deployed its long, dense columns, the Emperor Alexander and the King Frederick William rode through its ranks, encouraging their soldiers and receiving their enthusiastic acclamations. The two monarchs then placed themselves on an eminence commanding the battlefield, from which they could watch the fortunes of the day. Of Ney's corps the most advanced division was that of General Souham, a man who had grown grey in war, imposing in appearance by his great stature, cool, determined, and of undaunted courage. The divi-

sion was formed near Gross-Gorschen. Not till about ten o'clock was there any sign of the approaching storm, but at that hour the advanced sentries could see the long blue lines near the Flossgraben, which the old soldiers in the ranks recognised as regiments of the enemy, deploying from column of march. On the other side, near the Rippach, the glint of the sun on brass and steel showed the presence of the dragoons and *cuirassiers* of the Russian Imperial Guard, while the black clouds that wheeled and hovered near and far were the pulks of Cossacks, whose name even then was one of dread to Western Europe. To the young soldiers of France who had not

been three months under arms, it seemed that all was lost, and that it would be impossible for them to hold their ground against such odds till help came.

The fiery Blücher, though bearing the weight of seventy years, commanded the first line of the attack on the French with all the vigour and impetuosity of youth, with all the patriotic enthusiasm which animated the soldiers of Germany. Covered by the fire of twenty-four guns and supported on the left near Starsiedel by the Russian cavalry, his leading division advanced; but Souham stood fast with his men formed in squares, for, young as they were, they could not have been trusted in a looser formation. The French artillery, inferior in numbers, replied to the Prussian fire, but was unable to subdue the torrents of grape that tore through the French ranks, and whose every discharge was followed by the ominous order from Souham and his officers, "Close your ranks," as gaps were made in the serried masses. The conscripts fought like veterans, and, when the Prussian infantry charged with loud cries of "*Vaterland! Vaterland!*" repulsed them once and again, but, decimated by the ruthless artillery fire, threatened on their right by powerful squadrons, they gave way and fell back from Gross-Gorschen to Rahna and Klein-Gorschen. The cavalry, which had menaced them, thought to convert the retreat into a rout and swept down from Starsiedel; but General Girard's division, supported by the divisions of Generals Marchand, Ricard, and Brenier, received the hostile squadrons with so steady and deadly a fire that they drew rein and retired. The divisions of Souham and Girard then occupied Klein-Gorschen and Rahna, and for the time checked the further advance of the Prussian infantry.

Rallied in their new position, the brigades of Souham regained all their original steadiness, and, with Girard's division formed on their right, were, again prepared for vigorous resistance. The watercourses, enclosures, and ponds, which were the main features of the villages, became important means of defence, and the long-experienced generals of the French army knew well how to make the most of the advantages they offered. The general situation was changed, moreover, and fresh confidence put into the young soldiers by the arrival of Marshal Marmont, who, with his arm in a sling from a recent wound, debouched near Starsiedel with the divisions of Generals Campans and Bonnet. These two divisions were at once formed in a series of squares, and occupied all the ground between Girard's right and Starsiedel. Campans's division was composed entirely of

marines, who had been drafted from their service afloat and the seaport garrisons to swell the ranks of the field-army; and nobly did these men maintain the maritime honour of France in one of her mightiest conflicts ashore. As they came under the terrible fire of the Prussian batteries, they bore themselves proudly and unflinchingly giving back no step of ground and securing the right of the army with soldierly persistence. When the allied sovereigns and Blücher saw the new and firm attitude of their enemy, it became evident to them that the French had not been so much surprised as they had hoped would be the case, and that it would be no easy task to carry the villages now so strongly held. But Blücher, undaunted by any obstacles and recognising that victory could alone be gained by forcing the French centre, left their flanks to be neutralised by the allied cavalry, and hurled himself at the head of fresh troops—Ziethen's division, supported on right and left by two of d'York's divisions—against Klein-Gorschen and Rahna.

Furious was this second assault, and the battle became a series of independent struggles between detached bodies, in the defence and attack of each incident of the scene which offered a post of vantage. In houses, gardens, enclosures, across watercourses, from tree to tree in the groves, the stalwart Germans and the French recruits fought it out hand to hand. There was no time to load, and the issue was to be decided with the bayonet. Backwards and forwards the combatants swayed, but, bravely as they struggled, boys could not stand against men. Klein-Gorschen and Rahna were carried by Blücher and his sturdy followers, and the *débris* of the two divisions which had defended the villages fell back towards Kaya and Starsiedel. *Débris* they were indeed. When the roll was called, scarce a third of each company replied "Present." The centre of the French line was rudely shaken, but still Souham and Girard were able again to re-form under cover of Kaya, held by Brenier and Ricard, and Starsiedel, where Campans's marines and Bonnet's division still stood immovable and defiant.

It seemed as though the impassioned vehemence of Blücher, the patriotic ardour and courage of the soldiers who followed him, were destined to success in driving the great wedge of attack into the heart of the French army; but at this moment a new and tremendous force, though it was only the magnetic personality of one man, appeared in the field against them. Marshal Ney, whom we have seen with Napoleon near Leipsic, now arrived at a gallop to assume the command of the army corps, which had hitherto been battling without him. The presence of the hero of countless battlefields, the victor of Elchingen, the great Prince de la Moskowa, the noblest of the rear-guard in the dread retreat over the frozen steppes of Russia, was like a draught of strong wine to the men who were staggering under their enemy's fierce attack. The very aspect of the marshal's face, whose every feature told of uncompromising energy, the vivid lightning of his eye, the rudely-cut upturned nose, the massive dominant jaw, inspired confidence, and the athletic, powerful frame seemed a tower of strength which no force could overthrow.

Ney at once grasped his *corps d'armée* in his strong hand. Marchand's division he detached across the Flossgraben towards the hamlet of Eisdorf to threaten the enemy's right and to effect a junction with Macdonald, whose arrival on the field could not now be long delayed. He himself, at the head of the divisions of Brenier and Ricard, pressed forward to retake the villages which had been abandoned. But the Prussians had already left the villages behind them, and the line of French bayonets crashed into Blucher's men at the foot of the eminence on which Kaya stands. If the Prussians fought to restore the dignity of their country, so long ground beneath the heel of Napoleon, the French generals, officers, and men fought with equal desperation to maintain the glory of their loved France and reassert her predominance in Europe. But nothing could resist the leadership of Ney. Death passed him by on every hand, and, while others fell on his right and left, he seemed invulnerable. Forward he pressed and ever forward till at last the bloodstained ruins of Klein-Gorschen and Rahna were again in the possession of Brenier and Ricard, the relics of Souham's and Girard's divisions following hard on their forward track; and, despite every effort of Blücher, the Prussians were hurled back upon Gross-Gorschen.

The French supports began to close at last on the scene of conflict. Macdonald and Prince Eugène were following the east bank of the Flossgraben and approaching Eisdorf, the Guard was hurrying towards the north of Kaya, and though the head of Bertrand's columns was not yet in sight, his early arrival might be counted upon. Napoleon himself rode on to the field of one of the bloodiest engagements in modern war. The personal presence of the greatest general of the time was allowed by his adversaries to be worth at least ten thousand men; and his soldiers, believing that where he was defeat could not be, hailed his appearance as a presage of victory. Still the determination of Blücher and his resources were not exhausted, though division after division had crumbled to pieces in his hands, while they sacrificed themselves in following where he led. The Prussian Royal Guard and reserves had not yet been engaged, and Blücher called upon them in turn to conquer or die. On his right he sent two battalions across the Flossgraben to check the head of Macdonald's advancing columns. On his left he launched the cavalry

of the Royal Guard against Marmont's squares, and in the centre he placed himself at the head of the tall Pomeranian grenadiers to attempt a last attack on the position which had so long defied him. Again Frenchman and German closed in the shock of deadly strife. Against the furious charges of Prussian cavalry, supported by Wintzingerode's squadrons, Marmont's squares remained unbroken, like iron citadels, vomiting fire from their living walls. No check could be given on the right to Macdonald and Prince Eugène, but in the centre the four divisions of Ney's corps, already rudely handled and battle-weary, gave way before Blücher. Klein-Gorschen and Rahna were carried for the second time. The German leader was severely wounded in the assault, but, refusing to quit the field, the old warrior gave his men no breathing-space and pressed up the slope towards Kaya. Even there the French could not again rally in time, and the last village, the key of the position, was at last wrested from them.

The French centre was pierced, and, if the Russian army had at once followed in support of the conquering Prussians, the day would have been lost to Napoleon. But the movements of allies always lack unison, and the opportunity which had been gained by the determined gallantry of Blücher was lost by the inactivity of the Russian commanders. Napoleon's cool glance marked that the Prussian Guard, though for the time successful, was shaken by its advance, and that no fresh troops were behind them. Riding into the midst of the shattered bands of conscripts and exclaiming, "Young men, I have counted on you to save the empire, and are you flying?" he succeeded in restoring some order. Ricard's division had suffered less than the others, and was still in battle formation. To its head he sent Count Lobau, one of his most trusted generals, bidding him lead it again into the fight. It was a last despairing effort.

The emperor had no longer under his hand the eighty squadrons, led by the brilliant Murat, which, in similar circumstances, he had been able to launch at his foe at Eylau and Borodino. These had perished in the Russian snows. He was obliged to trust his fate to battalions of half-drilled, weakly, inexperienced boys, already shaken by heavy loss and worn out by fatigue. And the boys failed him not. Inflamed by the warrior spirit of their country, they responded gallantly to the appeals of their emperor and the leadership of Count Lobau. With the bayonet they fell upon the Prussians, who had so lately driven them back. The divisions of Souham and Grenier also rallied in their attenuated ranks under the mastery of Ney's adamantine energy, and again plunged into the fight. Welcome sound to French ears, the roar of guns was heard on their left flank. It was Macdonald, who at last was making his presence felt on the other side of the Flossgraben.

Far away on their right deep columns were deploying into fighting formation, relieving the pressure on Marmont's corps. Bertrand had arrived, and from both flanks the allies were exposed to a cross fire. Over a front of two leagues the carnage raged. Even the oldest of the warriors present had never seen an issue so bitterly contested, none that had demanded such a tribute of death. The last charge of Ney's corps carried all before it. The Prussian Guard reeled back, and Kaya, the key of the position, was lost to Blücher. A vast crescent of fire was now in front of the allied army, but still, if the centre of that crescent could be cut through, its horns could be held of comparatively little consequence. They must fall back if their connection was destroyed. Although 40,000 men had been expended by Blücher, there still remained the corps of Wittgenstein untouched, the corps of d'York, which had suffered little, and the infantry of the Russian Imperial Guard. It was six o'clock in the evening, and the effort must be made at once or not at all. Wittgenstein decided to make it, and led the fresh troops over the ground where lay the piles of French and German dead and wounded which marked where the tide of success had ebbed and flowed. Masses of cavalry supported the movement, and, under Wintzingerode, neutralised the French right. Macdonald's infantry had not yet been able to come into action, and the allied advance was, for a time, unchecked. But what is that long line of bearskins crowning the height stretching from Starsiedel to Kaya? what are those six steady masses in the rear? what is that huge battery whirling into action? It is the infantry and artillery of Napoleon's Imperial Guard, which has at last arrived. Sixteen battalions of the Young Guard are in columns of attack, under Dumoutier, supported by six battalions of the Old Guard. Druot is putting eighty guns into action. No one can conceive the paralysing effect upon a foe of the appearance of the invincible French Guard. Trained by twenty years of war—survivors of all the campaigns from the revolutionary times till the great successes of the empire—their eagles have always looked on victory, and, in fair field, they have never yet met their superiors. They have just arrived from Leipsic, and have been marshalled under Napoleon's own eye. Now their stately advance pauses to give Druot time to pour a shower of grape and cannon-balls on Wittgenstein and d'York, and now again they move forward with levelled bayonets and set, determined faces. Vain is now the bravery of Wittgenstein and d'York, vain the hopes of Alexander and Frederick William. Shattered by the combined artillery and infantry fire, their troops stand still, waver, recoil.

The steady squares on the French right throw back the cavalry of Wintzingerode, the serried columns in the centre, flanked by Druot's artillery and Macdonald's infantry which is now in line, press against the Russian battalions, and now the whole allied army must retreat, having permanently gained no foot of ground, no single military advantage during the long day of undaunted effort and patriotic devotion.

But though victory, after hovering doubtful over the combatants, at last rested with Napoleon, though his young army had proved its spirit equal to that of its predecessors which had marched resistless over Europe, no trophies of success could be gathered, no crowds of prisoners swelled the triumph as in the days of bygone conquests. The grand cavalry of the past had disappeared never to be replaced. The pursuit, which alone could have so much demoralised the allies as to render them incapable of future action, was impossible. The Russo-Prussian army retired unmolested, slowly, sullenly, defeated but not finally overmastered, again to gather strength and cohesion. Great and undoubted as was his victory at Lutzen, it was but the prelude to the succession of shocks, which left the edifice of Napoleon's Empire in crumbling ruins.

ALSO FROM LEONAUR
AVAILABLE IN SOFTCOVER OR HARDCOVER WITH DUST JACKET

A HISTORY OF THE FRENCH & INDIAN WAR *by Arthur G. Bradley*—The Seven Years War as it was fought in the New World has always fascinated students of military history—here is the story of that confrontation.

WASHINGTON'S EARLY CAMPAIGNS *by James Hadden*—The French Post Expedition, Great Meadows and Braddock's Defeat—including Braddock's Orderly Books.

BOUQUET & THE OHIO INDIAN WAR *by Cyrus Cort & William Smith*—Two Accounts of the Campaigns of 1763-1764: Bouquet's Campaigns by Cyrus Cort & The History of Bouquet's Expeditions by William Smith.

NARRATIVES OF THE FRENCH & INDIAN WAR: 2 *by David Holden, Samuel Jenks, Lemuel Lyon, Mary Cochrane Rogers & Henry T. Blake*—Contains The Diary of Sergeant David Holden, Captain Samuel Jenks' Journal, The Journal of Lemuel Lyon, Journal of a French Officer at the Siege of Quebec, A Battle Fought on Snowshoes & The Battle of Lake George.

NARRATIVES OF THE FRENCH & INDIAN WAR *by Brown, Eastburn, Hawks & Putnam*—Ranger Brown's Narrative, The Adventures of Robert Eastburn, The Journal of Rufus Putnam—Provincial Infantry & Orderly Book and Journal of Major John Hawks on the Ticonderoga-Crown Point Campaign.

THE 7TH (QUEEN'S OWN) HUSSARS: Volume 1—1688-1792 *by C. R. B. Barrett*—As Dragoons During the Flanders Campaign, War of the Austrian Succession and the Seven Years War.

INDIA'S FREE LANCES *by H. G. Keene*—European Mercenary Commanders in Hindustan 1770-1820.

THE BENGAL EUROPEAN REGIMENT *by P. R. Innes*—An Elite Regiment of the Honourable East India Company 1756-1858.

MUSKET & TOMAHAWK *by Francis Parkman*—A Military History of the French & Indian War, 1753-1760.

THE BLACK WATCH AT TICONDEROGA *by Frederick B. Richards*—Campaigns in the French & Indian War.

QUEEN'S RANGERS *by Frederick B. Richards*—John Simcoe and his Rangers During the Revolutionary War for America.

AVAILABLE ONLINE AT **www.leonaur.com**
AND FROM ALL GOOD BOOK STORES

ALSO FROM LEONAUR
AVAILABLE IN SOFTCOVER OR HARDCOVER WITH DUST JACKET

JOURNALS OF ROBERT ROGERS OF THE RANGERS *by Robert Rogers*—The exploits of Rogers & the Rangers in his own words during 1755-1761 in the French & Indian War.

GALLOPING GUNS *by James Young*—The Experiences of an Officer of the Bengal Horse Artillery During the Second Maratha War 1804-1805.

GORDON *by Demetrius Charles Boulger*—The Career of Gordon of Khartoum.

THE BATTLE OF NEW ORLEANS *by Zachary F. Smith*—The final major engagement of the War of 1812.

THE TWO WARS OF MRS DUBERLY *by Frances Isabella Duberly*—An Intrepid Victorian Lady's Experience of the Crimea and Indian Mutiny.

WITH THE GUARDS' BRIGADE DURING THE BOER WAR *by Edward P. Lowry*—On Campaign from Bloemfontein to Koomati Poort and Back.

THE REBELLIOUS DUCHESS *by Paul F. S. Dermoncourt*—The Adventures of the Duchess of Berri and Her Attempt to Overthrow French Monarchy.

MEN OF THE MUTINY *by John Tulloch Nash & Henry Metcalfe*—Two Accounts of the Great Indian Mutiny of 1857: Fighting with the Bengal Yeomanry Cavalry & Private Metcalfe at Lucknow.

CAMPAIGN IN THE CRIMEA *by George Shuldham Peard*—The Recollections of an Officer of the 20th Regiment of Foot.

WITHIN SEBASTOPOL *by K. Hodasevich*—A Narrative of the Campaign in the Crimea, and of the Events of the Siege.

WITH THE CAVALRY TO AFGHANISTAN *by William Taylor*—The Experiences of a Trooper of H. M. 4th Light Dragoons During the First Afghan War.

THE CAWNPORE MAN *by Mowbray Thompson*—A First Hand Account of the Siege and Massacre During the Indian Mutiny By One of Four Survivors.

BRIGADE COMMANDER: AFGHANISTAN *by Henry Brooke*—The Journal of the Commander of the 2nd Infantry Brigade, Kandahar Field Force During the Second Afghan War.

BANCROFT OF THE BENGAL HORSE ARTILLERY *by N. W. Bancroft*—An Account of the First Sikh War 1845-1846.

AVAILABLE ONLINE AT **www.leonaur.com**
AND FROM ALL GOOD BOOK STORES

ALSO FROM LEONAUR
AVAILABLE IN SOFTCOVER OR HARDCOVER WITH DUST JACKET

AFGHANISTAN: THE BELEAGUERED BRIGADE *by G. R. Gleig*—An Account of Sale's Brigade During the First Afghan War.

IN THE RANKS OF THE C. I. V *by Erskine Childers*—With the City Imperial Volunteer Battery (Honourable Artillery Company) in the Second Boer War.

THE BENGAL NATIVE ARMY *by F. G. Cardew*—An Invaluable Reference Resource.

THE 7TH (QUEEN'S OWN) HUSSARS: Volume 4—1688-1914 *by C. R. B. Barrett*—Uniforms, Equipment, Weapons, Traditions, the Services of Notable Officers and Men & the Appendices to All Volumes—Volume 4: 1688-1914.

THE SWORD OF THE CROWN *by Eric W. Sheppard*—A History of the British Army to 1914.

THE 7TH (QUEEN'S OWN) HUSSARS: Volume 3—**1818-1914** *by C. R. B. Barrett*—On Campaign During the Canadian Rebellion, the Indian Mutiny, the Sudan, Matabeleland, Mashonaland and the Boer War Volume 3: 1818-1914.

THE KHARTOUM CAMPAIGN *by Bennet Burleigh*—A Special Correspondent's View of the Reconquest of the Sudan by British and Egyptian Forces under Kitchener—1898.

EL PUCHERO *by Richard McSherry*—The Letters of a Surgeon of Volunteers During Scott's Campaign of the American-Mexican War 1847-1848.

RIFLEMAN SAHIB *by E. Maude*—The Recollections of an Officer of the Bombay Rifles During the Southern Mahratta Campaign, Second Sikh War, Persian Campaign and Indian Mutiny.

THE KING'S HUSSAR *by Edwin Mole*—The Recollections of a 14th (King's) Hussar During the Victorian Era.

JOHN COMPANY'S CAVALRYMAN *by William Johnson*—The Experiences of a British Soldier in the Crimea, the Persian Campaign and the Indian Mutiny.

COLENSO & DURNFORD'S ZULU WAR *by Frances E. Colenso & Edward Durnford*—The first and possibly the most important history of the Zulu War.

U. S. DRAGOON *by Samuel E. Chamberlain*—Experiences in the Mexican War 1846-48 and on the South Western Frontier.

AVAILABLE ONLINE AT **www.leonaur.com**
AND FROM ALL GOOD BOOK STORES

ALSO FROM LEONAUR
AVAILABLE IN SOFTCOVER OR HARDCOVER WITH DUST JACKET

THE 2ND MAORI WAR: 1860-1861 *by Robert Carey*—The Second Maori War, or First Taranaki War, one more bloody instalment of the conflicts between European settlers and the indigenous Maori people.

A JOURNAL OF THE SECOND SIKH WAR *by Daniel A. Sandford*—The Experiences of an Ensign of the 2nd Bengal European Regiment During the Campaign in the Punjab, India, 1848-49.

THE LIGHT INFANTRY OFFICER *by John H. Cooke*—The Experiences of an Officer of the 43rd Light Infantry in America During the War of 1812.

BUSHVELDT CARBINEERS *by George Witton*—The War Against the Boers in South Africa and the 'Breaker' Morant Incident.

LAKE'S CAMPAIGNS IN INDIA *by Hugh Pearse*—The Second Anglo Maratha War, 1803-1807.

BRITAIN IN AFGHANISTAN 1: THE FIRST AFGHAN WAR 1839-42 *by Archibald Forbes*—From invasion to destruction-a British military disaster.

BRITAIN IN AFGHANISTAN 2: THE SECOND AFGHAN WAR 1878-80 *by Archibald Forbes*—This is the history of the Second Afghan War-another episode of British military history typified by savagery, massacre, siege and battles.

UP AMONG THE PANDIES *by Vivian Dering Majendie*—Experiences of a British Officer on Campaign During the Indian Mutiny, 1857-1858.

MUTINY: 1857 *by James Humphries*—Authentic Voices from the Indian Mutiny-First Hand Accounts of Battles, Sieges and Personal Hardships.

BLOW THE BUGLE, DRAW THE SWORD *by W. H. G. Kingston*—The Wars, Campaigns, Regiments and Soldiers of the British & Indian Armies During the Victorian Era, 1839-1898.

WAR BEYOND THE DRAGON PAGODA *by Major J. J. Snodgrass*—A Personal Narrative of the First Anglo-Burmese War 1824 - 1826.

THE HERO OF ALIWAL *by James Humphries*—The Campaigns of Sir Harry Smith in India, 1843-1846, During the Gwalior War & the First Sikh War.

ALL FOR A SHILLING A DAY *by Donald F. Featherstone*—The story of H.M. 16th, the Queen's Lancers During the first Sikh War 1845-1846.

AVAILABLE ONLINE AT **www.leonaur.com**
AND FROM ALL GOOD BOOK STORES

ALSO FROM LEONAUR
AVAILABLE IN SOFTCOVER OR HARDCOVER WITH DUST JACKET

THE FALL OF THE MOGHUL EMPIRE OF HINDUSTAN *by H. G. Keene*—By the beginning of the nineteenth century, as British and Indian armies under Lake and Wellesley dominated the scene, a little over half a century of conflict brought the Moghul Empire to its knees.

LADY SALE'S AFGHANISTAN *by Florentia Sale*—An Indomitable Victorian Lady's Account of the Retreat from Kabul During the First Afghan War.

THE CAMPAIGN OF MAGENTA AND SOLFERINO 1859 *by Harold Carmichael Wylly*—The Decisive Conflict for the Unification of Italy.

FRENCH'S CAVALRY CAMPAIGN *by J. G. Maydon*—A Special Correspondent's View of British Army Mounted Troops During the Boer War.

CAVALRY AT WATERLOO *by Sir Evelyn Wood*—British Mounted Troops During the Campaign of 1815.

THE SUBALTERN *by George Robert Gleig*—The Experiences of an Officer of the 85th Light Infantry During the Peninsular War.

NAPOLEON AT BAY, 1814 *by F. Loraine Petre*—The Campaigns to the Fall of the First Empire.

NAPOLEON AND THE CAMPAIGN OF 1806 *by Colonel Vachée*—The Napoleonic Method of Organisation and Command to the Battles of Jena & Auerstädt.

THE COMPLETE ADVENTURES IN THE CONNAUGHT RANGERS *by William Grattan*—The 88th Regiment during the Napoleonic Wars by a Serving Officer.

BUGLER AND OFFICER OF THE RIFLES *by William Green & Harry Smith*—With the 95th (Rifles) during the Peninsular & Waterloo Campaigns of the Napoleonic Wars.

NAPOLEONIC WAR STORIES *by Sir Arthur Quiller-Couch*—Tales of soldiers, spies, battles & sieges from the Peninsular & Waterloo campaigns.

CAPTAIN OF THE 95TH (RIFLES) *by Jonathan Leach*—An officer of Wellington's sharpshooters during the Peninsular, South of France and Waterloo campaigns of the Napoleonic wars.

RIFLEMAN COSTELLO *by Edward Costello*—The adventures of a soldier of the 95th (Rifles) in the Peninsular & Waterloo Campaigns of the Napoleonic wars.

AVAILABLE ONLINE AT **www.leonaur.com**
AND FROM ALL GOOD BOOK STORES

ALSO FROM LEONAUR
AVAILABLE IN SOFTCOVER OR HARDCOVER WITH DUST JACKET

AT THEM WITH THE BAYONET *by Donald F. Featherstone*—The first Anglo-Sikh War 1845-1846.

STEPHEN CRANE'S BATTLES *by Stephen Crane*—Nine Decisive Battles Recounted by the Author of 'The Red Badge of Courage'.

THE GURKHA WAR *by H. T. Prinsep*—The Anglo-Nepalese Conflict in North East India 1814-1816.

FIRE & BLOOD *by G. R. Gleig*—The burning of Washington & the battle of New Orleans, 1814, through the eyes of a young British soldier.

SOUND ADVANCE! *by Joseph Anderson*—Experiences of an officer of HM 50th regiment in Australia, Burma & the Gwalior war.

THE CAMPAIGN OF THE INDUS *by Thomas Holdsworth*—Experiences of a British Officer of the 2nd (Queen's Royal) Regiment in the Campaign to Place Shah Shuja on the Throne of Afghanistan 1838 - 1840.

WITH THE MADRAS EUROPEAN REGIMENT IN BURMA *by John Butler*—The Experiences of an Officer of the Honourable East India Company's Army During the First Anglo-Burmese War 1824 - 1826.

IN ZULULAND WITH THE BRITISH ARMY *by Charles L. Norris-Newman*—The Anglo-Zulu war of 1879 through the first-hand experiences of a special correspondent.

BESIEGED IN LUCKNOW *by Martin Richard Gubbins*—The first Anglo-Sikh War 1845-1846.

A TIGER ON HORSEBACK *by L. March Phillips*—The Experiences of a Trooper & Officer of Rimington's Guides - The Tigers - during the Anglo-Boer war 1899 - 1902.

SEPOYS, SIEGE & STORM *by Charles John Griffiths*—The Experiences of a young officer of H.M.'s 61st Regiment at Ferozepore, Delhi ridge and at the fall of Delhi during the Indian mutiny 1857.

CAMPAIGNING IN ZULULAND *by W. E. Montague*—Experiences on campaign during the Zulu war of 1879 with the 94th Regiment.

THE STORY OF THE GUIDES *by G.J. Younghusband*—The Exploits of the Soldiers of the famous Indian Army Regiment from the northwest frontier 1847 - 1900.

AVAILABLE ONLINE AT **www.leonaur.com**
AND FROM ALL GOOD BOOK STORES

ALSO FROM LEONAUR
AVAILABLE IN SOFTCOVER OR HARDCOVER WITH DUST JACKET

ZULU:1879 *by D.C.F. Moodie & the Leonaur Editors*—The Anglo-Zulu War of 1879 from contemporary sources: First Hand Accounts, Interviews, Dispatches, Official Documents & Newspaper Reports.

THE RED DRAGOON *by W.J. Adams*—With the 7th Dragoon Guards in the Cape of Good Hope against the Boers & the Kaffir tribes during the 'war of the axe' 1843-48'.

THE RECOLLECTIONS OF SKINNER OF SKINNER'S HORSE *by James Skinner*—James Skinner and his 'Yellow Boys' Irregular cavalry in the wars of India between the British, Mahratta, Rajput, Mogul, Sikh & Pindarree Forces.

A CAVALRY OFFICER DURING THE SEPOY REVOLT *by A. R. D. Mackenzie*—Experiences with the 3rd Bengal Light Cavalry, the Guides and Sikh Irregular Cavalry from the outbreak to Delhi and Lucknow.

A NORFOLK SOLDIER IN THE FIRST SIKH WAR *by J W Baldwin*—Experiences of a private of H.M. 9th Regiment of Foot in the battles for the Punjab, India 1845-6.

TOMMY ATKINS' WAR STORIES: 14 FIRST HAND ACCOUNTS—Fourteen first hand accounts from the ranks of the British Army during Queen Victoria's Empire.

THE WATERLOO LETTERS *by H. T. Siborne*—Accounts of the Battle by British Officers for its Foremost Historian.

NEY: GENERAL OF CAVALRY VOLUME 1—1769-1799 *by Antoine Bulos*—The Early Career of a Marshal of the First Empire.

NEY: MARSHAL OF FRANCE VOLUME 2—1799-1805 *by Antoine Bulos*—The Early Career of a Marshal of the First Empire.

AIDE-DE-CAMP TO NAPOLEON *by Philippe-Paul de Ségur*—For anyone interested in the Napoleonic Wars this book, written by one who was intimate with the strategies and machinations of the Emperor, will be essential reading.

TWILIGHT OF EMPIRE *by Sir Thomas Ussher & Sir George Cockburn*—Two accounts of Napoleon's Journeys in Exile to Elba and St. Helena: Narrative of Events by Sir Thomas Ussher & Napoleon's Last Voyage: Extract of a diary by Sir George Cockburn.

PRIVATE WHEELER *by William Wheeler*—The letters of a soldier of the 51st Light Infantry during the Peninsular War & at Waterloo.

AVAILABLE ONLINE AT **www.leonaur.com**
AND FROM ALL GOOD BOOK STORES

ALSO FROM LEONAUR
AVAILABLE IN SOFTCOVER OR HARDCOVER WITH DUST JACKET

OFFICERS & GENTLEMEN *by Peter Hawker & William Graham*—Two Accounts of British Officers During the Peninsula War: Officer of Light Dragoons by Peter Hawker & Campaign in Portugal and Spain by William Graham .

THE WALCHEREN EXPEDITION *by Anonymous*—The Experiences of a British Officer of the 81st Regt. During the Campaign in the Low Countries of 1809.

LADIES OF WATERLOO *by Charlotte A. Eaton, Magdalene de Lancey & Juana Smith*—The Experiences of Three Women During the Campaign of 1815: Waterloo Days by Charlotte A. Eaton, A Week at Waterloo by Magdalene de Lancey & Juana's Story by Juana Smith.

JOURNAL OF AN OFFICER IN THE KING'S GERMAN LEGION *by John Frederick Hering*—Recollections of Campaigning During the Napoleonic Wars.

JOURNAL OF AN ARMY SURGEON IN THE PENINSULAR WAR *by Charles Boutflower*—The Recollections of a British Army Medical Man on Campaign During the Napoleonic Wars.

ON CAMPAIGN WITH MOORE AND WELLINGTON *by Anthony Hamilton*—The Experiences of a Soldier of the 43rd Regiment During the Peninsular War.

THE ROAD TO AUSTERLITZ *by R. G. Burton*—Napoleon's Campaign of 1805.

SOLDIERS OF NAPOLEON *by A. J. Doisy De Villargennes & Arthur Chuquet*—The Experiences of the Men of the French First Empire: Under the Eagles by A. J. Doisy De Villargennes & Voices of 1812 by Arthur Chuquet .

INVASION OF FRANCE, 1814 *by F. W. O. Maycock*—The Final Battles of the Napoleonic First Empire.

LEIPZIG—A CONFLICT OF TITANS *by Frederic Shoberl*—A Personal Experience of the 'Battle of the Nations' During the Napoleonic Wars, October 14th-19th, 1813.

SLASHERS *by Charles Cadell*—The Campaigns of the 28th Regiment of Foot During the Napoleonic Wars by a Serving Officer.

BATTLE IMPERIAL *by Charles William Vane*—The Campaigns in Germany & France for the Defeat of Napoleon 1813-1814.

SWIFT & BOLD *by Gibbes Rigaud*—The 60th Rifles During the Peninsula War.

AVAILABLE ONLINE AT **www.leonaur.com**
AND FROM ALL GOOD BOOK STORES

ALSO FROM LEONAUR
AVAILABLE IN SOFTCOVER OR HARDCOVER WITH DUST JACKET

ADVENTURES OF A YOUNG RIFLEMAN by Johann Christian Maempel—The Experiences of a Saxon in the French & British Armies During the Napoleonic Wars.

THE HUSSAR by Norbert Landsheit & G. R. Gleig—A German Cavalryman in British Service Throughout the Napoleonic Wars.

RECOLLECTIONS OF THE PENINSULA by Moyle Sherer—An Officer of the 34th Regiment of Foot—'The Cumberland Gentlemen'—on Campaign Against Napoleon's French Army in Spain.

MARINE OF REVOLUTION & CONSULATE by Moreau de Jonnès—The Recollections of a French Soldier of the Revolutionary Wars 1791-1804.

GENTLEMEN IN RED by John Dobbs & Robert Knowles—Two Accounts of British Infantry Officers During the Peninsular War Recollections of an Old 52nd Man by John Dobbs An Officer of Fusiliers by Robert Knowles.

CORPORAL BROWN'S CAMPAIGNS IN THE LOW COUNTRIES by Robert Brown—Recollections of a Coldstream Guard in the Early Campaigns Against Revolutionary France 1793-1795.

THE 7TH (QUEENS OWN) HUSSARS: Volume 2—1793-1815 by C. R. B. Barrett—During the Campaigns in the Low Countries & the Peninsula and Waterloo Campaigns of the Napoleonic Wars. Volume 2: 1793-1815.

THE MARENGO CAMPAIGN 1800 by Herbert H. Sargent—The Victory that Completed the Austrian Defeat in Italy.

DONALDSON OF THE 94TH—SCOTS BRIGADE by Joseph Donaldson—The Recollections of a Soldier During the Peninsula & South of France Campaigns of the Napoleonic Wars.

A CONSCRIPT FOR EMPIRE by Philippe as told to Johann Christian Maempel—The Experiences of a Young German Conscript During the Napoleonic Wars.

JOURNAL OF THE CAMPAIGN OF 1815 by Alexander Cavalié Mercer—The Experiences of an Officer of the Royal Horse Artillery During the Waterloo Campaign.

NAPOLEON'S CAMPAIGNS IN POLAND 1806-7 by Robert Wilson—The campaign in Poland from the Russian side of the conflict.

AVAILABLE ONLINE AT www.leonaur.com
AND FROM ALL GOOD BOOK STORES

ALSO FROM LEONAUR
AVAILABLE IN SOFTCOVER OR HARDCOVER WITH DUST JACKET

OMPTEDA OF THE KING'S GERMAN LEGION by *Christian von Ompteda*—A Hanoverian Officer on Campaign Against Napoleon.

LIEUTENANT SIMMONS OF THE 95TH (RIFLES) by *George Simmons*—Recollections of the Peninsula, South of France & Waterloo Campaigns of the Napoleonic Wars.

A HORSEMAN FOR THE EMPEROR by *Jean Baptiste Gazzola*—A Cavalryman of Napoleon's Army on Campaign Throughout the Napoleonic Wars.

SERGEANT LAWRENCE by *William Lawrence*—With the 40th Regt. of Foot in South America, the Peninsular War & at Waterloo.

CAMPAIGNS WITH THE FIELD TRAIN by *Richard D. Henegan*—Experiences of a British Officer During the Peninsula and Waterloo Campaigns of the Napoleonic Wars.

CAVALRY SURGEON by *S. D. Broughton*—On Campaign Against Napoleon in the Peninsula & South of France During the Napoleonic Wars 1812-1814.

MEN OF THE RIFLES by *Thomas Knight, Henry Curling & Jonathan Leach*—The Reminiscences of Thomas Knight of the 95th (Rifles) by Thomas Knight, Henry Curling's Anecdotes by Henry Curling & The Field Services of the Rifle Brigade from its Formation to Waterloo by Jonathan Leach.

THE ULM CAMPAIGN 1805 by *F. N. Maude*—Napoleon and the Defeat of the Austrian Army During the 'War of the Third Coalition'.

SOLDIERING WITH THE 'DIVISION' by *Thomas Garrety*—The Military Experiences of an Infantryman of the 43rd Regiment During the Napoleonic Wars.

SERGEANT MORRIS OF THE 73RD FOOT by *Thomas Morris*—The Experiences of a British Infantryman During the Napoleonic Wars-Including Campaigns in Germany and at Waterloo.

A VOICE FROM WATERLOO by *Edward Cotton*—The Personal Experiences of a British Cavalryman Who Became a Battlefield Guide and Authority on the Campaign of 1815.

NAPOLEON AND HIS MARSHALS by *J. T. Headley*—The Men of the First Empire.

AVAILABLE ONLINE AT **www.leonaur.com**
AND FROM ALL GOOD BOOK STORES

ALSO FROM LEONAUR
AVAILABLE IN SOFTCOVER OR HARDCOVER WITH DUST JACKET

COLBORNE: A SINGULAR TALENT FOR WAR by *John Colborne*—The Napoleonic Wars Career of One of Wellington's Most Highly Valued Officers in Egypt, Holland, Italy, the Peninsula and at Waterloo.

NAPOLEON'S RUSSIAN CAMPAIGN by *Philippe Henri de Segur*—The Invasion, Battles and Retreat by an Aide-de-Camp on the Emperor's Staff.

WITH THE LIGHT DIVISION by *John H. Cooke*—The Experiences of an Officer of the 43rd Light Infantry in the Peninsula and South of France During the Napoleonic Wars.

WELLINGTON AND THE PYRENEES CAMPAIGN VOLUME I: FROM VITORIA TO THE BIDASSOA by *F. C. Beatson*—The final phase of the campaign in the Iberian Peninsula.

WELLINGTON AND THE INVASION OF FRANCE VOLUME II: THE BIDASSOA TO THE BATTLE OF THE NIVELLE by *F. C. Beatson*—The final phase of the campaign in the Iberian Peninsula.

WELLINGTON AND THE FALL OF FRANCE VOLUME III: THE GAVES AND THE BATTLE OF ORTHEZ by *F. C. Beatson*—The final phase of the campaign in the Iberian Peninsula.

NAPOLEON'S IMPERIAL GUARD: FROM MARENGO TO WATERLOO by *J. T. Headley*—The story of Napoleon's Imperial Guard and the men who commanded them.

BATTLES & SIEGES OF THE PENINSULAR WAR by *W. H. Fitchett*—Corunna, Busaco, Albuera, Ciudad Rodrigo, Badajos, Salamanca, San Sebastian & Others.

SERGEANT GUILLEMARD: THE MAN WHO SHOT NELSON? by *Robert Guillemard*—A Soldier of the Infantry of the French Army of Napoleon on Campaign Throughout Europe.

WITH THE GUARDS ACROSS THE PYRENEES by *Robert Batty*—The Experiences of a British Officer of Wellington's Army During the Battles for the Fall of Napoleonic France, 1813 .

A STAFF OFFICER IN THE PENINSULA by *E. W. Buckham*—An Officer of the British Staff Corps Cavalry During the Peninsula Campaign of the Napoleonic Wars.

THE LEIPZIG CAMPAIGN: 1813—NAPOLEON AND THE "BATTLE OF THE NATIONS" by *F. N. Maude*—Colonel Maude's analysis of Napoleon's campaign of 1813 around Leipzig.

AVAILABLE ONLINE AT **www.leonaur.com**
AND FROM ALL GOOD BOOK STORES

ALSO FROM LEONAUR
AVAILABLE IN SOFTCOVER OR HARDCOVER WITH DUST JACKET

BUGEAUD: A PACK WITH A BATON by *Thomas Robert Bugeaud*—The Early Campaigns of a Soldier of Napoleon's Army Who Would Become a Marshal of France.

WATERLOO RECOLLECTIONS by *Frederick Llewellyn*—Rare First Hand Accounts, Letters, Reports and Retellings from the Campaign of 1815.

SERGEANT NICOL by *Daniel Nicol*—The Experiences of a Gordon Highlander During the Napoleonic Wars in Egypt, the Peninsula and France.

THE JENA CAMPAIGN: 1806 by *F. N. Maude*—The Twin Battles of Jena & Auerstadt Between Napoleon's French and the Prussian Army.

PRIVATE O'NEIL by *Charles O'Neil*—The recollections of an Irish Rogue of H. M. 28th Regt.—The Slashers—during the Peninsula & Waterloo campaigns of the Napoleonic war.

ROYAL HIGHLANDER by *James Anton*—A soldier of H.M 42nd (Royal) Highlanders during the Peninsular, South of France & Waterloo Campaigns of the Napoleonic Wars.

CAPTAIN BLAZE by *Elzéar Blaze*—Life in Napoleons Army.

LEJEUNE VOLUME 1 by *Louis-François Lejeune*—The Napoleonic Wars through the Experiences of an Officer on Berthier's Staff.

LEJEUNE VOLUME 2 by *Louis-François Lejeune*—The Napoleonic Wars through the Experiences of an Officer on Berthier's Staff.

CAPTAIN COIGNET by *Jean-Roch Coignet*—A Soldier of Napoleon's Imperial Guard from the Italian Campaign to Russia and Waterloo.

FUSILIER COOPER by *John S. Cooper*—Experiences in the 7th (Royal) Fusiliers During the Peninsular Campaign of the Napoleonic Wars and the American Campaign to New Orleans.

FIGHTING NAPOLEON'S EMPIRE by *Joseph Anderson*—The Campaigns of a British Infantryman in Italy, Egypt, the Peninsular & the West Indies During the Napoleonic Wars.

CHASSEUR BARRES by *Jean-Baptiste Barres*—The experiences of a French Infantryman of the Imperial Guard at Austerlitz, Jena, Eylau, Friedland, in the Peninsular, Lutzen, Bautzen, Zinnwald and Hanau during the Napoleonic Wars.

AVAILABLE ONLINE AT **www.leonaur.com**
AND FROM ALL GOOD BOOK STORES

ALSO FROM LEONAUR
AVAILABLE IN SOFTCOVER OR HARDCOVER WITH DUST JACKET

CAPTAIN COIGNET by *Jean-Roch Coignet*—A Soldier of Napoleon's Imperial Guard from the Italian Campaign to Russia and Waterloo.

HUSSAR ROCCA by *Albert Jean Michel de Rocca*—A French cavalry officer's experiences of the Napoleonic Wars and his views on the Peninsular Campaigns against the Spanish, British And Guerilla Armies.

MARINES TO 95TH (RIFLES) by *Thomas Fernyhough*—The military experiences of Robert Fernyhough during the Napoleonic Wars.

LIGHT BOB by *Robert Blakeney*—The experiences of a young officer in H.M 28th & 36th regiments of the British Infantry during the Peninsular Campaign of the Napoleonic Wars 1804 - 1814.

WITH WELLINGTON'S LIGHT CAVALRY by *William Tomkinson*—The Experiences of an officer of the 16th Light Dragoons in the Peninsular and Waterloo campaigns of the Napoleonic Wars.

SERGEANT BOURGOGNE by *Adrien Bourgogne*—With Napoleon's Imperial Guard in the Russian Campaign and on the Retreat from Moscow 1812 - 13.

SURTEES OF THE 95TH (RIFLES) by *William Surtees*—A Soldier of the 95th (Rifles) in the Peninsular campaign of the Napoleonic Wars.

SWORDS OF HONOUR by *Henry Newbolt & Stanley L. Wood*—The Careers of Six Outstanding Officers from the Napoleonic Wars, the Wars for India and the American Civil War.

ENSIGN BELL IN THE PENINSULAR WAR by *George Bell*—The Experiences of a young British Soldier of the 34th Regiment 'The Cumberland Gentlemen' in the Napoleonic wars.

HUSSAR IN WINTER by *Alexander Gordon*—A British Cavalry Officer during the retreat to Corunna in the Peninsular campaign of the Napoleonic Wars.

THE COMPLEAT RIFLEMAN HARRIS by *Benjamin Harris as told to and transcribed by Captain Henry Curling, 52nd Regt. of Foot*—The adventures of a soldier of the 95th (Rifles) during the Peninsular Campaign of the Napoleonic Wars.

THE ADVENTURES OF A LIGHT DRAGOON by *George Farmer & G.R. Gleig*—A cavalryman during the Peninsular & Waterloo Campaigns, in captivity & at the siege of Bhurtpore, India.

AVAILABLE ONLINE AT www.leonaur.com
AND FROM ALL GOOD BOOK STORES

ALSO FROM LEONAUR
AVAILABLE IN SOFTCOVER OR HARDCOVER WITH DUST JACKET

THE LIFE OF THE REAL BRIGADIER GERARD VOLUME 1—THE YOUNG HUSSAR 1782-1807 *by Jean-Baptiste De Marbot*—A French Cavalryman Of the Napoleonic Wars at Marengo, Austerlitz, Jena, Eylau & Friedland.

THE LIFE OF THE REAL BRIGADIER GERARD VOLUME 2—IMPERIAL AIDE-DE-CAMP 1807-1811 *by Jean-Baptiste De Marbot*—A French Cavalryman of the Napoleonic Wars at Saragossa, Landshut, Eckmuhl, Ratisbon, Aspern-Essling, Wagram, Busaco & Torres Vedras.

THE LIFE OF THE REAL BRIGADIER GERARD VOLUME 3—COLONEL OF CHASSEURS 1811-1815 *by Jean-Baptiste De Marbot*—A French Cavalryman in the retreat from Moscow, Lutzen, Bautzen, Katzbach, Leipzig, Hanau & Waterloo.

THE INDIAN WAR OF 1864 *by Eugene Ware*—The Experiences of a Young Officer of the 7th Iowa Cavalry on the Western Frontier During the Civil War.

THE MARCH OF DESTINY *by Charles E. Young & V. Devinny*—Dangers of the Trail in 1865 by Charles E. Young & The Story of a Pioneer by V. Devinny, two Accounts of Early Emigrants to Colorado.

CROSSING THE PLAINS *by William Audley Maxwell*—A First Hand Narrative of the Early Pioneer Trail to California in 1857.

CHIEF OF SCOUTS *by William F. Drannan*—A Pilot to Emigrant and Government Trains, Across the Plains of the Western Frontier.

THIRTY-ONE YEARS ON THE PLAINS AND IN THE MOUNTAINS *by William F. Drannan*—William Drannan was born to be a pioneer, hunter, trapper and wagon train guide during the momentous days of the Great American West.

THE INDIAN WARS VOLUNTEER *by William Thompson*—Recollections of the Conflict Against the Snakes, Shoshone, Bannocks, Modocs and Other Native Tribes of the American North West.

THE 4TH TENNESSEE CAVALRY *by George B. Guild*—The Services of Smith's Regiment of Confederate Cavalry by One of its Officers.

COLONEL WORTHINGTON'S SHILOH *by T. Worthington*—The Tennessee Campaign, 1862, by an Officer of the Ohio Volunteers.

FOUR YEARS IN THE SADDLE *by W. L. Curry*—The History of the First Regiment Ohio Volunteer Cavalry in the American Civil War.

AVAILABLE ONLINE AT **www.leonaur.com**
AND FROM ALL GOOD BOOK STORES

ALSO FROM LEONAUR
AVAILABLE IN SOFTCOVER OR HARDCOVER WITH DUST JACKET

LIFE IN THE ARMY OF NORTHERN VIRGINIA by *Carlton McCarthy*—The Observations of a Confederate Artilleryman of Cutshaw's Battalion During the American Civil War 1861-1865.

HISTORY OF THE CAVALRY OF THE ARMY OF THE POTOMAC by *Charles D. Rhodes*—Including Pope's Army of Virginia and the Cavalry Operations in West Virginia During the American Civil War.

CAMP-FIRE AND COTTON-FIELD by *Thomas W. Knox*—A New York Herald Correspondent's View of the American Civil War.

SERGEANT STILLWELL by *Leander Stillwell*—The Experiences of a Union Army Soldier of the 61st Illinois Infantry During the American Civil War.

STONEWALL'S CANNONEER by *Edward A. Moore*—Experiences with the Rockbridge Artillery, Confederate Army of Northern Virginia, During the American Civil War.

THE SIXTH CORPS by *George Stevens*—The Army of the Potomac, Union Army, During the American Civil War.

THE RAILROAD RAIDERS by *William Pittenger*—An Ohio Volunteers Recollections of the Andrews Raid to Disrupt the Confederate Railroad in Georgia During the American Civil War.

CITIZEN SOLDIER by *John Beatty*—An Account of the American Civil War by a Union Infantry Officer of Ohio Volunteers Who Became a Brigadier General.

COX: PERSONAL RECOLLECTIONS OF THE CIVIL WAR--VOLUME 1 by *Jacob Dolson Cox*—West Virginia, Kanawha Valley, Gauley Bridge, Cotton Mountain, South Mountain, Antietam, the Morgan Raid & the East Tennessee Campaign.

COX: PERSONAL RECOLLECTIONS OF THE CIVIL WAR--VOLUME 2 by *Jacob Dolson Cox*—Siege of Knoxville, East Tennessee, Atlanta Campaign, the Nashville Campaign & the North Carolina Campaign.

KERSHAW'S BRIGADE VOLUME 1 by *D. Augustus Dickert*—Manassas, Seven Pines, Sharpsburg (Antietam), Fredricksburg, Chancellorsville, Gettysburg, Chickamauga, Chattanooga, Fort Sanders & Bean Station.

KERSHAW'S BRIGADE VOLUME 2 by *D. Augustus Dickert*—At the wilderness, Cold Harbour, Petersburg, The Shenandoah Valley and Cedar Creek..

AVAILABLE ONLINE AT **www.leonaur.com**
AND FROM ALL GOOD BOOK STORES

ALSO FROM LEONAUR
AVAILABLE IN SOFTCOVER OR HARDCOVER WITH DUST JACKET

THE RELUCTANT REBEL by *William G. Stevenson*—A young Kentuckian's experiences in the Confederate Infantry & Cavalry during the American Civil War..

BOOTS AND SADDLES by *Elizabeth B. Custer*—The experiences of General Custer's Wife on the Western Plains.

FANNIE BEERS' CIVIL WAR by *Fannie A. Beers*—A Confederate Lady's Experiences of Nursing During the Campaigns & Battles of the American Civil War.

LADY SALE'S AFGHANISTAN by *Florentia Sale*—An Indomitable Victorian Lady's Account of the Retreat from Kabul During the First Afghan War.

THE TWO WARS OF MRS DUBERLY by *Frances Isabella Duberly*—An Intrepid Victorian Lady's Experience of the Crimea and Indian Mutiny.

THE REBELLIOUS DUCHESS by *Paul F. S. Dermoncourt*—The Adventures of the Duchess of Berri and Her Attempt to Overthrow French Monarchy.

LADIES OF WATERLOO by *Charlotte A. Eaton, Magdalene de Lancey & Juana Smith*—The Experiences of Three Women During the Campaign of 1815: Waterloo Days by Charlotte A. Eaton, A Week at Waterloo by Magdalene de Lancey & Juana's Story by Juana Smith.

TWO YEARS BEFORE THE MAST by *Richard Henry Dana. Jr.*—The account of one young man's experiences serving on board a sailing brig—the Penelope—bound for California, between the years 1834-36.

A SAILOR OF KING GEORGE by *Frederick Hoffman*—From Midshipman to Captain—Recollections of War at Sea in the Napoleonic Age 1793-1815.

LORDS OF THE SEA by *A. T. Mahan*—Great Captains of the Royal Navy During the Age of Sail.

COGGESHALL'S VOYAGES: VOLUME 1 by *George Coggeshall*—The Recollections of an American Schooner Captain.

COGGESHALL'S VOYAGES: VOLUME 2 by *George Coggeshall*—The Recollections of an American Schooner Captain.

TWILIGHT OF EMPIRE by *Sir Thomas Ussher & Sir George Cockburn*—Two accounts of Napoleon's Journeys in Exile to Elba and St. Helena: Narrative of Events by Sir Thomas Ussher & Napoleon's Last Voyage: Extract of a diary by Sir George Cockburn.

AVAILABLE ONLINE AT **www.leonaur.com**
AND FROM ALL GOOD BOOK STORES

ALSO FROM LEONAUR
AVAILABLE IN SOFTCOVER OR HARDCOVER WITH DUST JACKET

ESCAPE FROM THE FRENCH by *Edward Boys*—A Young Royal Navy Midshipman's Adventures During the Napoleonic War.

THE VOYAGE OF H.M.S. PANDORA by *Edward Edwards R. N. & George Hamilton, edited by Basil Thomson*—In Pursuit of the Mutineers of the Bounty in the South Seas—1790-1791.

MEDUSA by *J. B. Henry Savigny and Alexander Correard and Charlotte-Adélaïde Dard*—Narrative of a Voyage to Senegal in 1816 & The Sufferings of the Picard Family After the Shipwreck of the Medusa.

THE SEA WAR OF 1812 VOLUME 1 by *A. T. Mahan*—A History of the Maritime Conflict.

THE SEA WAR OF 1812 VOLUME 2 by *A. T. Mahan*—A History of the Maritime Conflict.

WETHERELL OF H. M. S. HUSSAR by *John Wetherell*—The Recollections of an Ordinary Seaman of the Royal Navy During the Napoleonic Wars.

THE NAVAL BRIGADE IN NATAL by *C. R. N. Burne*—With the Guns of H. M. S. Terrible & H. M. S. Tartar during the Boer War 1899-1900.

THE VOYAGE OF H. M. S. BOUNTY by *William Bligh*—The True Story of an 18th Century Voyage of Exploration and Mutiny.

SHIPWRECK! by *William Gilly*—The Royal Navy's Disasters at Sea 1793-1849.

KING'S CUTTERS AND SMUGGLERS: 1700-1855 by *E. Keble Chatterton*—A unique period of maritime history-from the beginning of the eighteenth to the middle of the nineteenth century when British seamen risked all to smuggle valuable goods from wool to tea and spirits from and to the Continent.

CONFEDERATE BLOCKADE RUNNER by *John Wilkinson*—The Personal Recollections of an Officer of the Confederate Navy.

NAVAL BATTLES OF THE NAPOLEONIC WARS by *W. H. Fitchett*—Cape St. Vincent, the Nile, Cadiz, Copenhagen, Trafalgar & Others.

PRISONERS OF THE RED DESERT by *R. S. Gwatkin-Williams*—The Adventures of the Crew of the Tara During the First World War.

U-BOAT WAR 1914-1918 by *James B. Connolly/Karl von Schenk*—Two Contrasting Accounts from Both Sides of the Conflict at Sea During the Great War.

AVAILABLE ONLINE AT **www.leonaur.com**
AND FROM ALL GOOD BOOK STORES

ALSO FROM LEONAUR
AVAILABLE IN SOFTCOVER OR HARDCOVER WITH DUST JACKET

IRON TIMES WITH THE GUARDS *by An O. E. (G. P. A. Fildes)*—The Experiences of an Officer of the Coldstream Guards on the Western Front During the First World War.

THE GREAT WAR IN THE MIDDLE EAST: 1 *by W. T. Massey*—The Desert Campaigns & How Jerusalem Was Won---two classic accounts in one volume.

THE GREAT WAR IN THE MIDDLE EAST: 2 *by W. T. Massey*—Allenby's Final Triumph.

SMITH-DORRIEN *by Horace Smith-Dorrien*—Isandlwhana to the Great War.

1914 *by Sir John French*—The Early Campaigns of the Great War by the British Commander.

GRENADIER *by E. R. M. Fryer*—The Recollections of an Officer of the Grenadier Guards throughout the Great War on the Western Front.

BATTLE, CAPTURE & ESCAPE *by George Pearson*—The Experiences of a Canadian Light Infantryman During the Great War.

DIGGERS AT WAR *by R. Hugh Knyvett & G. P. Cuttriss*—"Over There" With the Australians by R. Hugh Knyvett and Over the Top With the Third Australian Division by G. P. Cuttriss. Accounts of Australians During the Great War in the Middle East, at Gallipoli and on the Western Front.

HEAVY FIGHTING BEFORE US *by George Brenton Laurie*—The Letters of an Officer of the Royal Irish Rifles on the Western Front During the Great War.

THE CAMELIERS *by Oliver Hogue*—A Classic Account of the Australians of the Imperial Camel Corps During the First World War in the Middle East.

RED DUST *by Donald Black*—A Classic Account of Australian Light Horsemen in Palestine During the First World War.

THE LEAN, BROWN MEN *by Angus Buchanan*—Experiences in East Africa During the Great War with the 25th Royal Fusiliers—the Legion of Frontiersmen.

THE NIGERIAN REGIMENT IN EAST AFRICA *by W. D. Downes*—On Campaign During the Great War 1916-1918.

THE 'DIE-HARDS' IN SIBERIA *by John Ward*—With the Middlesex Regiment Against the Bolsheviks 1918-19.

AVAILABLE ONLINE AT **www.leonaur.com**
AND FROM ALL GOOD BOOK STORES

ALSO FROM LEONAUR
AVAILABLE IN SOFTCOVER OR HARDCOVER WITH DUST JACKET

FARAWAY CAMPAIGN *by F. James*—Experiences of an Indian Army Cavalry Officer in Persia & Russia During the Great War.

REVOLT IN THE DESERT *by T. E. Lawrence*—An account of the experiences of one remarkable British officer's war from his own perspective.

MACHINE-GUN SQUADRON *by A. M. G.*—The 20th Machine Gunners from British Yeomanry Regiments in the Middle East Campaign of the First World War.

A GUNNER'S CRUSADE *by Antony Bluett*—The Campaign in the Desert, Palestine & Syria as Experienced by the Honourable Artillery Company During the Great War.

DESPATCH RIDER *by W. H. L. Watson*—The Experiences of a British Army Motorcycle Despatch Rider During the Opening Battles of the Great War in Europe.

TIGERS ALONG THE TIGRIS *by E. J. Thompson*—The Leicestershire Regiment in Mesopotamia During the First World War.

HEARTS & DRAGONS *by Charles R. M. F. Crutwell*—The 4th Royal Berkshire Regiment in France and Italy During the Great War, 1914-1918.

INFANTRY BRIGADE: 1914 *by John Ward*—The Diary of a Commander of the 15th Infantry Brigade, 5th Division, British Army, During the Retreat from Mons.

DOING OUR 'BIT' *by Ian Hay*—Two Classic Accounts of the Men of Kitchener's 'New Army' During the Great War including *The First 100,000* & *All In It*.

AN EYE IN THE STORM *by Arthur Ruhl*—An American War Correspondent's Experiences of the First World War from the Western Front to Gallipoli-and Beyond.

STAND & FALL *by Joe Cassells*—With the Middlesex Regiment Against the Bolsheviks 1918-19.

RIFLEMAN MACGILL'S WAR *by Patrick MacGill*—A Soldier of the London Irish During the Great War in Europe including *The Amateur Army*, *The Red Horizon* & *The Great Push*.

WITH THE GUNS *by C. A. Rose & Hugh Dalton*—Two First Hand Accounts of British Gunners at War in Europe During World War 1- Three Years in France with the Guns and With the British Guns in Italy.

THE BUSH WAR DOCTOR *by Robert V. Dolbey*—The Experiences of a British Army Doctor During the East African Campaign of the First World War.

AVAILABLE ONLINE AT **www.leonaur.com**
AND FROM ALL GOOD BOOK STORES

ALSO FROM LEONAUR
AVAILABLE IN SOFTCOVER OR HARDCOVER WITH DUST JACKET

THE 9TH—THE KING'S (LIVERPOOL REGIMENT) IN THE GREAT WAR 1914 - 1918 *by Enos H. G. Roberts*—Mersey to mud—war and Liverpool men.

THE GAMBARDIER *by Mark Severn*—The experiences of a battery of Heavy artillery on the Western Front during the First World War.

FROM MESSINES TO THIRD YPRES *by Thomas Floyd*—A personal account of the First World War on the Western front by a 2/5th Lancashire Fusilier.

THE IRISH GUARDS IN THE GREAT WAR - VOLUME 1 *by Rudyard Kipling*—Edited and Compiled from Their Diaries and Papers—The First Battalion.

THE IRISH GUARDS IN THE GREAT WAR - VOLUME 1 *by Rudyard Kipling*—Edited and Compiled from Their Diaries and Papers—The Second Battalion.

ARMOURED CARS IN EDEN *by K. Roosevelt*—An American President's son serving in Rolls Royce armoured cars with the British in Mesopatamia & with the American Artillery in France during the First World War.

CHASSEUR OF 1914 *by Marcel Dupont*—Experiences of the twilight of the French Light Cavalry by a young officer during the early battles of the great war in Europe.

TROOP HORSE & TRENCH *by R.A. Lloyd*—The experiences of a British Lifeguardsman of the household cavalry fighting on the western front during the First World War 1914-18.

THE EAST AFRICAN MOUNTED RIFLES *by C.J. Wilson*—Experiences of the campaign in the East African bush during the First World War.

THE LONG PATROL *by George Berrie*—A Novel of Light Horsemen from Gallipoli to the Palestine campaign of the First World War.

THE FIGHTING CAMELIERS *by Frank Reid*—The exploits of the Imperial Camel Corps in the desert and Palestine campaigns of the First World War.

STEEL CHARIOTS IN THE DESERT *by S. C. Rolls*—The first world war experiences of a Rolls Royce armoured car driver with the Duke of Westminster in Libya and in Arabia with T.E. Lawrence.

WITH THE IMPERIAL CAMEL CORPS IN THE GREAT WAR *by Geoffrey Inchbald*—The story of a serving officer with the British 2nd battalion against the Senussi and during the Palestine campaign.

AVAILABLE ONLINE AT **www.leonaur.com**
AND FROM ALL GOOD BOOK STORES

www.ingramcontent.com/pod-product-compliance
Lightning Source LLC
Chambersburg PA
CBHW031619160426
43196CB00006B/197